IDENTIFYING TREES OF THE WEST

An All-Season Guide to Western North America

Lois DeMarco and Jay Mengel

STACKPOLE BOOKS

0 11557 01472 3

Published by
STACKPOLE BOOKS
5067 Ritter Road
Mechanicsburg, PA 17055
www.stackpolebooks.com

Printed in the United States of America

10 9 8 7 6 5 4 3 2 1

First edition

Cover photo by Kathe and Jack Frank.
Cover design by Caroline M. Stover.
All photographs by the authors unless otherwise credited.
Photo credits on page 403.

Library of Congress Cataloging-in-Publication Data

DeMarco, Lois, author.
  Identifying trees of the West : an all-season guide to western North America / Lois DeMarco and Jay Mengel. — First edition.
      pages cm
  Includes index.
  ISBN 978-0-8117-1472-3
  1. Trees—North America—Identification. I. Mengel, Jay, author. II. Title.
  QK110.D46 2015
  582.16097—dc23
                          2015033553

Contents

This book provides descriptions for many species of trees found in western North America from the eastern base of the Rocky Mountains to the Pacific coast. It is a companion guide to *Identifying Trees* by Michael D. Williams, which covers the trees of the East. Trees are an important part of global ecosystem health. Therefore, conserving them is in everyone's interest. The noted ecologist Baba Dioum said, "In the end, we will conserve only what we love. We will love only what we understand. We will understand only what we are taught." Hopefully by using this book you will learn to know and understand trees, then love them, and ultimately conserve them. Enjoy!

Acknowledgments

We would like to thank the staff at various National Park Service, National Forest Service, and state park visitor centers and offices who assisted us in our quest to locate trees.

Allison Loar, National Park Service Inventory and Monitoring Division, Ft. Collins, Colorado, provided inventory data from the NPSpecies database which was used to compile the National Park and Seashore Tree Lists, in the appendices.

Andrea Hille, Forest Silviculturist, Allegheny National Forest, provided review of parts of the book.

Jack and Kathe Frank, Kevin Elliott, Marilyn Darling, and Susan Penny provided photos for us to use.

Michael D. Williams (deceased) whose *Identifying Trees* provided us a framework to follow.

Mark Allison and Stackpole Books, for giving us the opportunity to pursue this undertaking.

How to Get the Most Out of This Book

This book is divided into three sections.

Part 1: Identification Basics provides the essentials needed as you begin your journey in identifying trees. Tree identification is more than being able to distinguish leaf, bark, and form characteristics. Having a basic understanding of how trees are named, classification, and the environmental factors that define where different species are found can help as you identify the trees around you. An introduction to leaf shapes and parts of a leaf, as well as a description of parts of a tree, is also included.

Part 2: Tree Guides includes a Leaf Identification Guide and Winter Identification Guide. These guides use a simplified step-by-step question-and-answer process that is very similar to detailed keys used by botanists to identify species. The questions are designed to help you narrow down the field of potential candidate species. Once you think you've made a successful identification, refer to the full species account included in Part 3.

Part 3: Species Accounts includes a detailed description and pictures of major identifying features, habitats, and ranges for the commonly found trees in the West.

There are three appendices.

The first is a glossary of terms used in this book.

The second is a listing of trees included in this book that are found in western national parks and seashores.

The third is a listing of references and useful websites for further tree identification.

PART ONE

Identification Basics

Identifying trees is one way of enjoying time spent in the outdoors. Whether you are in your backyard or a local park or visiting one of our national parks, being able to identify trees can help you develop a closer relationship with the environment around you. It can be challenging, but it is greatly rewarding when you are able to identify the trees you are looking at. As your knowledge base increases and your confidence in your identification skills improves, you will find even greater enjoyment of your time spent in the woods.

1

The Importance
of Place

There are two kinds of names assigned to trees: the common name and the scientific name. Common names often include a descriptor such as habitat (Subalpine Fir), locality (Pacific Yew), or commemoration (Engelmann Spruce), as well as the common name for the genus in the scientific name (for example, pine for *Pinus*). Common names are often regional or local in nature. They are sometimes confusing because the same common name can be used to describe two different trees—usually in different locations—and the same trees often have more than one common name.

Scientific names, on the other hand, are very specific and provide a standardized system that is used worldwide to uniquely identify any particular tree. Scientific names are in Latin and have two parts: a genus name and a species name. The genus is capitalized and the species is not; both are usually italicized. There may be numerous trees with the same genus name (for example, there are 22 trees included in this book that belong to the genus *Pinus*) but each one of those will have a different species name. Therefore, there will only be one tree with any particular pair of genus and species names (*Pinus monophylla, Pinus ponderosa, Pinus strobiformis,* and so on). Even within the scientific community, there is not always full agreement on how to name a particular tree because scientific names are sometimes subject to change. It is helpful to know both the scientific and common names to avoid confusion.

The trees in this book are identified by both the common and scientific names. There will be several common names listed when more than one name is used. The scientific names are those used by the U.S. Department of Agriculture, Natural Resource Conservation Service, Plants Database (http://plants .usda.gov) and are current as of December 17, 2014.

CLASSIFICATION

Trees are classified into two major plant groups: gymnosperms and angiosperms. Gymnosperms include the conifers (also called softwoods) and are trees that are most often evergreen, have leaves that are needlelike or scalelike, and produce seeds that are usually enclosed in some kind of cone. Pines, junipers, and Redwood are examples of gymnosperms.

Angiosperms are flowering plants that have seeds enclosed in some kind of fruit and include palms (trees with large, evergreen, lancelike or fan-shaped leaves, usually clustered at the top of the tree) and hardwoods (broadleaf trees that are usually deciduous with net-veined leaves, such as oaks, maples, and willows).

Gymnosperms and angiosperms are further divided into families. Families include one or more genera that have similar characteristics. Examples include Pinaceae (the Pine family, which includes all pines, spruce, and fir) or Betulaceae (the Birch family, which includes the alders and birches).

HABITAT

Habitat is an environment that is defined by the complex relationship of all the physical conditions in a particular area. These physical conditions or factors include climate, soil characteristics, geography, and even other living organisms. Trees of a particular species are found when the sum of these factors produces an environment that is best suited for their growth. For some species, just a minor change in the mix of these factors can make an area unsuitable for survival.

- Climate is the average weather over an extended period of time. It is temperature, precipitation, humidity, wind, light, and air quality that together create the conditions that either favor or hinder a tree's ability to survive from one growing season to the next.
- Soils provide a tree with the physical support, moisture, and nutrients needed to grow. The texture, depth, and structure of the soil determine how moisture and air are made available to roots. Soil chemistry determines what kinds of nutrients are available to the tree.
- Physical geography includes elevation, slope, aspect, land form, and land-water interface. All of these play a role in defining habitat for a species. Increases in elevation generally mean cooler temperatures, shorter growing seasons, shallower soils, and greater solar intensity. Aspect—the direction that a mountain's slope faces—affects air temperature and precipitation patterns. South- and west-facing slopes tend to be warmer and drier than north- or east-facing slopes. Land form can create microclimates that cause temperature and moisture differences. The land-water interface causes changes in temperature and humidity. Land areas near

large bodies of water are usually cooler in summer and warmer in winter. Some trees thrive only at streamside (riparian) areas where others cannot tolerate excess water.

- Other organisms can have a positive or negative effect on the growth and well-being of a tree as well as the quality of a habitat for a particular species. Overbrowsing by wildlife can cause trees to die or become malformed. Some wildlife species, including birds, are essential for seed dispersal for some trees. Parasitic growth such as mistletoe has little or no impact on many trees, but other parasites, viruses, or fungi can be deadly. Some trees have special relationships with particular fungi, and neither the tree nor the fungi will survive without the other. Competition between tree species can have dramatic effects. Some trees die if shaded out by taller species. Often, exotic, invasive species simply crowd out native tree species. Exotic insect species that have no natural enemies can severely compromise a tree's ability to survive.

RANGE

The natural range of a species, the area where the tree is known to live, is the geographical area where climatic and physical conditions are suitable for the existence of that species. Some species have extensive natural ranges whereas others are extremely limited. Natural ranges are continually changing in response to environmental change. As the earth has slowly warmed since the end of the last ice age 12,000 years ago, the natural range of many species has shifted northward or has been reduced in size.

Exotic species have often been planted in areas that are far from their natural range. When introduced to new areas that have favorable habitats, they can become naturalized and are able to develop, reproduce, and compete with native species.

In many instances, knowing a species' range can help with identification. The range description and range maps are provided.

ELEVATION, ASPECT, AND LATITUDE

The environmental conditions under which a particular tree is found can vary throughout its range. As you move from south to north, temperatures become colder and shifts in elevation and aspect requirements can change. For example, Sugar Pine grows best on cool mountain soils and is found at elevations of 4,000 to 10,000 feet in the southern portion of its range. As you move to more northern climates, Sugar Pine can be found from 2,000 to 8,000 feet in the central portion of its range, and from 1,000 to 5,000 feet in the northern portion.

Similarly, Quaking Aspen is found at different elevations and aspects over its range. In the southern portion of the range, the cooler north- and east-facing slopes at elevations above 10,000 feet provide the optimum growing conditions. Farther north, these conditions are often found on the warmer south- and west-facing slopes at elevations below 3,000 feet.

FOREST TYPES

Although each species has particular environmental needs that define its range, trees and other vegetation become grouped in communities that have similar growing requirements. Forest types are one way to describe the groupings of species that are found across the landscape. Having a general understanding of different forest zones and major forest types can be very helpful in developing a sense of what trees grow where. The forest type discussion provided here is based on the work of the Society of American Foresters' "Forest Types of North America."

Boreal Forest

The boreal forest spans the entire North American continent from the Atlantic Ocean to the Pacific Ocean in the northern latitudes. In the West, this includes inland areas of Canada and Alaska. Climates are cold and snowy, and growing seasons are short. Black Spruce and alders are found on wetter sites. Drier sites support White Spruce, Paper Birch, and Quaking Aspen. Lodgepole Pine is often found on burned-over areas.

Rocky Mountain Complex

The Rocky Mountains are found from Alberta and British Columbia south to northern New Mexico and form the Continental Divide, rising to over 14,000 feet above the Great Plains to the east and the Great Basin to the west. There are six major forest types based on changes in elevation and latitude as well as a riparian forest type in this complex.

- **Pinyon-Juniper Woodland.** Composed of Twoneedle Pinyon and several junipers (Oneseed, Rocky Mountain, Utah, or Alligator). Ponderosa Pine, Gambel Oak, and Cercocarpus may also be found. From 5,000 to 7,000 feet (in Utah, Arizona, and New Mexico).
- **Ponderosa Pine Forest.** Composed of Ponderosa Pine, Rocky Mountain Juniper, Gambel Oak, Quaking Aspen, and Lodgepole Pine. From 4,000 to 8,000 feet.
- **Aspen Grove.** Pure stands of aspen develop after catastrophic wildfire and other disturbances. From 5,600 feet to 11,000 feet.
- **Lodgepole Pine Forest.** In pure stands after catastrophic wildfire, but also found with spruce, fir, Douglas-fir, and Ponderosa Pine. From 8,500 to 10,000 feet.

Pinyon-Juniper Woodland

Aspen Grove

Lodgepole Pine Forest

Subalpine Forest

- **Spruce-Fir Forest.** Engelmann Spruce, Subalpine Fir, White Fir, Blue Spruce, Western White Pine, and Western Larch. Growing above 9,000 feet in the southern Rockies and at lower elevations in the north.
- **Subalpine Forest.** Bristlecone and Foxtail Pines, Limber Pine, Whitebark Pine, and Mountain Hemlock. At upper elevations just below timberline.
- **Riparian Forest.** Willows, alders, cottonwoods, hackberry, and Box-elder, along streams.

Pacific Coastal Complex

This includes four forest types in the mountains of British Columbia, Oregon, Washington, and northern California and three forest types in the coastal fog belt stretching from Alaska to central California.

- **Northwest Oak-Pine Forest.** Includes Oregon White Oak, Pacific Madrone, Knobcone Pine, Lodgepole Pine, and Ponderosa Pine. From southern Vancouver Island throughout the Willamette Valley of Oregon and south to California.
- **Northwest Riparian Forest.** Black Cottonwood, Red and White Alder, Oregon Ash, and up to 30 species of willow. Found along rivers.
- **Douglas-fir Forest.** Douglas-fir, Red Alder, Bigleaf Maple, Western Redcedar, Western Hemlock, Noble Fir, Silver Fir, Ponderosa Pine, Incense Cedar, Sugar Pine, Grand Fir, White Fir, Western White Pine, and Western Larch.
- **Subalpine Forest.** Found below timberline in mountain areas. Subalpine Fir, Whitebark Pine, Engelmann Spruce, Mountain Hemlock, and Alaska Cedar. Timberline is at 9,500 feet on Mount Shasta, in California; 5,500 feet in British Columbia; and 1,500 feet in southern Alaska.

Northwest Riparian Forest

- **Spruce-Hemlock Forest.** Sitka Spruce, Western Hemlock, Douglas-fir, Port Orford Cedar, Pacific Yew, Pacific Dogwood. Within 30 miles of the Pacific coast in areas of high precipitation and coastal fog.
- **Redwood Forest.** Redwood, Western Hemlock, Douglas-fir, Sitka Spruce, Bigleaf Maple, Tanoak, and California Laurel. In the coastal fog belt.
- **Closed-Cone Pine Forest.** Conifer species with limited range along the Pacific coast of California, including Bishop Pine, Sargent's Cypress, Monterey Pine, Monterey Cypress, Gowen Cypress, Coulter Pine, and Torrey Pine.

Douglas-fir Forest

Redwood Forest

Sierra Nevada Complex

Found in the Sierra Nevada, bordered by the Central Valley of California on the west and the Great Basin on the east. Forest types generally occur at lower elevations on the moist, western side of the range and at lower elevations in the southern end of the range as compared to the north. There are six broad forest types in this complex.

- **Oak-Pine Woodland.** Oregon White Oak, Interior Live Oak, California Live Oak, Blue Oak, and Valley Oak as well as Pacific Madrone, California Laurel, Incense Cedar, California Buckeye, California Walnut, and California Foothill Pine. Found throughout western California, mainly in sheltered valleys up to 5,000 feet.

Oak-Pine Woodland

Sagebrush-Pinyon Forest

- **Sagebrush-Pinyon Forest.** Singleleaf Pinyon and California Pinyon, on the dry eastern slopes of the Sierra Nevada, between 5,000 and 7,000 feet.
- **Mid-elevation Pine Forest.** On the western slope between 2,400 and 6,000 feet, it includes White Fir, California Black Oak, Incense Cedar, Sugar Pine, and Douglas-fir. On the eastern slope between 7,000 to 8,000 feet, it includes Jeffrey Pine as well as the species found on the western slope.
- **Giant Sequoia Grove.** Restricted to 75 groves on about 35,000 acres on the western slopes of the Sierra Nevada, Giant Sequoia are found here, along with Sugar Pine, White Fir, Incense Cedar, and California Black Oak.

Giant Sequoia Grove

Subalpine Forest

- **Montane Fir Forest.** At elevations from 6,000 to 8,200 feet on the western slopes, and 8,000 to 9,000 feet on eastern slopes, composed primarily of California Red Fir but also Western White Pine and Lodgepole Pine. White Fir is found at lower elevations, and Douglas-fir, along with Pacific Yew, Tanoak, and California Nutmeg, is found in the northern Sierra Nevada, at 4,000 to 5,000 feet.
- **Subalpine Forest.** At higher elevations, just below timberline, dominated by Mountain Hemlock, Western Juniper, Whitebark Pine, Limber Pine, Lodgepole Pine, Western White Pine, Foxtail Pine, and Great Basin Bristlecone Pine.

Southwest Dry Forest Complex
Extending from southern California to western Texas and into central Mexico, this region is characterized by low precipitation and vast deserts. There are four forest types—two found along rivers and two in the mountains.
- **Canyon and Riparian Forest.** Found along intermittent streams and arroyos in canyons and includes many species that are adapted to arid climates: California and Arizona Sycamore, California and Arizona Walnut, Arizona Cypress, Fremont Cottonwood, Narrowleaf Cottonwood, Bigtooth Maple, Boxelder, New Mexico Locust, Honey Mesquite, Blue and Yellow Paloverde, and Desert Ironwood.
- **Lower Rio Grande Forest.** Along the Rio Grande—areas with extremely low precipitation. An interesting mix of both eastern and western tree species. (Most of the trees found here are not included in this book.)

Canyon and Riparian Forest

- **Sky Island Forest.** Pine forests are found in the upper elevations (above 6,500 feet) in the mountains of southeastern Arizona and northern Mexico. These "sky islands" contain similar vegetation, although they are separated by drier, less-vegetated conditions on the lower slopes. Apache Pine, Southwestern White Pine, and Arizona Pine, as well as Douglas-fir, Engelmann Spruce, Limber Pine, Lodgepole Pine, and Quaking Aspen are found.
- **Madrean Foothill Forest.** In northern Mexico, between 4,500 and 8,000 feet. Trees include Mexican Pinyon, Arizona Pine, and Alligator Juniper as well as many oak species.

Madrean Foothill Forest

USEFUL ID TIPS

- Expect variability. A tree's appearance can differ from one site to another, even from one growing season to another. Trees growing in extreme conditions can take on malformed shapes or growth characteristics that differ from what is considered "normal."
- Leaves may vary—even on the same tree. Sometimes, more than one leaf shape will be found.
- The color of leaves changes throughout the growing season. Initially, leaves will be lemon-lime in color and become darker as the summer progresses. Most broadleaf trees change color in the fall before the leaves are shed, but some broadleaf trees retain leaves all year round.
- The bark, twigs, buds, and tree form can be used to identify trees when leaves are absent.
- Bark pattern changes as a tree ages. Older bark at the base of a tree tends to be thicker and rougher. Younger bark is usually thinner and smoother.
- Trees often have unique tastes or odors that can help in identification.
- Location is an important factor to consider in tree identification. Refer to range information to determine whether or not a particular species is found where you are located.
- This book provides descriptions for 127 species of the most common trees of the West. There are websites you can access for descriptions of trees not included in this book (see page 402).
- A magnifying glass or jeweler's loupe may help you see fine hair, glands, scales, and other features that are not visible to the naked eye.
- Be aware that some vegetation is poisonous and can cause skin irritation. See the discussion of Poison Ivy and Poison Oak on page 22.

2

Tree Structure and Kinds of Leaves

Becoming familiar with the parts of the tree will help you use the Species Accounts in Part 3.

Crown. The crown includes the branches, twigs, and leaves that make up the upper portion of the tree. The crown defines the shape or form of the tree. It may be rounded, conical, spirelike, or irregular. It may be just the top of a long trunk or can completely envelope the entire tree. The shape of the crown and how much of the trunk, or bole, it covers can offer significant identification clues.

Trunk. The trunk, or bole, is the main stem of the tree. The section of the bole that has no branches is said to be clear. Trees are "phototaxic," which means that growth occurs from the tip and not from the base. A mark at the 6 foot height of a tree will stay at 6 feet, but the tallest twig, the leader, will continue to grow higher. Most of the trunk is dead tissue. The outer bark is dead, as is the woody center. A thin layer of living tissue, called the cambium layer, is sandwiched between the bark and the bulk of the trunk, the woody center. The cambium layer has the xylem and phloem "tubes" that carry fluid and nutrients between the roots and leaves. Trees with swollen bases are said to be fluted or buttressed.

Leaves. Leaves are the green structures along twigs where photosynthesis occurs. They contain the chlorophyll that converts sunlight to the energy needed to feed the tree. Leaves can be scalelike (junipers and cedars), needlelike (pines), or broad and flat (oaks, maples, birches, and many more). Leaves that are shed annually are said to be deciduous; those that remain green all year are evergreen. The assorted shapes and arrangements of leaves are key identifiers.

Broad leaves can be simple (with just one leaflet) or compound (with several leaflets that make up a single leaf). Leaves can be either opposite or alternate, meaning they are either in pairs along the stem or are single leaves arranged spirally along the twig. The leaf edge—the margin—can be smooth, toothed, or lobed.

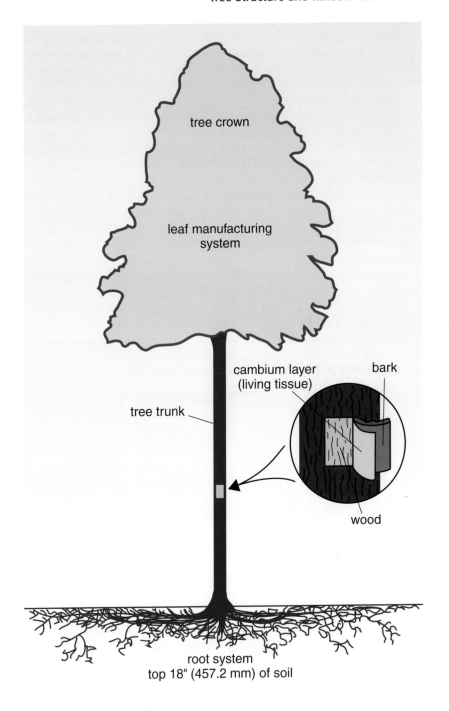

tree crown

leaf manufacturing
system

cambium layer
(living tissue)

bark

tree trunk

wood

root system
top 18" (457.2 mm) of soil

Bark. Bark is the smooth or corky outer covering of the trunk, branches, and twigs of a tree. Bark, especially in the larger trees, can be quite distinctive. The bark of most young trees is smooth, but as trees age, the dying exterior changes into varying forms. The corky roughening appears first at the base of the trunk and the bases of branches on some trees. Bark can be thick, thin, smooth, corky, shredded, or spongy. Thick bark can have deep fissures separating flat or rounded ridges. Bark color can be white, green, gray, brown, black, even purplish. The inner bark, the layer under the exposed bark, can also have characteristic color or odor that can help with identification.

Roots. Roots are the water- and nutrient-collecting mechanism of a tree. They are also the foundation that keeps the tree from toppling over. Most trees have dispersed root systems, usually about 18 inches deep, that spread out far from the base of the tree, collecting water and providing a base for support. Some trees have taproots that go deep into the soil, sometimes many times deeper than the tree is tall.

The first step in the identification process is asking yourself what kind of leaves you see. Are they needlelike, scalelike, or broad and flat?

NEEDLELIKE LEAVES
Needlelike leaves are long and slender. They get their name because they look like sewing needles. They may stand alone on a twig, grow in clusters, or be wrapped at the base in bundles of two to five needles each.

SCALELIKE LEAVES
Scalelike leaves are very small, overlapping one another like the scales of a fish. Juvenile scalelike leaves may stand erect and be prickly.

Tree Structure and Kinds of Leaves

BROAD AND FLAT LEAVES

Broad and flat leaves are broad, flat, and thin. They have many shapes and sizes, but all are much wider and longer than thick.

Broad and flat leaves have several unique properties that can be compared in order to identify the tree that produced them.

Simple or Compound

Broad and flat leaves may be either simple or compound. Simple leaves have a single leaf blade and stalk, or *petiole,* which is attached to the limb at the point called the *node.* Compound leaves have two or more leaf blades, called *leaflets,* attached to the petiole, which in turn is attached to the twig at the leaf node, where a bud will also be found. There are several kinds of compound leaves. Pinnately compound leaves have a central *leafstalk* (or rachis), with two or more leaflets; bipinnately compound leaves have a rachis that further divides into two or more side axes with two or more leaflets per side axis; palmately compound leaves have multiple leaflets attached at one point on a single leafstalk, like the fingers on a hand.

Opposite or Alternate

Broad and flat leaves may have either opposite or alternate arrangement along the twig. Simple or compound leaves attached directly across from one another at the same point (node) on the twig are said to have an opposite arrangement. Simple or compound leaves attached at offset, zigzag intervals, where the leaves are never straight across from one another along the stem, are said to have an alternate arrangement.

Broad and Flat Leaf Parts

Broad and flat leaves have distinguishing characteristics that can be used to separate one from the other. To help with identification, these different characteristics have all been given names.

- The farthermost point of the leaf away from the twig is called the *leaftip,* or *apex.*
- The closest point of the wide, flat portion of the leaf joining the leafstalk is called the *leaf base.*
- The *node* is the point where the leafstalk attaches to the twig.
- The stalk between the base of the leaf and the node is called the *petiole,* or *leafstalk.*
- On compound leaves, the portion of the stalk between leaflets is called the *rachis.*
- The large, flat, green portion of the leaf is called the *blade.*
- On compound leaves, the blades are often called *leaflets.*
- Leaf blades, veins, and stalks may be *pubescent,* having hair growing from their surfaces.

Simple Leaf Parts

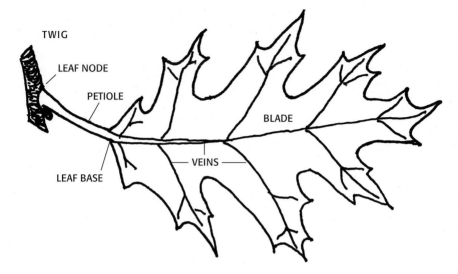

Compound Leaf Parts

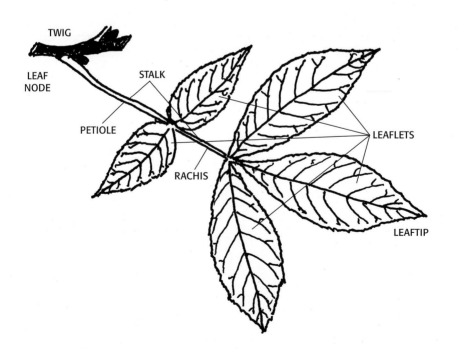

Leaf Margins

The edge of the broad and flat leaf or leaflet is called its *margin*. The margin may be either smooth or toothed. Teeth may be fine, or coarse, or both on the same edge. They may also be blunt.

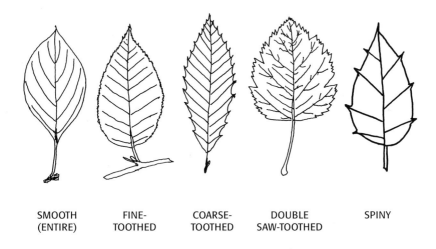

| SMOOTH (ENTIRE) | FINE-TOOTHED | COARSE-TOOTHED | DOUBLE SAW-TOOTHED | SPINY |

Broad and flat leaf margins may have dips, called *sinuses,* and bulges, called *lobes.* If the margins are continuous and unbroken, with no indentations, they are called *entire.*

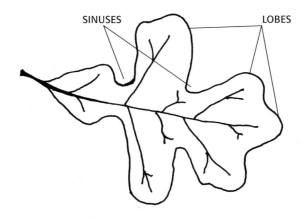

SINUSES   LOBES

Lobes and sinuses come in many different shapes that can be used to identify trees. The lobes may have either rounded or pointed ends, or they may have spiked ends, toothed edges, or both at the same time. The sinuses may be either rounded or V shaped.

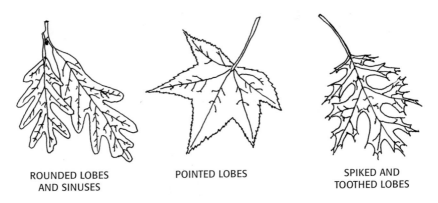

ROUNDED LOBES
AND SINUSES

POINTED LOBES

SPIKED AND
TOOTHED LOBES

Vein Patterns

Broad and flat leaves have different vein patterns that can be used to help with identification. Leaves may have a central vein running from base to point or notch, with secondary veins branching out at various points along the central vein, or they may have several major veins that spread up from a central point at the base of the leaf.

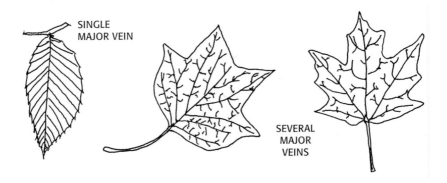

SINGLE
MAJOR VEIN

SEVERAL
MAJOR
VEINS

POISON IVY AND POISON OAK

"Leaves of three—let it be!"

It is extremely important to be able to identify poison ivy and poison oak in order to avoid the itchy rash that can result after contact with any part of either plant. It would be nice if there were signs that would indicate that the plants are present, but that is not usually the case, so you will need to rely on your own identification skills.

The rash caused by these plants is a result of a reaction to an oil they contain called urushiol. Contact with only a miniscule amount of urushiol is enough to cause significant outbreak of the rash for people who are allergic.

If you come in contact with either of these plants, you should immediately wash the area with rubbing alcohol or soap and water. Rinse well with water after washing. You don't actually have to come in contact with the plant to develop the rash. The urushiol can be on clothing or on your dog's fur and be transferred to the skin. If you develop a rash, applying wet compresses, calamine lotion, hydrocortisone creams, and other commercially available ointments may help reduce itching. In severe cases, medical help should be sought.

There are two kinds of poison ivy found in the West. Western Poison Ivy *(Toxicodendron rydbergii)* is found in every western state except California. Eastern Poison Ivy *(T. radicans),* common in the East, is found in only a few locations within the geographical area covered by this book: Pima, Santa Cruz, and Cochise Counties in Arizona and Jeff Davis and Brewster Counties in West Texas.

The two poison ivies are very similar except that Western Poison Ivy is an erect but low-growing shrub that does not attach itself and become a climbing vine like Eastern Poison Ivy. Eastern Poison Ivy is branching and has woody stems whereas Western Poison Ivy does not branch much

and the woody stems generally are limited to the base of the plant. Both plants have alternate, deciduous, compound leaves with three leaflets that can be 1 to 8 inches long and about half as wide. The leaflets can be quite varied but usually have coarse teeth on the margins. Green during spring and summer, the leaves turn an attractive red and/or yellow in the fall. The small, white flowers have five petals and grow in small clusters. The fruit is a tiny, white, dry, round seed that forms small clusters, like miniature grapes.

Pacific Poison Oak *(T. diversilobum)* bears a resemblance to the poison ivies in that it also has alternate, pinnately compound (usually three leaflets), deciduous leaves. The leaflets are very oaklike in appearance. The terminal leaflet tends to be larger than the lateral leaflets, which are slightly lobed on one side and not lobed on the other. Young leaflets are reddish green but soon turn completely green. In the fall, the leaves turn brilliant red or yellow. The flowers are small, yellow-green, and hang in clusters. These springtime flowers develop into clusters of white seeds with black striations. Pacific Poison Oak can grow as an erect shrub or a climbing vine.

PART TWO

Tree Guides

The Leaf Identification Guide and Winter Identification Guide provide step-by-step processes to identify trees, whether you are looking at them in the summer with the full complement of leaves or in winter, when leaves are no longer present. It will be most helpful if you have familiarized yourself with the terminology presented in Part 1 and the definitions provided in the glossary. Leaves are only one small piece of the puzzle needed to positively identify a tree. Tree form, bark, fruit, and a host of other features, including the natural range of the species, are all pieces of information you will need.

3

Leaf Identification Guide

U sing a leaf identification guide can be a quick and easy way to help identify a tree. By examining the leaf and considering a series of questions that focus on several characteristics, you make choices that lead you in the direction of identifying your tree. It is important that you understand the terminology in order to make the correct choices. Part 1 provides a description and examples of many of the leaf characteristics discussed in this section.

When you think you have identified your tree, compare your leaf to the picture included here. Remember there can be considerable variation in individual leaves and trees, so it is useful to refer to the complete description included in the Species Accounts (Part 3).

Even after careful consideration of the characteristics, you may find that the tree choices do not match your sample. If this happens, try again and make a different choice where you had a questionable selection. You may get a different answer and correctly identify your tree.

In the West, location is a critical element that can be used to help confirm your identification. The range—the geographical area where a particular species grows—as well as the elevation can help you in your final determination of your tree's identity.

A. If your sample leaves are needlelike or scalelike, go to *1. Needlelike or Scalelike Leaves* on page 27.
B. If your sample leaves are broad and flat, go to *2. Broad and Flat Leaves* on page 58.

1. NEEDLELIKE OR SCALELIKE LEAVES

a. If your sample leaves are scalelike, see *Scalelike Leaves* below.
b. If your sample leaves are single needles, go to *Single Needles* on page 37.
c. If your sample leaves are two, three, four, or five needles wrapped in each bundle, with a sheath at the base, go to *Bundled Needles* on page 46.

Scalelike Leaves

1. If your leaves form flat sprays, go to *Scalelike Leaves with Flat Sprays* on page 28.
2. If your leaves do not form flat sprays, go to *Scalelike Leaves Not in Flat Sprays* on page 30.

Scalelike Leaves with Flat Sprays
Compare your sample with the following trees:
> *Alaska Cedar, Incense Cedar, Port Orford Cedar, Western Redcedar, MacNab's Cypress*

ALASKA CEDAR page 132
Scales are very small ($^1/_{16}$ to $^1/_8$ inch), opposite, bright yellow-green, prominently pointed, and often pointing outward. The leaves form flat sprays with tips that tend to droop, often straight down. From coastal southeast Alaska, southwest Canada to Oregon and Washington, at sea level in northern areas and from 2,000 to 7,000 feet in elevation farther south.

INCENSE CEDAR page 134
Scales are $^1/_8$ to $^1/_2$ inch long, opposite, in four rows, shiny, and yellow-green. Side scales are keeled, have long points, and overlap as they cover the twig. Leaves form flat sprays and are aromatic when crushed. The $^3/_4$-inch to $1^1/_2$-inch leathery, pendantlike cones have six paired scales. From western Oregon through northern and central California along the Nevada border, also in Baja California. In California, at 1,000 to 5,000 feet in elevation; in Nevada, from 3,500 to 7,000 feet.

PORT ORFORD CEDAR page 136

Scales are very small (¹/₁₆ inch), opposite, in four rows, yellow-green to blue-green, blunt, and form flat, lacy sprays. Twigs are narrow and covered tightly with flattened scales, which on close inspection show white stripes that form an X. Found in the fog belt of the Coast Ranges in southern Oregon and northern California, from sea level to elevations of 2,000 to 7,000 feet.

WESTERN REDCEDAR page 138

Scales are ¹/₁₆ to ¹/₈ inch long, opposite, shiny, dark yellow-green or dark green, in rows of four, and on close inspection show butterflylike markings. Scales form flat sprays that are often long, droopy, almost fernlike, and stringy. The foliage is aromatic. From southeast Alaska, along the coast to northern California, also in western Montana and Idaho, northward into Alberta and British Columbia. At 3,000 feet in elevation in the north and 7,000 feet in the Rockies.

MACNAB'S CYPRESS page 144
Scales are tiny, $^1/_{16}$ long, dull gray-green, opposite, and form flat sprays. This is the only cypress with flat sprays. The scales are fragrant and have a gland dot that produces resin. The most widespread cypress in California—found in the Coast Ranges, northern mountains, and the Sierra Nevada.

Scalelike Leaves Not in Flat Sprays
Compare your sample with the following trees:
> *Arizona Cypress, Gowen Cypress, Monterey Cypress, Sargent's Cypress, Alligator Juniper, California Juniper, Drooping Juniper, Oneseed Juniper, Rocky Mountain Juniper, Utah Juniper, Western Juniper, Redwood, Giant Sequoia*

ARIZONA CYPRESS page 140
Scales are tiny, $^1/_{16}$ inch long, dull gray-green, keeled, somewhat pointed, and tightly hug the stem. Most scales have a gland dot that produces a whitish resin. They have a disagreeable odor when crushed. From the Trans-Pecos to southern California, rare and local, at elevations from 2,500 to 6,600 feet.

GOWEN CYPRESS page 142

Scales are tiny, less than $^{1}/_{16}$ inch long, opposite, in four rows. Leaves are usually bright green and do not have a gland dot. Found in coastal Redwood forests in northwest and central California, usually near sea level.

MONTEREY CYPRESS page 146

Scales are slightly more than $^{1}/_{16}$ inch long, blunt, bright green, and usually do not have a gland dot. Cones are larger than other cypresses (1 to $1^{3}/_{8}$ inches) and are longer than wide. Two native groves are found within Point Lobos State Natural Reserve and the Del Monte Forest at Point Cypress.

SARGENT'S CYPRESS page 148

Scales are tiny, $^1/_{16}$ inch long, opposite, dull green, some with gland dots. Found in the foothills and slopes of the Coast Ranges of California, up to 3,000 feet.

ALLIGATOR JUNIPER page 170

Scales are opposite, $^1/_{16}$ to $^1/_8$ inch long, blue-green to silver-green, with sharp points, in four rows that form slender, four-angled twigs. They have a gland dot and often a whitish resin drop. Checkered bark resembles the hide of an alligator. Found in the Trans-Pecos to northern Arizona, also in Mexico, at elevations from 4,500 to 8,000 feet.

CALIFORNIA JUNIPER page 172

Scalelike leaves are $^1/_{16}$ to $^1/_8$ inch long, usually in threes, blunt, forming stiff, rounded twigs. Scales do not usually overlap. They are light green and have a gland dot. California Juniper is found in hotter, drier areas than other junipers because of its ability to withstand heat and drought. In the mountains of California, especially southwestern California, into northern Baja California, also in extreme southern Nevada and western Arizona, at elevations from 1,000 to 5,000 feet.

DROOPING JUNIPER page 174

Scales are opposite, $^1/_{16}$ to $^1/_8$ inch long, yellow-green, with long, pointed, spreading tips, in four rows that form slender, drooping twigs. In the Chisos Mountains of the Trans-Pecos and Mexico, at elevations from 4,500 to 7,000 feet. In the U.S., it is found only in Big Bend National Park, in Texas.

ONESEED JUNIPER page 176
Scales are opposite, ¹/₁₆ inch long, green to dark-green, with a gland dot, in four rows that form short, stout, crowded twigs. Scales do not overlap. From central Colorado through New Mexico and west to central Arizona, at elevations from 3,000 to 7,000 feet.

ROCKY MOUNTAIN JUNIPER page 178
Scales are opposite, ¹/₁₆ inch long, bluish to dark green, in four rows that form slender, four-angled twigs. Scales are somewhat pointed. Foliage droops at the ends of branches. From central British Columbia and generally southeast through the Rockies to southeastern New Mexico, at elevations from 5,000 to 7,500 feet.

UTAH JUNIPER page 180
Scales are usually opposite, $^1/_{16}$ inch long, light yellow-green, in four rows that form stout twigs. Short-pointed scales are usually without a gland dot. Found in Nevada, east to Wyoming, south to western New Mexico, and west to southern California, at elevations from 3,000 to 8,000 feet. Also found along the south rim of the Grand Canyon, in Arizona.

WESTERN JUNIPER page 182
Scales are $^1/_{16}$ inch long, often in threes, dark gray-green, and form stout, rounded twigs. Gland dots are noticeable. From central and southeast Washington to southern California, at elevations to 10,000 feet.

REDWOOD page 228

Redwoods have two kinds of leaves. On the tips of new growth, stems, and the flower/cone-bearing branches, scalelike leaves are $^1/_4$ inch long, pointed, keeled, and encircle the twig. In addition, single needlelike leaves are $^3/_8$ to $^3/_4$ inch long, dark green above and whitish green beneath, flat, slightly stiff, pointed at the tip, and in two rows on older twigs. The longer needles are twisted and blunt near the bases. Found along the Pacific coast in a narrow band 25 to 40 miles wide, from sea level to 3,000 feet, in the fog belt that runs from extreme southwestern Oregon to just south of San Francisco Bay.

GIANT SEQUOIA page 230

Scales are $^1/_8$ to $^1/_4$ inch long, blue-green, somewhat oval-shaped, and can either be spreading or tightly covering drooping twigs. These enormous trees are found on fewer than 25,000 acres, almost all of which are protected on state and federal land holdings in scattered groves on western slopes of the Sierra Nevada, from 4,500 to 8,000 feet in elevation.

Single Needles

1. If the single needles are flexible, flat, and soft, see *Flexible Single Needles* below.
2. If the single needles are not soft and flexible but stiff or sharp, go to *Stiff Single Needles* on page 43.

Flexible Single Needles

Compare your sample with the following trees:

> *California Red Fir, Grand Fir, Noble Fir, Pacific Silver Fir, Subalpine Fir, White Fir, Douglas-fir, Bigcone Douglas-fir, Mountain Hemlock, Western Hemlock, Redwood, Pacific Yew*

CALIFORNIA RED FIR page 154

Needles are $3/4$ to $1^3/8$ inches long and four sided, usually with a point at the tip. They appear crowded toward the upper side of the branches. On new shoots, they are silvery white; on older twigs, silvery blue to dark blue-green with whitish lines on all sides. In the Cascade Mountains of southwest Oregon and south to the Coast Ranges of California, also in central California in the Sierra Nevada. At elevations to 4,500 feet in the north, 5,000 to 9,000 feet in the south.

GRAND FIR page 156

Needles are $3/4$ to 2 inches long, spread in two rows that are nearly at right angles, with the upper and lower needs being shorter than the lateral needles. This arrangement distinguishes Grand Fir from other firs. Needles are flat and flexible, with a shiny dark green upper surface, silvery white below. On upper twigs, the needles appear to be crowded and curve upward. Southwest British Columbia south to California along the Pacific coast. Also inland in the Rocky Mountain region to central Idaho. Found at elevations to 1,500 feet along the coast and up to 6,000 feet inland.

NOBLE FIR page 158

Needles are 1 to $1^5/8$ inches long, blue-green with white lines, and tend to curve upward on branches and appear crowded. On cone-bearing branches, needles are four sided and pointed compared to those on the flexible non-cone-bearing or sterile branches, which are comparatively flat and rounded. Found in the Cascade Mountains and Coast Ranges in Washington, Oregon, and very northern California, from 3,500 to 7,000 feet, infrequently from 200 to 8,900 feet.

PACIFIC SILVER FIR page 160

Needles are ³/₄ to 1¹/₂ inches, crowded at the ends of twigs, and pointed forward in two rows. They curve upward on top branches. The upper sides of the needles are shiny, dark green, and grooved; needles are silvery white beneath. Along the Pacific coast from southeast Alaska to Oregon at elevations from 1,000 to 5,000 feet; also found locally in California.

SUBALPINE FIR page 162

Needles are 1 to 1³/₄ inches long, flat, spreading at right angles, appear crowded, and curve upward on the higher branches. Needles are pale blue-green, with white lines on both surfaces. From central Yukon and southeast Alaska to New Mexico, at sea level in the most northern settings and higher elevations from 2,000 to 12,000 feet in the southern extent of its range.

WHITE FIR page 164

Needles are 1¹/₂ to 3 inches long, flat and flexible, with almost no stalk, in two rows, at nearly right angles to the stem, and often curved upward on the higher branches. They are light blue-green to bluish green with whitish lines on both surfaces. Tips can either be short pointed, rounded, or even notched. From southeast Idaho to New Mexico, west to California and into the Baja, and north to southwest Oregon. At elevations from 5,500 to 11,000 feet in the south, to 2,000 feet in the north.

DOUGLAS-FIR page 152

Needles are ³/₄ to 1¹/₄ inches long, yellow-green to blue-green, and either in two rows or standing out from all sides of the twig. Needles are flat, flexible, and have tips that are usually rounded. The upper side is grooved; the underside has fine, parallel white lines on either side of the midrib. The needle has a small post at the base where it attaches to the twig. From British Columbia southward through all the western states; along the coast, from sea level to 2,000 feet in the north and up to 6,000 feet in the south; inland, above 2,000 feet in the north and up to 8,000 to 10,000 feet in the south.

BIGCONE DOUGLAS-FIR page 150

Needles are ³/₄ to 1¹/₄ inches long, blue-green, generally in two rows, and sharply pointed. Found in the mountains of southern California, from 900 to 8,000 feet, well south of the range of Douglas-fir.

MOUNTAIN HEMLOCK page 166

Needles are ¹/₄ to 1 inch long, blue-green with white lines on all surfaces, flattened, and grooved above and rounded beneath. They are blunt tipped and grow from all sides of the twigs or are crowded on the upper sides of short twigs. Needles have thin stalks that are attached to the stems with small pegs. Along the Pacific coast from southern Alaska to British Columbia, in the mountains south to central California, also in the Rocky Mountains in southeast British Columbia to northern Idaho and northeast Oregon. At elevations up to 3,500 feet in Alaska, 5,500 to 11,000 feet in the south.

WESTERN HEMLOCK page 168

Needles are $^1/_4$ to $^3/_4$ inch long, dark green, grooved above, with two faint white lines beneath, flat and uniform in width for their entire length, forming flat sprays. They are rounded or blunt at the tip and have very short basal stalks. Found in coastal areas from southwest Alaska to northwest California, also in the Rocky Mountains from southeast British Columbia to northern Idaho and northwest Montana. At elevations to 2,000 feet in coastal areas, up to 6,000 feet inland.

REDWOOD page 228

Redwoods have both scalelike and single, needlelike leaves. **Full key description on page 36.**

PACIFIC YEW page 242

Needles are $^1/_2$ to $^3/_4$ inch long, linear, dark yellow-green to blue-green above, paler with two whitish lines beneath, odorless, flat, soft, and short pointed at both ends. They are generally in two rows and spirally arranged on the twig. From southeastern Alaska, along the coast to Monterey Bay, California. Also found in the Sierra Nevada and from British Columbia and Washington to the western slopes of the Rockies in Montana and Idaho, up to 8,000 feet in elevation.

Stiff Single Needles

Compare your sample with the following trees:

> *Western Larch, California Nutmeg, Singleleaf Pinyon, Blue Spruce, Engelmann Spruce, Sitka Spruce, White Spruce*

WESTERN LARCH page 184

Needles are 1 to 1³/₄ inches long, pale green, three angled, and arranged in clusters of several needles on short spurs. They turn brilliant yellow before being shed in the fall. From southern British Columbia to northwest Oregon and central Idaho, at elevations from 2,000 to 5,500 feet in the north and to 7,000 feet in the south.

CALIFORNIA NUTMEG page 186

Needles are 1 to 2¹/₄ inches long, in rows of two, flat, stiff, and slightly curved, with a long sharp point at the tip, almost stalkless at the base. They are shiny dark green above, with two whitish lines beneath. They have a disagreeable odor when crushed. Found in the mountains of central and northern California, from 3,000 to 6,000 feet in elevation, and near sea level along the coast.

SINGLELEAF PINYON page 224
Needles are 1 to $2^{1}/_{4}$ inches long, dull gray-green, with whitish lines. They are stout, stiff, and sharp pointed, can be either straight or slightly curved, and resinous. Found in the Great Basin Region in Nevada, southern California, and northern Baja California, from 3,500 to 7,000 feet.

BLUE SPRUCE page 234
Needles are $^{3}/_{4}$ to $1^{1}/_{4}$ inches long, dull green to blue-green, with whitish lines, spreading from all sides of the twig. They are four angled (four sided) and sharp to the touch, stiff, with very short leafstalks; they have a pungent odor when crushed. Found in the Rocky Mountains from western Wyoming to Arizona and New Mexico, from 6,000 to 11,000 feet in elevation.

ENGELMANN SPRUCE page 236

Needles are ⁵/₈ to 1 inch long, four sided, dark or blue-green, with whitish lines. They are often blunt and are slender and flexible. They tend to be pointed forward on the stem rather than at a right angle and encircle all sides of the twig from short, peglike leafstalks. They have a skunklike odor when crushed. From central British Columbia and southwest Alberta southeast to New Mexico, at elevations of 1,500 to 12,000 feet in British Columbia and Alberta, and 9,000 to 12,000 feet in the central and southern Rockies.

SITKA SPRUCE page 238

Needles are ⁵/₈ to 1 inch long, bright yellow-green above, blue-green and waxy below. They are flattened, slighty keeled, and have a very sharp point. Needles extend outward at right angles from all sides of the twig. Found along the west coast from northern California, northward, within 30 miles of the Pacific coast and in the foggy rain forest.

WHITE SPRUCE page 240

Needles are ¹/₂ to ³/₄ inch long, four sided, blue-green, and waxy. The tip is pointed but not sharp to the touch. Needles crowd the upper side of the branch. When crushed, they have a pungent odor. From the northernmost limits of tree cover in northern Canada and Alaska, east to Labrador, south to Maine, and west to Montana and British Columbia, from sea level to 5,000 feet in elevation.

Bundled Needles

If the needles are bundled together with two, three, four, or five needles to a bundle, see *Two Needles per Bundle* below, *Three Needles per Bundle* on page 49, *Four Needles per Bundle* on page 53, or *Five Needles per Bundle* on page 53.

Two Needles per Bundle

Compare your sample with the following trees:

> *Bishop Pine, Lodgepole Pine, Rocky Mountain Ponderosa Pine, Twoneedle Pinyon*

BISHOP PINE page 190
Needles are 4 to 6 inches long, yellow-green or dull green, rigid, and slightly flattened, with a blunt point. Found in widely scattered groves along the California coastline from northern California to the Baja, from sea level to 1,000 feet.

LODGEPOLE PINE page 204
Needles are 1 to 3 inches long, yellow-green to dark green, stout, and often twisted. In Alaska and British Columbia from sea level to 2,000 feet; in Oregon and Washington up to 6,000 feet; in California up to 11,500 feet; and in the Rocky Mountains from 6,000 to 11,000 feet.

ROCKY MOUNTAIN PONDEROSA PINE page 208

There are several varieties of Ponderosa Pine. The Rocky Mountain variety (var. *scopulorum*) usually has two needles per bundle; needles are 4 to 8 inches long, yellow-green to dark gray-green, stout, flexible, with a turpentine odor when crushed. Found in the Rocky Mountains in southwest North Dakota, Montana, Idaho, and south to Arizona, New Mexico, and western Texas. (See also *Three Needles per Bundle* on page 49.)

TWONEEDLE PINYON page 226

Needles are $^3/_4$ to 2 inches long, light green, and stout. They may be tightly pressed against each other and look like one needle. Occasionally, there may be one needle or three needles per bundle. Broadly distributed in the southern Rocky Mountains from Utah and Colorado south to New Mexico and Arizona, from 5,000 to 7,000 feet.

Three Needles per Bundle

Compare your sample with the following trees:
> *Apache Pine, California Foothill Pine, Coulter Pine, Jeffrey Pine, Knobcone Pine, Monterey Pine, Ponderosa Pine, Mexican Pinyon*

APACHE PINE page 188

Needles are 8 to 12 inches long, dull green, and stout. They appear crowded at the ends of very stout twigs, sometimes drooping or spreading widely. Rarely in bundles of two or five. From southeastern Arizona and southwest New Mexico south into Mexico, at elevations of 5,000 to 8,200 feet.

CALIFORNIA FOOTHILL PINE page 194

Needles are 8 to 12 inches long, gray-green, many with white lines, flexible, slender, and drooping. Brown cones are 6 to 10 inches long and weigh more than 1 pound, bending downward from long stalks. Distinctive gray cast makes this tree identifiable from a distance. Found in the Coast Ranges and western slopes of the Sierra Nevada in California, at elevations from 1,000 to 3,000 feet.

COULTER PINE page 196
Needles are 8 to 12 inches long, light gray-green with many white lines, rigid, sharp pointed, appearing crowded at the ends of stout brown twigs. Cones are very large and can weigh 4 to 6 pounds when green. From central to southern California and northern Baja California, from 3,000 to 6,000 feet in elevation.

JEFFREY PINE page 198
Needles are 5 to 10 inches long, light gray-green or blue-green, with white lines on all surfaces, stout, stiff, and twisted. They sometimes grow in bundles of two or three on the same tree. Crushed needles and twigs have a pleasant scent, like vanilla, lemon, or pineapple. From southwest Oregon through the Sierra Nevada, especially on the eastern slopes, to western Nevada and southern California, from 6,000 to 9,000 feet.

KNOBCONE PINE page 200
Needles are 3 to 7 inches long, yellow-green, slender, and rigid. In the mountains of southwestern Oregon along the Coast Ranges, into northern and central California, at elevations from 1,000 to 4,000 feet.

MONTEREY PINE page 206
Needles are 4 to 6 inches long, shiny green, slender, and flexible. Relatively rare, this tree is found in isolated locations in central California in the fog belt to about 6 miles inland to 1,000 feet in elevation.

PONDEROSA PINE page 208

There are several varieties of Ponderosa Pine. Ponderosa Pine (var. *ponderosa*) usually has three needles per bundle; needles are 4 to 8 inches long, yellow-green to dark gray-green, stout, and flexible, with a turpentine odor when crushed. Found in the mountains of the Pacific Coast region from southern British Columbia to southern California and western Nevada from sea level to 7,600 feet in elevation. (See also Ponderosa Pine in *Two Needles per Bundle* on page 48.)

MEXICAN PINYON page 220

Needles are 1 to 2¹/₂ inches long, green, with white lines on several surfaces, slender, and flexible. Rarely, needles are two per bundle. From the Trans-Pecos and southeast Arizona south into central Mexico, from 5,000 to 7,500 feet.

Four Needles per Bundle
Compare your sample with *Parry Pinyon*:

PARRY PINYON page 222
Needles are 1 to $2^1/4$ inches long, bright green with whitish lines on inner surfaces, sharp pointed, stout, and stiff. Limited in range; found in southern California and Baja California, from 4,000 to 6,000 feet.

Five Needles per Bundle
Compare your sample with the following trees:
> *Bristlecone Pine, Foxtail Pine, Great Basin Bristlecone Pine, Limber Pine, Southwestern White Pine, Sugar Pine, Torrey Pine, Western White Pine, Whitebark Pine*

BRISTLECONE PINE page 192
Needles are $3/4$ to $1^1/2$ inches long, bright blue-green, some having small drops of white resin on the outer surface and a noticeable groove. Needles are stout, stiff, and clustered at the ends of twigs, creating a bushy, foxtail appearance. Found on high ridges and slopes in Colorado, northern New Mexico, and northern Arizona, from 7,500 to 11,200 feet.

FOXTAIL PINE page 192

Needles are ³/₄ to 1¹/₂ inches long, bright blue-green, with no groove. Needles are stout, stiff, and clustered at the ends of twigs, creating a bushy, foxtail appearance. Found in the mountains of northern California and the Sierra Nevada, from 5,000 to 11,500 feet.

GREAT BASIN BRISTLECONE PINE page 192

Needles are ³/₄ to 1¹/₂ inches long, bright blue-green, with a few white resin deposits. Needles are stout, stiff, and clustered at the ends of twigs, creating a bushy, foxtail appearance. Needles are not grooved. Found in Utah, Nevada, and eastern California, at elevations from 5,600 to 11,200 feet.

LIMBER PINE page 202

Needles are 2 to 3¹/₂ inches long, light to dark green, with fine white lines on all surfaces, slender, and clustered at the ends of twigs. Twigs are extremely flexible and tough and can be tied in knots. From Alberta southward through the Rocky Mountains and into southern California, at elevations from 4,000 to 10,000 feet in the north, up to 11,800 feet in California.

SOUTHWESTERN WHITE PINE page 210

Needles are 2¹/₂ to 3¹/₂ inches long, with a sheath that sheds in the first season. Bright green, with white lines on inner surfaces, they are slender and finely toothed near the tip. From the Trans-Pecos to east-central Arizona to northern Mexico, at elevations from 6,300 to 9,900 feet.

SUGAR PINE page 212

Needles are $2^3/4$ to 4 inches long, blue-green to gray-green, often silvery, with white lines on all surfaces. They are thin, stiff, pointed, and spirally twisted. Cones are huge and can be as long as 26 inches and 4 to 5 inches in diameter when open. In the mountains of western Oregon south through the Sierra Nevada and into southern California, extending into northern Baja California, at altitudes of 1,000 to 5,000 feet in the north, 2,000 to 8,000 feet in the Sierra Nevada, and 4,000 to 10,000 feet in the south.

TORREY PINE page 214

Needles are 8 to 13 inches long, dark gray-green, with white lines, stiff, stout, and crowded in large clusters at the ends of very stout twigs. This is the rarest of North American pines, with only a few thousand trees, most of which are found in Torrey Pines State Natural Reserve, in California.

WESTERN WHITE PINE page 216

Needles are 2 to 4 inches long, waxy, blue-green, with two to six rows of fine white lines on the lower side, and are straight, slender, and flexible. Needles persist for three or four years. Found along the Pacific coast from southwest British Columbia through the mountains of California to the Sierra Nevada, also in the northern Rocky Mountains from British Columbia southeast to Idaho and northwest Montana. In the north from sea level to 3,500 feet; from 6,000 to 10,000 feet in the south.

WHITEBARK PINE page 218

Needles are 1 to $2^3/4$ inches long, dull green, with faint white lines on all sides, stiff, pointed, with clusters crowded together at the ends of twigs. From central British Columbia south to central California and from Alberta through Montana, Idaho, and Wyoming, at elevations from 4,500 to 7,000 feet in the north, 8,000 to 12,000 feet in the south.

2. BROAD AND FLAT LEAVES

a. If your broad, flat leaves are large and fan shaped, go to *Large Fan-shaped Leaves* on page 59.

b. If your leaves are in an opposite arrangement and are simple, go to *Opposite Simple Leaves* on page 60.

c. If your leaves are in an opposite arrangement and are compound, go to *Opposite Compound Leaves* on page 64.

d. If your leaves are in an alternate arrangement and are simple, go to *Alternate Simple Leaves* on page 68.

e. If your leaves are in an alternate arrangement and are compound, go to *Alternate Compound Leaves* on page 90.

Large Fan-shaped Leaves

Compare your sample with *California Fan Palm*:

CALIFORNIA FAN PALM page 354

Numerous evergreen fan-shaped leaves spread at the top of the tree. Leafstalks are 3 to 5 feet long, stout, and have hooked spines along the edges. Gray-green leaf blades are 3 to 5 feet in diameter, split into many narrow, folded, leathery segments. Leaf margins are frayed with threadlike fibers. Old, dead leaves hang down and form a thatchlike layer against the trunk. Southeast California, southwest Arizona, and northern Baja California, from 3,000 to 5,000 feet.

Opposite Simple Leaves

Compare your sample with the following trees:
> *Pacific Dogwood, Tasmanian Eucalyptus, Bigleaf Maple, Bigtooth Maple, Rocky Mountain Maple, Vine Maple, Wavyleaf Silktassel, Desert Willow*

PACIFIC DOGWOOD page 290

Simple untoothed leaves are opposite, $2^1/_2$ to $4^1/_2$ inches long and $1^1/_4$ to $2^3/_4$ inches wide, elliptical or egg-shaped, with slightly wavy edges. There are five or six long, curved veins on each side of the midvein. Green leaves are shiny and nearly hairless above, paler, with woolly hair beneath. Leaves turn bright orange or red in autumn. Showy, off-white flowers are 4 to 6 inches in diameter. From southwestern British Columbia to western Oregon, and in the mountains to southern California, from sea level to 6,000 feet in elevation.

BIGLEAF MAPLE page 318

Simple lobed leaves are opposite, 8 to 12 inches in diameter, and usually have five lobes. Including the long leafstalk, the length can be 16 to 24 inches. The tips of the lobes and leaf are bluntly pointed, but the sinuses are rounded. Leaves are dark green above, paler beneath. Leafstalks join the leaf blade in an inverted V. Generally a coastal tree found at sea level to 1,000 feet in British Columbia, and from 3,000 to 7,000 feet in the southern part of its range in southern California and the Sierra Nevada.

TASMANIAN EUCALYPTUS page 298

Simple untoothed leaves are both opposite and alternate (on the same tree), 4 to 12 inches long and 1 to 2 inches wide, narrowly elliptical, slightly curved, with a long-pointed tip. Leaves have smooth margins. Thick, leathery leaves are dull green and hairless on both surfaces. On young growth, leaves are opposite, more oval shaped, and have a blue or whitish bloom on the lower surface. Alternate leaves are found on older twigs. Found in coastal California.

BIGTOOTH MAPLE page 320

Simple lobed leaves are opposite, 2 to $3^{1}/_{4}$ inches long and wide, with three broad lobes and two smaller basal lobes with a few blunt teeth. There are three or five main veins. Leaves are shiny dark green above, paler with fine hairs beneath, and turn red or yellow in autumn. Found from southeast Idaho to northern Arizona, and east to southern New Mexico and the Trans-Pecos at elevations of 4,000 to 7,000 feet.

ROCKY MOUNTAIN MAPLE

page 322
Simple lobed leaves are opposite, $1^1/_2$ to $4^1/_2$ inches in length and width, and palmately veined, with three main veins. The leaf has three, sometimes five, short-pointed lobes with a double sawtoothed edge. In some instances, the lobes are so deep that the leaf is divided into a palmately compound leaf with the leaflets joining together at the hairless reddish leafstalk. The leaves are glossy dark green above, paler beneath. From southeast Alaska through British Columbia into western Oregon and Washington, also found throughout the Rockies from British Columbia, Idaho, and Montana to Arizona and New Mexico. Close to sea level in the north and from 5,000 to 9,000 feet in the south.

VINE MAPLE page 324

Simple lobed leaves are opposite, $2^1/_2$ to $4^1/_2$ inches wide and long, the outline of which almost forms a circle. There are 7 to 11 long, pointed lobes that are double sawtoothed, each lobe having a main vein that extends from a notched leaf base. Leaves are bright green above, paler beneath, with tufts of hair along the vein angles. They turn orange and red in the autumn. Long leafstalks have enlarged bases. The single fruits are paired and spread almost horizontally with reddish wings when young. Along the Pacific coast from southwest British Columbia to northern California, to 5,000 feet in elevation.

WAVYLEAF SILKTASSEL page 362

Simple untoothed leaves are opposite, 2 to $3^1/4$ inches long, and elliptical or egg shaped. Leaf margins are wavy and uneven. Leaves are leathery, dark shiny green, and hairless above; paler and covered with a coat of wool-like hair beneath. Found along the coast from southern Oregon to southern California, to 2,000 feet in elevation.

DESERT WILLOW page 289

Simple untoothed leaves are both opposite and alternate (on the same tree), linear, 3 to 6 inches long and $1/4$ to $3/8$ inch wide, long, and narrow. They are very long pointed at each end and can be straight or slightly curved. They have smooth margins, are light green, and can be hairy or sticky. Showy, bell-shaped flowers appear in 4-inch clusters from late spring to early summer. They are $1^1/4$ inches long and wide, whitish, with purple or pink edges and a yellow throat. From the Trans-Pecos and New Mexico west to southwest Utah and southern California, from 1,000 to 5,000 feet in elevation.

Opposite Compound Leaves

Compare your sample with the following trees:
> *California Ash, Fragrant Ash, Oregon Ash, Velvet Ash, California Buckeye, Blue Elderberry, Red Elderberry, Boxelder*

CALIFORNIA ASH page 250

Pinnately compound leaves are opposite and only $1^1/2$ to $4^1/2$ inches long. There are three to seven paired leaflets that are coarsely sawtoothed, $3/4$ to $1^1/2$ inches long, $1/4$ to $5/8$ inch wide. Leaflets are elliptical or obovate, short pointed at the base, either blunt or short pointed at the tip. They are dark green above and paler beneath. Found in California and northern Baja California, up to 3,500 feet in elevation.

FRAGRANT ASH page 252

Pinnately compound leaves are opposite, 3 to 7 inches long. There are usually seven leaflets, $1^1/2$ to $2^1/2$ inches long and $1/2$ to $3/4$ inch wide, paired with a single leaflet at the end. Leaflets are lancelike or oval and can be sharply sawtoothed or smooth on the margin. They are shiny dark green above, paler with some hairs beneath when young. White, fragrant, $5/8$-inch flowers with four petals form in branched clusters, 3 to 4 inches long. This is the only ash with white flower petals found east of California. Limited distribution at scattered locations from southern Texas through New Mexico and Arizona.

OREGON ASH page 254

Pinnately compound leaves are opposite, 5 to 12 inches long. There are five to nine stalkless leaflets, 2 to 5 inches long, 1 to 1½ inches wide, paired, with a single leaflet at the tip. Leaflets are elliptical and pointed; margins are smooth or slightly sawtoothed. Leaflets are light green above, paler and often hairy beneath. Coastal British Columbia southward to the San Francisco Bay, also along the western slopes of the Sierra Nevada, up to 3,000 feet in elevation.

VELVET ASH page 256

Pinnately compound leaves are opposite, 3 to 6 inches long. There are usually five short-stalked leaflets (sometimes up to nine), 1 to 3 inches long, ³/₈ to 1½ inches wide, paired, with a single leaflet at the tip. Leaflets are lancelike to elliptical, with points at the ends, and have either slightly wavy teeth or untoothed margins. They are shiny green above, paler with soft hairs beneath (sometimes hairless). The Trans-Pecos across southern New Mexico and Arizona and into southern California, from 2,500 to 7,500 feet in elevation.

CALIFORNIA BUCKEYE page 266

Palmately compound leaves are opposite, 6 to 10 inches in diameter, the outline of which nearly forms a circle. Typically, five stalked leaflets are joined together at the long main leafstalk, like fingers on a hand, and are 3 to 6 inches long and 1 to 2 inches wide. The leaflets have sharp points and fine-toothed edges. They are dark green above, paler below, with whitish hair. Fragrant flowers form showy white to rose-colored clusters that are 4 to 8 inches long. They bloom in late spring or early summer. Found only at lower elevations in California in the coastal mountains and in the Sierra Nevada, below 4,000 feet.

BLUE ELDERBERRY page 292

Pinnately compound leaves are opposite, 5 to 7 inches long. There are three to five leaflets, 1 to 5 inches long and $^3/_8$ to $1^1/_2$ inches wide, paired with a single leaflet at the tip. Leaflets are elliptical and pointed at the tip with an asymmetrical base and have edges that are finely sawtoothed with sharp teeth. Green above and paler below, the leaflets are slightly thick and leathery. During periods of drought, they turn yellow. Small $^1/_4$-inch yellow or white flowers form flat-topped clusters on the terminal branches. The clusters remain upright and can bloom throughout the year. Found throughout the West from western Alberta and southern British Columbia, south to northwest Mexico and the Trans-Pecos, at elevations to 5,000 feet.

RED ELDERBERRY page 294

Pinnately compound leaves are opposite, 5 to 10 inches long. There are five or seven individual leaflets, 2 to 5 inches long and 1 to 2 inches wide, paired, with a single leaflet at the tip. Leaflets are oval or lancelike, with a pointed tip and sometimes asymmetrical base, and have a toothed edge with teeth varying from fine to coarse. Leaflets are green, with very few hairs above, paler and hairy beneath. Small, creamy white flowers form in upright, ball-like clusters up to 4 inches in diameter. Coastal from southern Alaska to central California, up to 2,000 feet in elevation.

BOXELDER page 264

Pinnately compound leaves are opposite, 4 to 10 inches long, with three to seven leaflets that are 2 to 5 inches long and up to 3 inches wide. The leaflets are attached to the main leafstalk by short stalks. Leaflets are pointed at the tip but display considerable individual variability in shape, ranging from oval to lancelike. All are coarse toothed and may have one or more lobes. They are light green and smooth above, paler beneath with some light fuzz, notably along the leaf veins. Widely scattered throughout the Southwest, found from sea level to 8,000 feet.

Alternate Simple Leaves

1. If your leaves do not have lobes, see *Alternate Simple Leaves without Lobes* below.
2. If your leaves have lobes, go to *Alternate Simple Leaves with Lobes* on page 87.

Alternate Simple Leaves without Lobes

a. If your leaf has smooth, toothless margins, go to *Alternate Simple Leaves with Smooth Margins* on page 69.
b. If your leaf has fine teeth along the margins, go to *Alternate Simple Leaves with Fine-toothed Margins* on page 74.

c. If your leaf has coarse teeth along the margins, go to *Alternate Simple Leaves with Coarse-toothed Margins* on page 80.

d. If your leaf has double sawtoothed margins, go to *Alternate Simple Leaves with Double Sawtoothed Margins* on page 82.

e. If your leaf has smooth margins with spiny teeth, go to *Alternate Simple Leaves with Spiny Teeth* on page 84.

Alternate Simple Leaves with Smooth Margins

Compare your sample with the following trees:

Curl-leaf Cercocarpus, Giant Chinquapin, Tasmanian Eucalyptus, Netleaf Hackberry, California Laurel, Arizona Madrone, Pacific Madrone, Texas Madrone, Gray Oak, Silverleaf Oak, Desert Willow, Scouler's Willow

CURL-LEAF CERCOCARPUS page 272

Simple untoothed leaves are ever-green, alternate, $1/2$ to $1^1/4$ inches long, but only $3/8$ inch wide, elliptical, with smooth margins that are curled under. There are very prominent, grooved midveins on the leaves, but side veins are barely evident. The leaves are thick and leathery, shiny and dark green above, pale with fine hairs beneath, and clustered in groups at the ends of branchlets. Throughout the Great Basin and surrounding area, from 5,000 to 9,000 feet.

GIANT CHINQUAPIN page 280
Simple untoothed leaves are evergreen, alternate, 2 to 5 inches long
and ⁵/₈ to 1¹/₂ inches wide, lancelike
with a sharp point, smooth margins,
and slightly turned-under edges.
Leaves are thick and leathery, shiny
dark green with scales above, having
tiny yellow scales beneath. Leaves
turn yellow before falling. Along the
Pacific coast from southwest Washington to central California, also in
the Sierra Nevada of central California, from sea level to 1,500 feet elevation. The shrub form is found to
6,000 feet elevation.

TASMANIAN EUCALYPTUS page 298
There are both opposite and alternate leaves found on the same tree. **Full key
description on page 61.**

NETLEAF HACKBERRY page 300
Simple untoothed leaves are alternate, 1 to 2¹/₂ inches long and ³/₄ to 1¹/₂
inches wide, in two rows. Leaves are usually ovate, with a short or long point.
The base is asymmetrical and either rounded or slightly notched. Thick, dark
green leaves have three main veins and sometimes coarse teeth. Undersides are
yellow-green with a pronounced network of raised veins and slightly hairy. Its
gray, warty bark is this tree's most distinguishing characteristic. From Kansas
to central Texas, west through New Mexico and Arizona, with more scattered
occurrences in California, Oregon, Washington, Idaho, Utah, and Colorado, at
elevations from 1,500 to 6,000 feet.

CALIFORNIA LAUREL page 306

Simple untoothed leaves are evergreen, alternate, 2 to 5 inches long and $^1/_2$ to $1^1/_2$ inches wide, elliptical to lancelike, having a short-pointed to blunt tip and usually a V-shaped base. Thick, leathery leaves have a smooth, toothless margin that may turn under slightly. Leaves are shiny dark green to yellow-green above, pale and hairless beneath. When crushed, leaves give off a strong, camphorlike odor. Found from the Coos Bay area of southern Oregon along the coastal mountains and in the southern Sierra Nevada to the southern border of California. Found up to 1,500 feet in the north, from 2,000 to 6,000 feet in the south.

ARIZONA MADRONE page 312

Simple untoothed leaves are evergreen, alternate, $1^1/_2$ to 3 inches long, $^1/_2$ to 1 inch wide, lancelike, with a V-shaped base and pointed tip. Leaves are thick and stiff, shiny light green above, paler beneath. Whitish twigs have fine hairs when young and turn red-brown. Jug-shaped flowers can be white or pink and are found in branched clusters at the ends of twigs. The smooth bark is a distinctive red. Found in southeast Arizona, extreme southwest New Mexico, and northwest Mexico, at elevations from 4,000 to 8,000 feet.

PACIFIC MADRONE page 314

Simple untoothed leaves are ever-green, alternate, 2 to 5 inches long and 1 to 3 inches wide, oval to oblong, with blunt tips. Leaf margins are usually smooth, although some-times can be finely to coarsely toothed on vigorous growth. Thick, leathery leaves are shiny dark green on upper surfaces, paler or whitish beneath. Leaves are shed in the summer of their second year, turning red before falling. The slender twigs are green, red, or brown. Large clusters of small, bell-shaped, white flowers appear in early spring. The smooth bark is a dis-tinctive red. In coastal areas from southwest British Columbia through Washington and Oregon to southern California, also in the Sierra Nevada and on Santa Cruz Island, at eleva-tions up to 5,000 feet.

TEXAS MADRONE page 316

Simple untoothed leaves are evergreen, alternate, 1 to $3^1/2$ inches long, $5/8$ to $1^1/2$ inches wide, elliptical, with blunt tips and uneven bases. Thick, stiff leaves can be wavy or sometimes sawtoothed, shiny green above and slender and slightly hairy beneath. Slender leafstalks are hairy. Red twigs are covered with dense hairs when young and turn dark reddish brown and develop scales. Jug-shaped flowers can be white or pinkish and are found in upright, branched clusters at the ends of twigs. The smooth bark is a distinctive red. From central Texas, the Trans-Pecos, and southeast New Mexico, at elevations from 2,000 to 6,000 feet.

GRAY OAK page 344

Simple untoothed leaves are alternate, $^3/_4$ to 2 inches long and $^3/_8$ to $^3/_4$ inches wide, elliptical to ovate, sometimes with a few short teeth toward the tip, slightly thickened or rigid. The base can be notched or rounded. Leaves are gray-green or blue-green, shiny, and slightly hairy above, dull and finely hairy with slightly raised veins beneath. The Trans-Pecos through New Mexico to central Arizona, at elevations from 5,000 to 7,000 feet.

SILVERLEAF OAK page 350

Simple untoothed leaves are evergreen, alternate, 2 to 4 inches long, lancelike, with a sharp-pointed tip, rounded at the base, with smooth margins that may be rolled under. Leaves are thick, leathery, shiny yellow-green above, with dense, woolly hairs beneath. The Trans-Pecos to southeastern Arizona and northern Mexico, from 5,000 to 6,000 feet in elevation.

DESERT WILLOW page 289
There are both opposite and alternate leaves found on the same tree. **Full key description on page 63.**

SCOULER'S WILLOW page 382
Simple untoothed leaves are alternate, 2 to 5 inches long, and $1/2$ to $1^1/2$ inches wide, elliptical to oval, widest at the tip, with a short, blunt point. Leaf margins can be smooth or have sparse, wavy teeth. Leaves are dark green above, whitish with gray or red hair beneath. Central Alaska south to Idaho and California and east to the Black Hills of South Dakota; also in the mountains of southern New Mexico, at elevations to 10,000 feet.

Alternate Simple Leaves with Fine-toothed Margins

Compare your sample with the following trees:
> *White Alder, Cascara Buckthorn, Birchleaf Cercocarpus, Bitter Cherry, Black Cherry, Chokecherry, Black Cottonwood, Narrowleaf Cottonwood, Quaking Aspen, Goodding's Willow, Pacific Willow*

WHITE ALDER page 248
Simple toothed leaves are alternate, 2 to $3^1/2$ inches long and $1^1/2$ to 2 inches wide, oval to nearly round in shape, with fine teeth. There are 9 to 12 pairs of parallel veins coming from the midvein. Leaves are dull, dark green, nearly hairless above, and may have tiny gland dots; light yellow-green and slightly hairy beneath. Found in Washington and western Idaho, south through the Coast Ranges of California and in the Sierra Nevada, to western Nevada and southern California. From sea level up to 8,000 feet elevation, but generally below 5,000 feet.

CASCARA BUCKTHORN page 268
Simple toothed leaves are alternate, 2 to 6 inches long and 1 to $2^1/2$ inches wide, oblong to oval, with a finely toothed or wavy margin. There are 10 to 15 parallel side veins prominently raised on the underside. The leaf is dull green and nearly hairless above, paler and slightly hairy beneath. Young plants can be evergreen. Found within a few hundred miles of the Pacific coast from British Columbia to northern California and also in the Rockies in northern Idaho, Washington, and Montana, at elevations to 5,000 feet.

BIRCHLEAF CERCOCARPUS page 270
Simple toothed leaves resemble birch leaves and are alternate, evergreen, 1 to $1^1/4$ inches long and $3/8$ to $1/2$ inch wide, elliptical, broadly rounded, and finely toothed toward the tip, with five to eight parallel side veins. Leaves are dark green above, pale green or grayish and slightly hairy beneath. From southern Oregon to Baja California and into Arizona, from 3,500 to 6,500 feet.

BITTER CHERRY page 274

Simple toothed leaves are alternate, 1 to $2^{1}/_{2}$ inches long and $^{3}/_{8}$ to $1^{1}/_{2}$ inches wide, elliptical or oblong, short pointed at the base, rounded or blunt at the tip. Margins are finely sawtoothed. Leaves are dark green above, paler and sometimes hairy beneath. From British Columbia, Washington, and western Montana, south to southwest New Mexico and southern California, to 9,000 feet in elevation.

BLACK CHERRY page 276

Simple toothed leaves are alternate, 2 to 5 inches long and $1^{1}/_{4}$ to 2 inches wide, having one or two dark red glands at the base, elliptical, with margins that are finely sawtoothed with teeth that are curved or blunt. Slightly thickened leaves are shiny dark green above, paler beneath, with dense pale or reddish-brown hairs along the midvein. The Trans-Pecos through New Mexico and Arizona, from 4,500 feet to 7,500 feet in elevation.

CHOKECHERRY page 278

Simple toothed leaves are alternate, $1^{1}/_{2}$ to $3^{1}/_{4}$ inches long, and egg shaped or elliptical, with a U- or heart-shaped base and 8 to 11 side veins. Leaf margins have fine, sharp-pointed teeth. Leaves are dark green and shiny above, lighter and some-times hairy, especially along the mid-vein, beneath. The leafstalk is often reddish. Widespread over much of the northern half of the U.S. and Canada and scattered throughout all the west-ern states. Found up to 8,000 feet in elevation.

BLACK COTTONWOOD
page 282

Simple toothed leaves are alternate, 3 to 6 inches long and 2 to 4 inches wide, somewhat triangular in shape, with a pointed tip and rounded base. The margin has fine, wavy, rounded teeth. Leaves are dark green and smooth above and a contrasting rusty brown, silver white, or paler green beneath. Leafstalks are $1^{1}/_{2}$ to 3 inches long, have a round cross-section, and tend to be hairy. From Alaska along the Pacific coast to the Baja; also found throughout the Rockies in Alberta, Montana, Idaho, Oregon, and Washington; and scat-tered through Nevada. At sea level to 2,000 feet in the north, to 9,000 feet in the south.

NARROWLEAF COTTONWOOD page 286

Simple toothed leaves are alternate, 2 to 5 inches long and $^1/_2$ to 1 inch wide, willowlike, lancelike, with a long narrow tip and rounded base with short leafstalks. Leaf margins are finely sawtoothed. Leaves are shiny green above and paler beneath; they turn a dull yellow in fall. Southern Alberta south through the Rocky Mountains to the Mexican border, at elevations from 3,000 to 8,000 feet.

QUAKING ASPEN page 258

Simple toothed leaves are alternate, $1^1/_2$ to 3 inches long, somewhat rounded, with an acute point, rounded base, and rounded teeth along the margin. Leaves are lustrous green above and paler beneath; they turn brilliant golden yellow in fall. Leafstalks are flat. Across North America from Alaska to Newfoundland, south through British Columbia, and in the Rocky Mountains south to southern Arizona and New Mexico from sea level to 10,000 feet.

GOODDING'S WILLOW page 378
Simple toothed leaves are alternate, 2 to 5 inches long, $^3/_8$ to $^3/_4$ inch wide, lance shaped, often with a slight curve to one side and a long point. Leaf margins are finely sawtoothed. Leaves are dark shiny green above and lighter green beneath. The Trans-Pecos west through New Mexico and Arizona to northern California at elevations to 5,000 feet.

PACIFIC WILLOW page 380
Simple toothed leaves are alternate, 2 to 5 inches long, $^1/_2$ to 1 inch wide, narrow, and generally oblong or lancelike, with very long points and a rounded base. They are finely sawtoothed, initially hairy, becoming hairless. Leaves are shiny green above, white beneath. Leafstalks are slender. From central and southeast Alaska east to Saskatchewan and south to southern New Mexico and southern California, mostly in the mountains, at elevations to 8,000 feet.

Alternate Simple Leaves with Coarse-toothed Margins

Compare your sample with the following trees:

> *Siberian Elm, Black Hawthorn, Fremont Cottonwood, Saskatoon Serviceberry, Tanoak*

SIBERIAN ELM page 296

Simple toothed leaves are alternate, $^3/_4$ to 2 inches long and $^1/_2$ to 1 inch wide, oval, with a slightly asymmetrical, blunt base, and a sharp tip. Leaves are slightly thickened, have a sawtoothed margin and many straight side veins. They are dark green above, paler beneath. Leaves turn yellow in autumn. From Minnesota south to Kansas and west to Utah, from 1,000 to 5,000 feet in elevation.

BLACK HAWTHORN page 302

Simple toothed leaves are alternate, 1 to 3 inches long and $^5/_8$ to 2 inches wide, oval, and tend to be broader near the sharp-pointed tip. Leaf margins are sawtoothed, but some teeth have deeper cuts that create a lobed appearance. Leaves are dark green above, paler beneath. The base of the leaf is long, narrow, and pointed. Shiny, red, slender twigs are hairless and may have straight, sometimes curved, strong, 1-inch spines. From southern Alaska throughout British Columbia and as far south as central California, and farther east between Saskatchewan and New Mexico. Near sea level in the north, up to 6,000 feet elevation in the south.

FREMONT COTTONWOOD
page 284
Simple toothed leaves are alternate, 2 to 3 inches long and wide, triangular, short pointed, and nearly straight across at the base, with short, irregular curved teeth. Leaves are thick, shiny yellow-green, with long, flattened leafstalks. They turn bright yellow in the fall. Southwest Colorado to California, south to the Mexican border, at elevations to 6,500 feet.

SASKATOON SERVICEBERRY
page 360
Simple toothed leaves are alternate, $3/4$ to 2 inches in diameter, almost round, with coarse teeth above the middle of the leaf. Seven to nine straight veins are visible on each side of the midvein. Leaves are dark green above, lighter and hairy beneath. From coastal Alaska to northern California and east to western Minnesota, at elevations to 6,000 feet.

TANOAK page 370
Simple toothed leaves are evergreen, alternate, $2^1/2$ to 5 inches long, $^3/4$ to $2^1/2$ inches wide, and generally oblong or lancelike. Leaf margins are wavy, with coarse teeth and can be curled under. They are leathery and shiny dark green above, brownish and covered with woolly hair, especially in the spring, beneath. In the fall, leaves become more bluish white and lose much of their pubescence. From southern Oregon to southern California along the Coast Ranges, also in the Sierra Nevada; at sea level to 5,000 feet elevation.

Alternate Simple Leaves with Double Sawtoothed Margins
Compare your sample with the following trees:
> *Arizona Alder, Red Alder, Paper Birch, Water Birch*

ARIZONA ALDER page 244
Simple toothed leaves are alternate, $1^1/2$ to $3^1/4$ inches long, 1 to $1^1/2$ inches wide, elliptical, and have seven to ten nearly parallel side veins. The margins are double sawtoothed. Leaves are dark green and essentially hairless above, paler and covered with fine hair beneath. Tufts of reddish fuzz are found in the angles between the veins. From Arizona and southwest New Mexico, from 4,500 to 7,500 feet elevation.

RED ALDER page 246

Simple toothed leaves are alternate, 3 to 6 inches long and 1½ to 3 inches wide, oval, with 10 to 15 pairs of straight, parallel side veins. Leaf margins turn under slightly and have a deeply double sawtoothed edge. Leaves are dark green above, paler with rusty fuzz on the midrib and major veins beneath. The short, ¼- to ½-inch leafstalk is grooved. Found within 50 miles of the Pacific coast from Alaska to California but also in some interior areas of Washington and Idaho, below 2,500 feet elevation.

PAPER BIRCH page 260

Simple toothed leaves are alternate, 2 to 4 inches long and 1½ to 2 inches wide, oval, with a long point. They are coarsely double sawtoothed and have a rounded base. Leaves are smooth and dull, dark green above, paler and light green and nearly hairless beneath. Leaves turn light yellow in the fall. Widespread across Canada and Alaska but also found in northern Washington, Idaho, and western Montana, to 4,000 feet in elevation.

WATER BIRCH page 262
Simple toothed leaves are alternate, 1 to 2 inches long, ³/₄ to 1 inch wide, ovate, pointed at the tip, with rounded leaf bases, and four or five pairs of parallel side veins coming from the midvein. Margins are double sawtoothed. Leaves are dark green above, paler yellow-green with tiny gland dots beneath. From British Columbia to southern Manitoba in Canada, and across the northern tier states from Washington to North Dakota and south to central California, Nevada, Arizona, and New Mexico, at elevations to 8,000 feet.

Alternate Simple Leaves with Spiny Teeth

Compare your sample with the following trees:
Arizona White Oak, California Live Oak, Canyon Live Oak, Emory Oak, Interior Live Oak

ARIZONA WHITE OAK page 330
Simple toothed leaves are evergreen, alternate, 1¹/₂ to 3 inches long, ³/₄ to 1¹/₂ inches wide, and oblong. Leaf margins are somewhat wavy and spiny. They are dull blue-green, have sunken veins, and are hairless above, with hairs and raised veins beneath. Leaves are shed in the spring as new ones develop. The Trans-Pecos, New Mexico, and Arizona, also in Mexico, from 5,000 to 7,500 feet in elevation.

CALIFORNIA LIVE OAK page 336

Simple toothed leaves are evergreen, alternate, $3/4$ to 3 inches long and $1/2$ to $1^1/2$ inches wide, hollylike, oblong or elliptical, and may be either short pointed or rounded at each end. Edges turn under and have spiny teeth. Thick, leathery leaves are shiny green above and yellow-green and sometimes hairy beneath. Coast Ranges from central California to Baja California, from sea level to 4,500 feet elevation.

CANYON LIVE OAK page 338

Simple toothed leaves are evergreen, alternate, 1 to 3 inches long and $1/2$ to $1^1/2$ inches wide, elliptical or oval shaped. Hollylike leaves on sprouts or young trees have a spiny or prickly leaf margin whereas leaves on older trees have smooth margins. Initially, thick, leathery leaves are shiny, yellow-green, and hairy above, turning dark blue-green and hairless in the second year, persisting for three or four years. From southwest Oregon through the Coast Ranges and the Sierra Nevada to Baja California, at elevations of 1,000 to 6,000 feet, and from east to central and southern Arizona and southwestern New Mexico, at elevations of 5,500 to 7,500 feet.

EMORY OAK page 340

Simple toothed leaves are evergreen, alternate, 1 to 2^1/$_2$ inches long and ^{3}/$_8$ to 1 inch wide, somewhat lancelike, with a short, spiny point at the tip. Margins can be smooth but most are wavy with a few short, spiny teeth. Nearly hairless leaves are shiny yellow-green on both surfaces, thick, stiff, and leathery. Leaves are shed in the spring as new leaves develop. The Trans-Pecos to central Arizona and south to northwest Mexico, at elevations from 4,000 to 8,000 feet.

INTERIOR LIVE OAK page 346

Simple toothed leaves are evergreen, alternate, 1 to 2 inches long and ^{1}/$_2$ to 1^1/$_4$ inches wide. The hollylike leaves are elliptical to lancelike, thick, leathery, with a sharp point at the tip and often thick, spiny teeth on the margins. The hairless leaves are shiny dark green above, light yellow with a dense network of veins beneath. They remain on the tree for two years. Found in California on Mount Shasta and southward, primarily in the foothills of the Sierra Nevada and along the Coast Ranges, from 1,000 feet to 5,000 feet elevation.

Alternate Simple Leaves with Lobes
Compare your sample with the following trees:
> *Blue Oak, California Black Oak, Gambel Oak, Oregon White Oak, Valley Oak, Arizona Sycamore, California Sycamore*

BLUE OAK page 332
Simple lobed leaves are alternate, $1^1/4$ to 4 inches long and $^3/4$ to $1^3/4$ inches wide, elliptical or oblong, with rounded or blunt ends. Leaves have short leafstalks and can be lobed, shallowly indented, or unlobed, with untoothed or toothed margins. They are thin yet firm, pale blue-green, almost hairless above, and paler and somewhat hairy beneath. Interior valleys from northern to southern California in the Coast Ranges and the Sierra Nevada, from 3,000 to 3,500 feet.

CALIFORNIA BLACK OAK
page 334
Simple lobed leaves are alternate, 3 to 8 inches long and 2 to 5 inches wide, elliptical, with five to seven deep lobes that are bristled at the tips. Leaves are dark green above, paler green and often hairy beneath. Leaves have 1- to 2-inch leafstalks. From southern Oregon south along the Pacific coast and in the Sierra Nevada to southern California, from 1,000 to 8,000 feet in elevation.

GAMBEL OAK page 342

Simple lobed leaves are alternate, 2 to 6 inches long and 1¼ to 2½ inches wide, elliptical or oblong, rounded at the tip and pointed at the base, with short leafstalks. Leaves have five to nine rounded lobes and deep sinuses. They are slightly leathery and shiny green above, lighter with soft hairs beneath, turning yellow or red in the fall. From northern Utah east to southern Wyoming, south to west Texas and southern Arizona, at elevations from 5,000 to 8,000 feet.

OREGON WHITE OAK page 348

Simple lobed leaves are alternate, 4 to 6 inches long and 2 to 4 inches wide, oblong or obovate, and either rounded or blunt at both ends. Margins are smooth and slightly rolled under. The leaf has five to seven lobes that are blunt or slighty toothed, separated by deep, narrow sinuses. Leaves are leathery, dark green, and smooth above, pale green with orange-brown hair beneath. The leafstalk is ¾ inch long and hairy. British Columbia southward to central California in the Coast Ranges and the Sierra Nevada, at elevations up to 3,000 feet in the north and from 1,000 to 5,000 feet in the south.

VALLEY OAK page 352

Simple lobed leaves are alternate, 2 to 4 inches long and 1¼ to 2½ inches wide, oblong or elliptical, with 7 to 11 deep lobes with sinuses that go halfway to the midvein. The lobes are rounded, and the larger lobes are notched at the end. Leaves are dark green and nearly hairless above, paler with fine hairs beneath, and have short leafstalks. From northern to southern California from the Sierra Nevada to the coast, up to 5,000 feet in elevation. Also found on Santa Cruz and Catalina Islands.

ARIZONA SYCAMORE page 366

The simple lobed leaves are alternate, 6 to 9 inches long and wide, star shaped, with three or five long, narrow, sharp-pointed lobes with sinuses that extend nearly halfway into the leaf. They have five main veins. Leaf margins are wavy and may have a few large teeth. Leaves are light green above, lighter and hairy beneath. Found in Arizona, southwest New Mexico, and northwest Mexico, from 2,000 to 6,000 feet in elevation.

CALIFORNIA SYCAMORE page 368

Simple lobed leaves are alternate, 6 to 9 inches long and wide, star shaped, with five long, narrow, sharp-pointed lobes with sinuses that extend nearly halfway into the leaf. Leaf margins are wavy and may have a few large teeth. Leaves are light green above, lighter and hairy beneath. Found in the Sierra Nevada and California Coast Ranges and Baja California, to 4,000 feet.

Alternate Compound Leaves

1. If your sample is pinnately compound, see *Alternate Pinnately Compound Leaves* below.
2. If your sample is bipinnately compound, go to *Alternate Bipinnately Compound Leaves* on page 94.

Alternate Pinnately Compound Leaves

Compare your sample with the following trees:

   Desert Ironwood, Black Locust, New Mexico Locust, Western Soapberry, Arizona Walnut, Little Walnut, Northern California Walnut

DESERT IRONWOOD page 304
Pinnately compound leaves are alternate, 1 to 2^1/$_4$ inches long, with two to ten pairs of tiny, oblong leaflets that have rounded tips and short-pointed bases. Blue-green leaflets are thick and have short stalks. The southwest corner of Arizona, southeast California, and northwest Mexico, to 2,500 feet in elevation.

BLACK LOCUST page 308
Pinnately compound leaves are alternate, 6 to 14 inches long, with 7 to 19 paired leaflets that are 1^1/$_2$ to 2 inches long and ^{1}/$_2$ to ^{3}/$_4$ inch wide. They can be elliptical or oval shaped, with smooth margins and a small bristled tip. Leaf surfaces are a dull, dark blue-green above, paler beneath. Leaves turn yellow in fall. There are pairs of stout, ^{1}/$_4$- to ^{1}/$_2$-inch spines at leaf nodes. Originally, Black Locust was found in the East, but it has become naturalized throughout the U.S. and southern Canada.

NEW MEXICO LOCUST
page 310
Pinnately compound leaves are alternate, 4 to 10 inches long, with 13 to 21 paired, elliptical leaflets that are $^1/_2$ to $1^1/_2$ inches long and $^1/_4$ to 1 inch wide. Pale blue-green leaflets are rounded at the ends and have a tiny bristle at the tip. They are finely hairy when young with short stalks. There are pairs of stout, brown, $^1/_4$- to $^1/_2$-inch spines at leaf nodes. Southeast Nevada to central and southern Colorado, south to western Texas, and west to southeast Arizona, at elevations from 4,000 to 8,500 feet.

WESTERN SOAPBERRY
page 364
Pinnately compound leaves are alternate, 5 to 8 inches long, with 11 to 19 paired leaflets that are nearly opposite, $1^1/_2$ to 3 inches long and $^3/_8$ to $^3/_4$ inch wide. Leaflets have very short stalks, are curved, lancelike, and have a toothless margin and pointed tip. Leathery leaflets are dull green above, hairy with noticeable veins beneath. From Missouri south to Louisiana and then westward to southern New Mexico and Arizona and north to Colorado, at elevations to 6,000 feet.

ARIZONA WALNUT page 372

Pinnately compound leaves are alternate, 7 to 14 inches long, with 9 to 13 lancelike leaflets that are 2 to 4 inches long, slightly wavy, and coarsely sawtoothed. The yellow-green leaves are hairy when young, becoming hairless. Found in central Texas west to Arizona and south into Mexico, at elevations from 2,000 to 7,000 feet.

LITTLE WALNUT page 374

Pinnately compound leaves are alternate, 8 to 13 inches long, and have 11 to 25 narrow, lancelike leaflets that are 2 to 3 inches long. Leaves are sharp pointed, usually curvy, with finely sawtoothed edges, and yellow-green. Leafstalks on leaflets are very short. From southwest Kansas through Oklahoma and Texas and southward into northeastern New Mexico, at elevations from 1,500 to 4,000 feet.

NORTHERN CALIFORNIA WALNUT page 376

Pinnately compound leaves are alternate, 7 to 12 inches long, with 15 to 19 leaflets, $2^1/2$ to 4 inches long, with sawtoothed margins. The leafstalk is covered with soft hair. Green, stalkless leaflets are shiny on upper surfaces, paler and hairy below, with a tuft of hair along leaf veins. Found only in central California, at elevations to 500 feet.

Alternate Bipinnately Compound Leaves

Compare your sample with the following trees:

Honey Mesquite, Velvet Mesquite, Blue Paloverde, Yellow Paloverde

HONEY MESQUITE page 326

Bipinnately compound leaves are alternate, 3 to 8 inches long. The main stem splits in two, with each side stem having 7 to 17 pairs of short, $3/8$- to $1^1/4$-inch, stalkless, narrow, oblong leaflets, which are yellow-green and nearly hairless. From eastern Texas and southwest Oklahoma west to southwest Utah and southern California, to 4,500 feet in elevation. Also naturalized as far north as Kansas and southeast Colorado.

VELVET MESQUITE page 328
Bipinnately compound leaves are alternate, 5 to 6 inches long. The main stem splits into 1 or 2 pairs of side stems, with each side stem having 15 to 20 pairs of $1/4$- to $1/2$-inch, narrow, oblong leaflets that are dull green and stalkless. Southwest New Mexico west to central Arizona and northwest Mexico, from 500 to 5,500 feet in elevation.

BLUE PALOVERDE page 356
Bipinnately compound leaves are alternate, few, and scattered, appearing in spring and quickly shed. Leaves are 1 inch long and have a short main stem that forks into two side stems. Each side stem has two or three pairs of oblong leaflets that are $1/4$ inch long and pale blue-green. Flowers are $3/4$ inch wide with five bright yellow petals. The largest petals may have a few red spots. Two-inch clusters of four to five flowers cover the tree in spring. Trees may reflower in late summer. Southeast California and central and southern Arizona, also northwest Mexico, at elevations up to 4,000 feet.

YELLOW PALOVERDE page 358

The bipinnately compound leaves are alternate, few, and scattered, appearing in spring and quickly shed. Leaves are 1 inch long and have a short main stem that forks into two side stems. Each side stem has three to seven pairs of tiny elliptical leaflets that are pale yellow-green. Twigs are short, stout, and end in a 2-inch-long straight spine. Clusters of flowers that are $1/2$ inch wide with five petals (three are pale yellow and the two largest are white or cream colored) appear in spring. From Arizona to southeast California and northwest Mexico, at elevations from 500 to 4,000 feet.

4

Winter Identification Guide

Identifying deciduous trees (trees that lose their leaves) in winter can be challenging; there are characteristics other than leaves, however, that can be used to help in identification. If your sample tree has needles, scales, or persistent leaves, the Leaf Identification Guide should be used. If not, the Winter Identification Guide can help.

The winter guide is similar to the leaf guide. To use it, you will need to examine your tree and consider a series of questions that focus on several characteristics (opposite or alternate arrangement, leaf scars, bark, thorns, and so on) to help you narrow down the field of possible candidates. Then, within the field of candidates, other identifying characteristics are described, and the geographic range where the species is typically found is outlined. It is important that you understand the terminology in order to make correct choices. Chapter 1 and the Glossary provide descriptions and examples of many of the characteristics discussed in this guide.

There may be other clues that can help with identification of your sample. Fallen leaves and fruit can be considered (be aware, however, that this material could be from neighboring trees). Persistent leaves or fruit may be evident. If the characteristics seem to match, refer to the full Species Account for more in-depth descriptions.

Even after careful consideration of the questions, you may find that the tree choices do not match your sample. Do not be discouraged! If this happens, try again, making a different choice where you had a questionable selection. You may get a different answer and correctly identify your tree.

First determine the arrangement of your tree. Is it opposite or alternate?

A. If your tree is opposite, go to *1. Opposite* on page 99.

B. If your tree is alternate, go to *2. Alternate* on page 105.

1. OPPOSITE

Trees with opposite arrangements are divided into those with shield-shaped leaf scars and those with crescent-shaped leaf scars. Skilled botanists would look at whether the leaf scars encircle the twig as well as the number and size of structures within the leaf scar. That kind of detailed analysis is beyond the scope of this book. Therefore, further identification will rely upon more general tree descriptions that include bark, characteristics particular to the species (buds, twigs, and so on), tree size, and the range where the species is typically found.

If the leaf scars are shield shaped, go to *a. Shield-shaped Leaf Scars* on page 100.

If the leaf scars are thin and crescent shaped, go to *b. Crescent-shaped Leaf Scars* on page 101.

Shield-shaped Leaf Scars

Compare your sample with the following trees:
California Ash, Velvet Ash, California Buckeye, Blue Elderberry, Red Elderberry

CALIFORNIA ASH page 250
The light gray bark is rough and scaly. A small tree up to 20 feet tall. Found in California and northern Baja California, up to 3,500 feet in elevation.

VELVET ASH page 256
The bark is gray and smooth when young, developing scaly ridges separated by deep furrows with age. A small tree up to 40 feet tall. Found in the Trans-Pecos across southern New Mexico, Arizona, and into southern California, from 2,500 to 7,500 feet in elevation.

CALIFORNIA BUCKEYE page 266
The smooth, thin bark is light gray. Reddish brown twigs are stout, with a tacky, resinous terminal bud. A small tree up to 40 feet tall. Found only at lower elevations in California in the coastal mountains and the Sierra Nevada, below 4,000 feet.

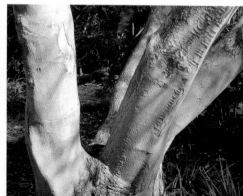

BLUE ELDERBERRY page 292
The bark is light gray or brown and furrowed into a loose, woven pattern of long, scaly ridges. There are no terminal buds. A small tree up to 25 feet tall. Throughout the West from western Alberta and southern British Columbia, south to northwest Mexico and the Trans-Pecos, at elevations to 5,000 feet.

RED ELDERBERRY page 294
The bark is smooth, light to dark gray or brown, and with age may become broken into scaly plates separated by shallow fissures. There are no terminal buds. A small tree up to 20 feet. Coastal from southern Alaska to central California, up to 2,000 feet in elevation.

Crescent-shaped Leaf Scars

Compare your sample with the following trees:
Fragrant Ash, Oregon Ash, Boxelder, Pacific Dogwood, Bigleaf Maple, Bigtooth Maple, Rocky Mountain Maple, Vine Maple

FRAGRANT ASH page 252
The smooth gray bark becomes fissured with scaly ridges. A small tree up to 20 feet. Limited distribution at scattered locations from southern Texas through New Mexico and Arizona.

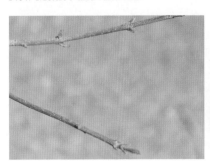 

OREGON ASH page 254

The bark is dark gray to gray-brown and typical of most ashes—with an interwoven, diamond-shaped lace pattern made up of winding ridges with flat tops and sharp edges. The terminal bud is small. A medium-size tree up to 80 feet in height. Coastal British Columbia southward to the San Francisco Bay and along the western slopes of the Sierra Nevada, up to about 3,000 feet in elevation.

BOXELDER page 264

The light brown bark is thin and has narrow ridges between furrows that form a lacelike pattern. The bark is coarser in older trees. The green to purplish green twigs are stout, with small but noticeable lenticels, and covered with a waxy haze. Terminal buds are roundish, with four overlapping scales. A medium-size tree up to 60 feet in height. Widely scattered throughout the Southwest, where it can be found from sea level to 8,000 feet.

PACIFIC DOGWOOD page 290

Thin bark is reddish brown, generally smooth, with thin, scaly plates at the base of the trunk. Young twigs are slender, green, and hairy, turning dark red or black. Small, dry, berrylike fruit may persist. A small tree up to 50 feet in height. Southwestern British Columbia to western Oregon and in the mountains to southern California, from sea level to 6,000 feet in elevation.

BIGLEAF MAPLE page 318

The bark is light gray-brown and smooth on smaller trunks, darkening and becoming furrowed with flat plates as the tree ages. The terminal buds are blunt and have many scales. The winged fruit may persist into winter. A medium-size tree up to 75 feet in height. Generally, a coastal tree found at sea level to 1,000 feet in British Columbia, and from 3,000 to 7,000 feet in the southern part of its range in southern California in the Sierra Nevada.

BIGTOOTH MAPLE page 320

The thin bark can be gray or brown and is either smooth or scaly. A small tree up to 40 feet in height. It is found from southeast Idaho to northern Arizona, and east to southern New Mexico and western Texas, at elevations of 4,000 to 7,000 feet.

ROCKY MOUNTAIN MAPLE page 322
The thin, smooth bark is brown or gray. A small tree up to 30 feet in height. From southeast Alaska through British Columbia into western Oregon and Washington. Also found throughout the Rockies from British Columbia, Idaho, and Montana to Arizona and New Mexico. Close to sea level in the north and from 5,000 to 9,000 feet in the southern part of its range.

VINE MAPLE page 324
The bark can be brown or gray and smooth or finely fissured. The tree has a short trunk, often with several leaning branches that twist or turn from the base, giving it a sprawling, vinelike appearance. Slender twigs are green to reddish brown, often with a whitish bloom. A small tree to 25 feet in height. Along the Pacific coast from southwest British Columbia to northern California, to 5,000 feet in elevation.

2. ALTERNATE

Of the deciduous trees with alternate arrangement, most exhibit very distinctive characteristics that can be used to make a fairly certain identification. Eight species that have less-specific characteristics are grouped at the end of this section.

a. If your sample has thorns, go to *Thorns* on page 107.

b. If your sample has white bark, cream-colored bark with green and brown mottling, shiny brown bark with lenticels, or mottled bark, go to *Distinctive Bark* on page 111.

c. If your sample has spur branches generally less than 2 inches long, from which the leaves, needles, and fruit grow, go to *Spur Branches* on page 114.

d. If your sample has multiple terminal buds, go to *Multiple Terminal Buds* on page 116.
e. If your sample has persistent fruit, go to *Persistent Fruit* on page 119.

f. If your sample has large, raised, three-lobed leaf scars, go to *Large, Raised, Three-lobed Leaf Scars* on page 124.
g. There are eight remaining species that can be identified by differences in the size and color of twigs and by the buds. If your sample does not fit into any of the above descriptions, go to *Remaining Species* on page 125.

Thorns

1. If your sample has paired thorns, see *Paired Thorns* below.
2. If your sample has single thorns, go to *Single Thorns* on page 109.

Paired Thorns

Compare your sample with the following trees:

> *Black Locust, New Mexico Locust, Honey Mesquite, Velvet Mesquite*

BLACK LOCUST page 308

Thick, light gray bark is deeply furrowed, with interlacing ridges. Reddish brown twigs are somewhat zigzagged and have stout, paired spines at nodes, $^1/4$ to $^1/2$ inch long. Two- to four-inch-long, dark brown, narrow, oblong pods mature in autumn and persist into winter. They contain four to eight flattened, beanlike seeds. A medium-size tree to 60 feet in height. Originally, Black Locust was found in the East, but it has become naturalized throughout the U.S. and southern Canada.

NEW MEXICO LOCUST page 310
Thick, light gray bark has shallow furrows and flat, scaly ridges. Brown twigs have rust-colored hair when young and stout, brown, $^1/_4$- to $^1/_2$-inch, paired spines. Fruit is a $2^1/_2$- to $4^1/_2$-inch-long, narrowly oblong, flat, brown pod that holds three to eight flattened, beanlike, brown seeds. A small tree to 25 feet in height. Southeast Nevada to central and southern Colorado, south to western Texas, and west to southeast Arizona, at elevations from 4,000 to 8,500 feet.

HONEY MESQUITE page 326
The rough, thick, dark brown bark has shreddy plates separated by fissures. Stout twigs are zigzagged and have pairs of yellowish thorns, $^1/_4$ to 1 inch long, growing from slightly swollen nodes. A small tree to 20 feet in height, or a shrub. From eastern Texas and southwest Oklahoma west to southwest Utah and southern California, to 4,500 feet in elevation. Also naturalized as far north as Kansas and southeast Colorado.

VELVET MESQUITE page 328
Young bark is gray, smooth, and thin. The dark brown older bark is thick and has vertical fissures separating long, flat plates. Light brown twigs are slightly zigzagged, covered with fine velvety hair, with paired thorns (¹/₄ to 1 inch) growing from enlarged nodes. A small tree to 40 feet in height. Southwest New Mexico west to central Arizona and northwest Mexico, from 500 to 5,500 feet in elevation.

Single Thorns
Compare your sample with the following trees:
Black Hawthorn, Blue Palovere, Yellow Paloverde

BLACK HAWTHORN page 302
The smooth bark is brown or gray but may become broken into scales. Shiny red, slender twigs are hairless and may have straight, sometimes curved, 1-inch spines. A small tree to 30 feet in height. From southern Alaska, throughout British Columbia and as far south as central California, and farther east between Saskatchewan and New Mexico. Near sea level in the north, up to 6,000 feet elevation in the south.

BLUE PALOVERDE page 356

The smooth bark on the trunk and branches is blue-green. The base of larger trees becomes brown and scaly. The smooth twigs are blue-green, can be slightly zigzagged, and have a short, straight, slender spine at each node. A small tree to 30 feet in height. Southeast California and central and southern Arizona, also northwest Mexico, at elevations up to 4,000 feet.

YELLOW PALOVERDE page 358

The smooth bark on the trunk and branches is yellow-green. Twigs are short, stout, and end in a 2-inch-long, straight spine. Yellowish brown fruits develop as 2- to 3-inch thin pods ending in a long, narrow point and constricted between seeds. They persist through the winter. A small tree to 25 feet in height. From Arizona to southeast California and northwest Mexico, from 500 to 4,000 feet in elevation.

Distinctive Bark

There are five distinctive bark patterns that can be used to identify sample trees: white bark that peels; gray, warty bark; smooth, greenish white or cream-colored bark; white bark with mottled green and brown patches; and shiny bark with lenticels.

White Bark that Peels

Compare your sample with *Paper Birch*:

PAPER BIRCH page 360

The bark is dark brown when young but quickly becomes chalky or creamy white, with long, horizontal lines that separate into papery strips. A medium-size tree to 70 feet in height. Widespread across Canada and Alaska but also found in northern Washington, Idaho, and western Montana, to 4,000 feet in elevation.

Gray, Warty Bark

Compare your sample with *Netleaf Hackberry:*

NETLEAF HACKBERRY page 300

The bark is initially gray and smooth but becomes fissured, with large, corky warts. A small tree to a height of 50 feet. From Kansas to central Texas, west through New Mexico and Arizona, with more scattered occurrences in California, Oregon, Washington, Idaho, Utah, and Colorado, at elevations from 1,500 to 6,000 feet.

Smooth, Greenish White or Cream-colored Bark
Compare your sample with *Quaking Aspen*:

QUAKING ASPEN page 258
On young trees, the bark is smooth, greenish white, or cream colored. Bark on older trees becomes dark brown or gray with furrowed, long, flat-topped ridges toward the base. A medium-size tree to a height of 60 feet, often found growing in groves. Across North America from Alaska to Newfoundland, south through British Columbia, and in the Rocky Mountains south to southern Arizona and New Mexico, from sea level to 10,000 feet.

White Bark with Mottled Green and/or Brown Patches
Compare your sample with the following trees:
Arizona Sycamore, California Sycamore

ARIZONA SYCAMORE page 366
Smooth, white bark develops peeling, brownish flakes and becomes mottled with shades of white, green, and brown. Bark at the base of larger trees becomes rough and furrowed, turning dark brown or gray. Stout trunks branch near the base, often forming clumps up to 10 feet in diameter. The crown is broad and irregular, with crooked, spreading branches. A medium-size tree to a height of 80 feet. Found in Arizona, southwest New Mexico, and northwest Mexico, from 2,000 to 6,000 feet in elevation.

CALIFORNIA SYCAMORE page 368
Smooth, white bark develops peeling flakes and becomes mottled with shades of white, green, and brown. Bark at the base of larger trees becomes rough and

furrowed, turning dark brown or gray. Stout trunks branch near the base, often forming clumps up to 10 feet in diameter. Slender, brown twigs are zigzagged, have noticeable ring scars, and are hairy when young. A medium-size tree to a height of 80 feet. Found in the Sierra Nevada, California Coast Ranges, and Baja California, to 4,000 feet.

Shiny Bark with Lenticels
Compare your sample to the following trees:
  Water Birch, Bitter Cherry, Black Cherry

WATER BIRCH page 262
Bark is red-brown, shiny, smooth, and has white, horizontal lenticels. Unlike that of Paper Birch, this bark does not peel. Catkins are sometimes persistent. A small tree to a height of 25 feet. From British Columbia to southern Manitoba in Canada and across the northern tier states from Washington to North Dakota and south to central California, Nevada, Arizona, and New Mexico, at elevations to 8,000 feet.

BITTER CHERRY page 274

The smooth, shiny bark is dark reddish brown, with conspicuous horizontal lenticels and a very bitter taste. Slender twigs are shiny red and hairy when young. A small tree to a height of 20 feet. Found in British Columbia, Washington, and western Montana, south to southwest New Mexico and southern California, to 9,000 feet in elevation.

BLACK CHERRY page 276

The bark is initially dark gray and smooth, with conspicuous horizontal lenticels. With age, it becomes fissured, with shiny, platelike scales with upturned edges, exposing a reddish brown inner bark. Slender twigs are reddish brown and hairless; they have a bitter taste. A medium-size tree to a height of 60 feet. From the Trans–Pecos through New Mexico and Arizona, from 4,500 feet to 7,500 feet in elevation.

Spur Branches

Compare your sample to the following trees:
   Bitter Cherry, Western Larch, Saskatoon Serviceberry

BITTER CHERRY page 274

Bitter Cherry has short spur branches found on shiny, red, slender twigs. **Full key description above.**

WESTERN LARCH page 184

Western Larch is the only conifer that sheds its needles in winter. Younger trees have reddish brown, scaly bark. On older trees, the bark is 4 to 6 inches thick and develops flat plates divided by deep fissures. Short $1/4$-inch spurs remain on twigs after the needles drop in the fall; needles persist on the ground beneath the tree. Twigs are stout, initially hairy, but soon turning orange-brown and hairless. Persistent cones are 1 to $1^1/2$ inches long, oblong, on a short stalk, and purplish red to reddish brown. A very large tree to a height of 180 feet. From southern British Columbia to northwest Oregon and central Idaho, at elevations from 2,000 to 5,500 feet in the north and to 7,000 feet in the south.

SASKATOON SERVICEBERRY page 360

The thin bark can be gray or brown. It is often smooth but can also develop slight fissures. Small, pointed buds are deep red. Bud scales usually have a fringe of white hair. A small tree to a height of 30 feet. From coastal Alaska to northern California and east to western Minnesota, at elevations to 6,000 feet.

Multiple Terminal Buds

Compare your sample with the following trees:
Cascara Buckthorn, Blue Oak, California Black Oak, Gambel Oak, Gray Oak, Oregon White Oak, Valley Oak

CASCARA BUCKTHORN page 268

Has smooth, thin, gray or brown bark that may develop thin, scaly, vertical ridges. The bark is very bitter to the taste. Gray twigs are slender and hairy when young, with scaleless buds covered with woolly hair. A close look at the bud may reveal small leaf edges. Young plants can be evergreen. A small tree to a height of 40 feet. Within a few hundred miles of the Pacific coast from British Columbia to northern California and also in the Rockies in northern Idaho, Washington, and Montana, at elevations to 5,000 feet.

BLUE OAK page 332

The light gray bark is thin, with fissures separating narrow, scaly plates. Twigs are hairy. A medium-size tree to a height of 60 feet. Interior valleys from northern to southern California in the Coast Ranges and the Sierra Nevada, from 3,000 to 3,500 feet.

CALIFORNIA BLACK OAK page 334

The bark is smooth and brown on younger trunks but dark brown on older trunks, with irregular plates and ridges separated by deep furrows. A medium-size tree to a height of 80 feet. Twigs are sometimes hairy and end in clusters of $1/4$-inch long, pointed, hairless buds. From Southern Oregon south along the coast and in the Sierra Nevada to southern California, from 1,000 to 8,000 feet in elevation.

GAMBEL OAK page 342

The rough, gray bark is thick, with flat, scaly plates, and deeply furrowed. A medium-size tree to a height of 70 feet. Found in northern Utah east to southern Wyoming, south to west Texas and southern Arizona, at elevations from 5,000 to 8,000 feet.

GRAY OAK page 344

The light gray bark has fissures separating flat plates that can become shaggy. Twigs are stout and hairy. A medium-size tree to a height of 60 feet. Found in the Trans-Pecos through New Mexico to central Arizona, at elevations from 5,000 to 7,000 feet.

OREGON WHITE OAK page 348

The bark of younger stems is smooth. The bark on older trunks is gray or gray-brown and has narrow, shallow fissures that separate flat, scaly ridges. Twigs are stout, and young ones are covered with a dense, orange-red pubescence. Twigs are tipped with clusters of $1/4$- to $1/2$-inch long, fuzz-covered buds. A medium-size tree to a height of 70 feet. Found from British Columbia southward to central California in the Coast Ranges and the Sierra Nevada, at elevations up to 3,000 feet in the north and from 1,000 to 5,000 feet in the south.

VALLEY OAK page 352

The light gray or brown bark has deep, vertical and horizontal fissures that break the bark into small, thick, flat blocks so that it resembles the hide of an alligator. Twigs tend to droop and are slender and hairy, ending in clusters of ¹/₄-inch hairy, scale-covered, pointed buds. It is a large, sprawling tree, to a height of 125 feet. From northern to southern California, up to 5,000 feet elevation, from the Sierra Nevada to the coast. Also found on Santa Cruz and Catalina Islands.

Persistent Fruit

1. If the fruit is conelike, go to *Conelike Fruit* on page 120.
2. If the fruit is beanlike, go to *Beanlike Fruit* on page 121.
3. If the fruit is berrylike, go to *Berrylike Fruit* on page 123.

Conelike Fruit

Compare your sample with the following trees:
> *Arizona Alder, Red Alder, White Alder, Western Larch*

ARIZONA ALDER page 244

The thin, dark gray bark is smooth but with age becomes scaly or checkered with fissures. Brown twigs have fine hair when they are young. The pith is three angled. Persistent $^1/_2$- to $^3/_4$-inch, hard, brown cones are found in clusters of three to eight. A medium-size tree to a height of 80 feet. From Arizona and southwest New Mexico, from 4,500 to 7,500 feet elevation.

RED ALDER page 246

The smooth, thin bark is pale gray to blue-gray and sometimes has thin, wart-like growths. In larger trees, the bark breaks up into large, flat plates. The inner bark is bright reddish brown. Twigs are slender and covered with gray hair when young and may be somewhat three angled. The pith is also somewhat triangular. Persistent $^1/_2$- to 1-inch cones are found in groups of four to eight on short stalks. A medium-size tree to a height of 120 feet. Found within 50 miles of the Pacific coast from Alaska to California, also in some interior areas of Washington and Idaho, below 2,500 feet elevation.

WHITE ALDER page 248
Light brown or gray, smooth bark divides into irregular, scaly plates with age. The straight trunk supports an open, rounded crown that can be quite showy in winter, when the golden male catkins are in bloom. The slender twigs are orange-red, and the buds are on short stalks. Small female cones are $^3/_8$ to $^3/_4$ inch long. They remain clustered in groups of three to seven on the twigs, developing hard, black scales that remain closed until early spring. The nuts mature by late summer. A medium-size tree to a height of 80 feet. Found in Washington and western Idaho, and then south through the Coast Ranges of California and in the Sierra Nevada to western Nevada and southern California. From nearly sea level in the northern part of its range and up to 8,000 feet elevation in the south, but generally below 5,000 feet.

WESTERN LARCH page 184
Western Larch has 1- to $1^1/_2$-inch-long oblong cones, purplish red to reddish brown, that are persistent and may remain on the tree for many years. **Full key description on page 115.**

Beanlike Fruit
Compare your sample with the following trees:
    Desert Willow, Black Locust, New Mexico Locust, Yellow Paloverde

DESERT WILLOW page 289
Young bark is initially smooth. Older bark is dark brown, coarse, and furrowed into scaly ridges. The tree is often forked, with an open crown. Brown twigs are very slender, sometimes hairy or sticky. The dark brown fruit is a 4- to 8-inch-long, $^1/_4$-inch-diameter capsule that matures in early autumn, splitting in half and remaining attached to the tree through winter. A small tree to a height of 25 feet. The Trans-Pecos and New Mexico west to southwest Utah and southern California, from 1,000 to 5,000 feet in elevation.

BLACK LOCUST page 308
Narrow, dark brown, oblong pods are 2 to 4 inches long. They mature in autumn and persist into winter. **Full key description on page 107.**

NEW MEXICO LOCUST page 310
Narrow, oblong, flat, brown pods are $2^1/_2$ to $4^1/_2$ inches long and contain three to eight beanlike seeds. **Full key description on page 108.**

YELLOW PALOVERDE page 358
Two- to three-inch yellow-brown pods remain on the tree during winter. **Full key description on page 110.**

Berrylike Fruit
Compare your sample with *Western Soapberry*:

WESTERN SOAPBERRY page 364
The light gray bark becomes furrowed with scaly ridges. The crown is rounded, formed with upright branches. Yellow-green twigs may be hairy and have no terminal bud. Pith is solid. Berrylike, $^{3}/_{8}$- to $^{1}/_{2}$-inch-diameter, nearly transparent, leathery fruits turn from yellow-orange to black and remain on the tree through winter. Fruits have a single, hard seed. A small tree to a height of 40 feet. Also grows as a spreading shrub. From Missouri south to Louisiana and then westward to southern New Mexico and Arizona and north to Colorado, at elevations to 6,000 feet.

Large, Raised, Three-lobed Leaf Scars

Compare your sample with the following trees:
Arizona Walnut, Little Walnut, Northern California Walnut

ARIZONA WALNUT page 372
Has gray-brown bark that is initially smooth but becomes thicker as it develops ridges separated by deep furrows. Stout twigs are brown and have large, raised, shield-shaped leaf scars and chambered pith. The fruits are walnuts, 1 to 1¹/₂ inches in diameter, with a thin, hairy brown husk and thick, grooved shell. A small tree to a height of 50 feet. From central Texas west to Arizona and south into Mexico, at elevations from 2,000 to 7,000 feet.

LITTLE WALNUT page 374
The gray bark is smooth when young but with age turns darker and becomes deeply furrowed. Slender twigs are gray and have large, raised, shield-shaped leaf scars and brown, chambered pith. Fruits are ¹/₂ to ³/₄ inch in diameter, with a thick, hard, grooved shell and very small edible seed. A small tree to a height of 30 feet. From southwest Kansas through Oklahoma and Texas and southward into northeastern Mexico, at elevations from 1,500 to 4,000 feet.

NORTHERN CALIFORNIA WALNUT page 376

Gray-brown bark is broken into long plates separated by narrow ridges. Twigs are stout, brown, and occasionally hairy, with large, raised, shield-shaped leaf scars and a chambered pith. Fruits are $1^{1}/_{2}$ to 2 inches in diameter and have a thin husk and thick, dark brown shell that is nearly smooth. The seed is edible and matures in early fall. A medium-size tree to a height of 70 feet. Central California, at elevations to 500 feet.

Remaining Species

If your sample has stout, light-colored twigs, consider *Black Cottonwood* or *Fremont Cottonwood.*

If your sample has slender, light-colored twigs and long-pointed buds, consider *Narrowleaf Cottonwood* or the *Willow* species.

If your sample has slender, dark-colored twigs, consider *Chokecherry* or *Siberian Elm.*

CHOKECHERRY page 278

Bark is gray-brown, generally smooth but may be scaly, with shallow fissures. The tree has a short trunk that quickly breaks into many spreading branches. Brown twigs are thin and have a very bitter taste. There are no spur branches. Rounded bud scales are hairless. A small tree to a height of 20 feet. The tree is widespread over much of the northern half of the U.S. and Canada and scattered throughout all the western states. Found up to 8,000 feet in elevation.

BLACK COTTONWOOD page 282

On younger stems, the bark is brownish yellow or gray and smooth. On older trunks, the coarse bark has flat-topped, scaly ridges separated by deep vertical fissures. These vertical fissures are separated by horizontal fissures every several inches. Brown twigs are slender to stout and slightly angular. The pointed terminal buds are noticeably larger ($3/4$ inch) than the lateral buds ($1/2$ inch). When crushed, the buds are fragrant. A large tree to a height of 150 feet. From Alaska along the Pacific coast to the Baja and also throughout the Rockies in Alberta, Montana, Idaho, Oregon, and Washington and scattered through Nevada. Found at sea level to 2,000 feet in the north, to 9,000 feet in the south.

FREMONT COTTONWOOD page 284

Young bark is gray and smooth with shallow fissures. Older trees have thick, rough bark that is gray and deeply furrowed. Stout twigs are light green and hairless. A medium-size tree to a height of 80 feet. Southwest Colorado to California, south to the Mexican border at elevations to 6,500 feet.

NARROWLEAF COTTONWOOD page 286

Smooth yellow-green bark develops gray-brown furrows and ridges. Narrow, pointed buds are resinous with shiny scales and a balsam odor. A small tree to a height of 50 feet. Southern Alberta south through the Rocky Mountains to the Mexican border at elevations from 3,000 to 8,000 feet.

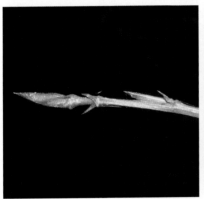

SIBERIAN ELM page 296

Bark can be gray or brown and is deeply furrowed. The tree has an open, rounded crown made up of spreading branches. Twigs are slightly zigzagged, nearly hairless, and greenish brown. In winter, flower buds are nearly black, enlarged, and visible from a distance. A medium-size tree to a height of 60 feet. From Minnesota south to Kansas and west to Utah from 1,000 to 5,000 feet in elevation.

GOODDING'S WILLOW
page 378

Bark is gray-brown to black and has deep furrows, with thick, scaly ridges. The tree tends to grow in clumps, with one or more straight and leaning trunks, and has a spreading, irregular crown. Slender twigs are grayish brown and detach easily from the base. A medium-size tree to a height of 80 feet. From the Trans-Pecos, west through New Mexico and Arizona to northern California, at elevations to 5,000 feet.

PACIFIC WILLOW page 380

Bark can be gray or brown and develops flat ridges separated by deep, rough furrows. The tree has a crooked trunk with an open, irregular crown and can also grow as a thicket-forming shrub. Twigs can be a shiny red, brown, or yellow. A small tree to a height of 50 feet. From central and southeast Alaska east to Saskatchewan and then south to southern New Mexico and southern California, mostly in the mountains, at elevations to 8,000 feet.

SCOULER'S WILLOW page 382

Gray bark is thin and smooth, becoming dark brown and developing flat ridges separated by fissures. The tree has a straight trunk and rounded crown. Stout twigs are yellow to reddish brown. A true pussy willow, its flowers appear in spring before leaf-out. A small tree to a height of 50 feet. From central Alaska south to Idaho and California and east to the Black Hills of South Dakota, also in the mountains of southern New Mexico, at elevations to 10,000 feet.

PART THREE

Species Accounts

This section presents a detailed description and photos for the 127 species included in this book. The key features that are depicted in the accompanying photos are described in the text for easy reference. Many accounts include interesting facts that will add to your knowledge base. The specific features, relative measurements, range and distribution information, and photographs should allow you to make a positive identification of your sample tree.

This section is in two parts: conifers and hardwoods. Trees are in alphabetical order, grouped by genus name.

CONIFERS

CEDAR

Four different genera, all members of the Cypress family, are grouped together and commonly called cedar. ("True cedars," however, are members of the *Cedrus* genus of the Pine family and are not native to North America.) The four cedars included here are tall, stately trees with narrow, conical crowns and scalelike leaves that form flat sprays.

Alaska Cedar, *Callitropsis nootkatensis*
Alaska Yellow Cedar, Nootka Cypress

Alaska Cedar is a medium-size evergreen that grows to a height of 60 to 90 feet with a diameter from 2 to 3 feet. The bark on young trees is gray-brown, thin, and shredded, becoming thin, narrow, and flattened, with interlacing ridges on older trees. The base of the trunk is broadly buttressed, often fluted, with a rapidly tapering bole that is clear of branches for up to half its length. The crown is narrow and conical, with numerous drooping branches.

The scalelike leaves are very small, only $^1/_{16}$ to $^1/_8$ inch long, opposite, bright yellow-green, prominently pointed, and often pointing outward. The leaves form flat sprays, with tips that tend to droop, often straight down. Twigs are relatively stout and may be flat or four angled. The $^1/_2$-inch cones are ball shaped, reddish brown, with four or six rounded scales that have a prominent, pointed tip.

The largest Alaska Cedars are found on the islands of southeastern Alaska and British Columbia near tidewater. At timberline, trees can be reduced to a sprawling, even prostrate, shrub on unprotected sites. The tree is most commonly found with other conifers and does best on moist sites. It is very tolerant of shade.

Features: Alaska Cedar is an extremely long-lived species and often reaches 1,000 years in age. The growth-ring count on one specimen showed the age to be 3,500 years. The durable wood has a pleasing scent and is used for furniture and paneling and in boat making.

Range: From coastal southeast Alaska, southwest Canada to Oregon and Washington, from sea level in the north and from 2,000 to 7,000 feet in elevation farther south.

Incense Cedar, *Calocedrus decurrens*

Incense Cedar is a medium-size evergreen that grows to 100 feet in height with a diameter of 3 to 4 feet. The bark on younger trees is smooth and gray-green or scaly and tinged with red. On older trees, the 3- to 8-inch-thick bark is yellowish brown to cinnamon red and appears fibrous, with very irregular, deep furrows separated by shreddy ridges. The crowns of younger trees are conical to columnar and can cover nearly half the trunk. Older trees have an irregularly angled and buttressed trunk. Mistletoe and witches'-broom growth often deforms the crown.

The scalelike leaves are $\frac{1}{8}$ to $\frac{1}{2}$ inch long, opposite, in four rows, shiny, and yellow-green. Side scales are keeled, have long points, and overlap as they cover the twig. Leaves form flat sprays and are very aromatic when crushed. The reddish twigs are many branched and generally flat. The $\frac{3}{4}$- to $1\frac{1}{2}$-inch leathery, pendantlike cones have six paired scales. Cone scales are vase shaped. Two of the scales enlarge and, when partially open, look like a duck's bill.

Incense Cedar prefers cooler, moist sites and does not do well in drought-prone zones. It is never found in pure stands but can make up to 50 percent of some mixed-conifer forests. The thick bark makes this tree somewhat resistant to fire. Trees can live to 500 years.

Features: The durable, fragrant wood is used for cedar chests, fencing, and shingles. The wood is also used for pencils because it can be sharpened without splintering. The tree is planted as an ornamental. Native Americans used the branches and twigs in sweat baths and also in remedies for colds and stomach ailments.

Range: Western Oregon through northern and central California along the Nevada border, also in Baja California. In California, it is found at 1,000 to 5,000 feet in elevation; in Nevada, from 3,500 to 7,000 feet.

Port Orford Cedar, *Chamaecyparis lawsoniana*
Lawson False-cypress, Lawson Cypress,
Oregon White-cedar, Oregon-cedar

Port Orford Cedar is a large to very large evergreen that grows to heights of 140 to 180 feet with diameters of 4 to 6 feet. The silvery brown bark may be 10 inches thick on older trees and is very coarse and fibrous, with ridges separated by deep, irregular fissures. The short, narrow, conical crown is made up of short, horizontal, drooping branches. Some large trees have a cypresslike buttressed base, and the trunk can be limbless for 150 feet.

Scalelike leaves are very small, only $^1/_{16}$ inch long, opposite, in four rows, yellow-green to blue-green, blunt, and form flat, lacy sprays. Twigs are narrow and covered tightly with scales, which on close inspection show white stripes forming an X. The cones are small, $^3/_8$-inch diameter, reddish brown balls that have three pairs of bracts, giving the cone a plated appearance. Cones often have a bloom.

Port Orford Cedar grows best in areas with high atmospheric moisture and deep soil but can tolerate drier conditions. It forms pure stands around Coos Bay, Oregon, but elsewhere is found mixed with other conifers. It will grow rapidly in burned-over areas and does well in shade and sunlight. Trees will eventually die off when growing in dense understory, however. They mature in 300 to 350 years and can live to 500.

Features: The lumber from Port Orford Cedar is used for building construction, boats, fence posts, and matchwood. The aromatic wood is used for woodenware. Entire logs are exported to Japan for use in temples and shrines. Many cultivars have been developed for ornamental plantings around the world. Unfortunately, the tree is vulnerable to root rot, which may affect the future of the species.

Range: Found in the fog belt of the Coast Ranges in southern Oregon and northern California from sea level to elevations of 2,000 to 7,000 feet; also on Mount Shasta, in California.

Western Redcedar, *Thuja plicata*
Giant Arborvitae, Canoe Cedar

Western Redcedar is a very large evergreen that grows to heights over 200 feet with diameters of over 8 feet on favorable sites. The largest known specimen is 250 feet in height and 21 feet in diameter. The thin bark, $^1/_2$ to 1 inch thick, is cinnamon red on younger trees and turns gray with age. The bark is fibrous and shredded. The trunk tapers from a sometimes buttressed and/or fluted base and ends in a narrow, conical, oftimes irregular, forked crown. Branches are horizontal or drooping. The ends of the branches have an upward turn that looks like a hook.

The scalelike leaves are opposite, $^1/_{16}$ to $^1/_8$ inch long, shiny, dark yellow-green or green, in rows of four, and on close inspection show butterflylike markings. Scales form flat sprays that are often long, droopy, almost fernlike, and stringy. The foliage is very aromatic. Twigs are branching but stay in flat, fanlike, jointed sprays. Small, brown cones ($^1/_2$ inch) are in upright clusters on short, curved stems. The 10 to 12 paired, thin but coarse, leathery, pointed cone scales carry two or three winged seeds.

Western Redcedar requires wetter sites and is found along rivers, in swamps, or on moist slopes and flats. It is sometimes found in bogs. Though infrequently found in pure stands, it often constitutes over half of mixed stands of other conifers and sometimes cottonwoods.

Features: Western Redcedar is an important commercial timber species in the Northwest, with a notable resistance to rot. It is the primary source of wood shingles in the U.S. and Canada, and is also used for fence posts, telephone poles, boats, outdoor furniture, and decking.

Range: From southeast Alaska, along the coast to northern California, also in western Montana and Idaho, northward into Alberta and British Columbia. At 3,000 feet in the north and 7,000 feet in the Rocky Mountains.

CYPRESS

There are seven species of cypress found from southwest Oregon through coastal northern and central southern California. Arizona Cypress has the broadest range, extending from west Texas to southern California, but it is rare within that range. Six other species—MacNab's, Gowen, Sargent's, and Monterey, as well as Tecate and Modoc (not covered here)—have very limited distribution within California.

Cypresses are evergreen trees or shrubs that often have conical or irregularly shaped crowns; shreddy bark; tiny, scalelike leaves; and small, hard, round or oval cones. They can be very difficult to distinguish from each other. As well, cypress vegetation is easily confused with that of junipers. Juniper fruits are fleshy and berrylike, however—quite different from cypress cones.

Arizona Cypress, *Hesperocyparis arizonica*

Arizona Cypress is a small evergreen that grows to a height of 50 to 65 feet with diameters of 15 to 30 inches. The bark on younger stems can be reddish brown and broken into thin, irregular scales. On older trees, the bark is gray to black and becomes furrowed, fibrous, and peeling. Short, stout, horizontal branches form a conical crown that covers more than half the length of a tapered bole.

Scalelike leaves are tiny, $^1/_{16}$ inch long, dull gray-green, keeled, somewhat pointed, and tightly hug the stem. Most scales have a gland dot that produces a whitish resin. Twigs have a disagreeable odor when crushed. They are four angled, thin, and branch at relatively wide, almost right, angles. The $^3/_4$- to $1^1/_4$-inch round, woody cones are divided by six to eight shieldlike cone scales, each with a small point. Old cones are often retained.

Arizona Cypress is found on coarse, gravelly soil on mountain slopes and in coves with northern exposures. On dry canyon walls and sterile sites, the trees are dwarfed. It normally is found in open, clear forests but occasionally with live oak, pinyons, junipers, and Arizona Pine. These are slow-growing trees. Those of less than 1 foot in diameter can be 100 years old; larger trees can be 400 years old.

Range: The Trans-Pecos to southern California, rare and local, at elevations from 2,500 to 6,600 feet.

Gowen Cypress, *Hesperocyparis goveniana*

Gowen Cypress is a small evergreen that grows to a height of 30 feet with a diameter from 6 to 18 inches. The grayish brown bark is initially smooth but becomes rougher, more fibrous, and shredded with age. The tree has an open, spreading crown. Scalelike leaves are opposite, in four rows, less than $1/16$ inch long. Leaves are usually bright green and do not have a gland dot. Twigs are four angled and slender. Grayish brown cones are nearly round, have a point, and are less than $3/4$ inch in diameter. They have six to ten rounded, hard cone scales. Seeds are dull brown to shiny black and $1/8$ inch long.

Range: Gowen Cypress is found in coastal Redwood forests in northwest and central California, usually near sea level.

MacNab's Cypress, *Hesperocyparis macnabiana*

MacNab's Cypress is a small evergreen that grows to a height of 30 feet with a diameter up to 1 foot. The gray bark is roughened by shallow furrows separating scaly ridges. The spreading crown is wider than it is tall. The dull gray-green, opposite, scalelike leaves are tiny ($^1/_{16}$ inch) and formed in flat sprays (this is the only cypress with flat sprays). The scales are fragrant and have a gland dot that oozes resin. The round cones are $^3/_4$ to 1 inch in diameter, gray or brown, with six to eight cone scales, each with a noticeable point. The tree is found on dry, rocky soils in foothills and lower mountain ranges up to 2,600 feet. Wood is used for fence posts.

Range: MacNab's Cypress is the most widespread cypress in California and is found in the Coast Ranges, northern mountains, and the Sierra Nevada.

Monterey Cypress, *Hesperocyparis macrocarpa*

Monterey Cypress is a medium-size evergreen tree that grows to a height of 60 to 80 feet with a diameter between 2 and 4 feet. It has rough, fibrous, gray bark and a straight trunk and symmetrical crown when growing on protected sites. When growing on more exposed sites subject to high winds, it develops a gnarled, windswept form. Blunt, scalelike leaves are opposite, in four rows, and slightly more than $1/16$ inch long. They are bright green and usually do not have a gland dot. Twigs are stout and four angled. Brown, oval cones are 1 to $1^3/8$ inches long with 8 to 12 pointed, rounded, hard scales that remain closed and attached. There are many shiny, brown, irregularly shaped seeds. The windswept trees along the California coast are favorite photography subjects.

Range: Two native groves of Monterey Cypress are found within the Point Lobos State Natural Reserve and the Del Monte Forest at Point Cypress. The tree is planted extensively as an ornamental and a windbreak along the California coastline.

Sargent's Cypress, *Hesperocyparis sargentii*

Sargent's Cypress is a small evergreen that grows to a height of 30 to 50 feet with a diameter up to 3 feet. The thick, rough bark is shades of gray to dark brown, with furrows and fibrous ridges appearing to twist around the trunk. The crown has a narrow point compared to the very wide base, creating a profile that looks like an equilateral triangle. Leaves are dull green, tiny ($^1/_{16}$ inch) scales, some with gland dots. Scales are in opposite rows, forming four-angled, stout twigs that branch in random directions. Round cones are $^3/_4$ to 1 inch in diameter and very irregular, covered with six to eight pimply looking, rough scales.

Range: Sargent's Cypress is found in the foothills and slopes of the Coast Ranges of California, up to 3,000 feet elevation.

DOUGLAS-FIR

Douglas-fir are members of the Pine family and differ from the "true firs" by the leaf base and how it attaches to the twig.

Bigcone Douglas-fir, *Pseudotsuga macrocarpa*
Bigcone Spruce

Bigcone Douglas-fir is a medium-size evergreen that grows to a height of 40 to 80 feet with a diameter of 1 to 3 feet. The dark reddish brown bark is thick, with wide, scaly ridges separated by deep furrows. The straight, tapering trunk is mostly hidden by branches that form a broad, pyramidal crown.

Needlelike leaves are ³/₄ to 1¹/₄ inches long, blue-green, generally in two rows, and sharply pointed. The twigs are dark reddish brown and may be slightly hairy when young. Thin twigs often droop and are tipped with a pointed bud that is dark brown, hairless, and scaly. Cones are 4 to 6 inches long and are tapered at the tip. The rounded cone scales have long, three-pointed bracts that extend well past the cone scales.

Bigcone Douglas-fir is a somewhat isolated species found in canyons and on dry slopes in mixed-conifer forests, and in chaparral, with live oak.

Features: Bigcone Douglas-fir is not a significant commercial timber tree; it is used for Christmas trees, however. When recovering from fire damage, the tree sprouts vigorously from the trunk and branches. It has much larger cones than Douglas-fir.

Range: Found in the mountains in southern California, well south of the range of Douglas-fir, from 900 to 8,000 feet.

Douglas-fir, *Pseudotsuga menziesii*

Douglas-fir is an important component of western forests and has two distinct varieties. Coast Douglas-fir (var. *menziesii*) is a very large evergreen tree that grows to heights of 180 to 250 feet with a diameter of 4 to 6 feet, although it can reach heights of 325 feet and diameters of 8 to 10 feet. (The tallest known Douglas-fir was 385 feet and had a diameter of 15 feet.) Coast Douglas-fir is the largest tree in the Pacific Northwest. A smaller form, Rocky Mountain Douglas-fir (var. *glauca*), is found in the Rockies and grows to a height of 130 feet and a diameter of 3 feet. The bark on young stems of both varieties is smooth with resin blisters and can be 6 inches to 24 inches thick on older trees, where it divides into reddish brown ridges separated by deep fissures. It often becomes corky. The long, clear bole is topped with a pointed, rounded or irregular, flat crown.

Needlelike leaves are ³/₄ to 1¹/₄ inches long, yellow-green to blue-green, and either in two rows or standing out from all sides of the twig. Needles are flat, flexible, and have tips that are usually rounded. The topside is grooved; the underside has fine, parallel, white lines on either side of the midrib. The needle has a small post at the base where it attaches to the twig. The slender twigs are orange but turn brown and are hairy. Pointed buds are dark red, conical, and scaly. Elongated, 2- to 4-inch, reddish brown, egg-shaped cones hang down and have a bract that tends to point up or out from the cone. Bracts have three lobes, with the center lobe being the longest.

Rocky Mountain Douglas-fir tends to be more blue-green than Coast Douglas-fir. Its cones are generally less than 3 inches long, and the bracts extend from the cones more so than on the coastal trees.

Coast Douglas-fir grows best on rich, well-drained soils. Young-growth Douglas-fir forms pure stands but develops into mixed stands with other conifers depending on the region. Rocky Mountain Douglas-fir also grows well on moist sites but is tolerant of drought.

Range: From British Columbia southward through the western states. Along the coast, from sea level to 2,000 feet in the north and up to 6,000 feet in the south; inland above 2,000 feet in the north and up to 8,000 to 10,000 feet in the south.

FIR

Firs, members of the Pine family, are sometimes referred to as "true firs" to distinguish them from other firlike trees, such as Douglas-fir, which are in a different genus. True firs have single needlelike leaves that are attached to the twigs with a suction-cup–like base and are usually flat and soft to the touch. The cones stand erect on branches and disintegrate when mature.

California Red Fir, *Abies magnifica*
Red Fir, Silvertip

California Red Fir is a very large evergreen that grows to a height of 150 to 180 feet and from 4 to 5 feet in diameter. The bark is smooth and white on young trees. On older trees, it is very thick (4 to 6 inches) and has rounded, reddish brown ridges separated by deep furrows. The reddish color makes California Red Fir easily distinguishable from other firs. Short, horizontal branches form an open, conical crown that is sometimes rounded at the top.

The needlelike leaves are ³/₄ to 1³/₈ inches long, four sided, usually with a point at the tip. Needles appear crowded toward the upper side of the branches. On new shoots, they are silvery white; on older twigs, silvery blue to dark blue-green, with whitish lines on all sides. Stout twigs are light brown and finely hairy when young. Purplish brown cones are fairly large—6 to 9 inches long and 2 to 3¹/₄ inches in diameter. They stand erect on upper branches and are cylindrical in shape. Cone scales have fine hairs. The yellowish bracts, shorter than the scales, are hidden from view. Seeds are ¹/₂ to ³/₄ inch long and have large, reddish purple wings.

California Red Fir grows best on cool, moist, gravelly, or sandy soil in protected ravines and gulches or on mountain slopes. It can be found in pure stands at higher elevations and also at timberline. It is often found in mixed stands with other conifers. It commonly reaches 250 to 350 years of age.

Features: Early settlers used the scented boughs as bedding by overlapping the branches. On higher elevations, in exposed settings, the tops of California Red Fir are often broken off by high winds. The larger upper branches often grow into the crown position, creating an easily identifiable silhouette.

Range: Found in the Cascade Mountains of southwest Oregon, south to the Coast Ranges of California, also in central California in the Sierra Nevada, at elevations up to 4,500 feet in the north, and from 5,000 to 9,000 feet in the south.

Grand Fir, *Abies grandis*
Lowland White Fir, Lowland Fir

Grand Fir is a large to very large evergreen that grows to heights of 140 to 160 feet with diameters of 2 to 4 feet in coastal forests. Trees in the Rocky Mountains are somewhat smaller reaching heights up to 120 feet and 3 feet in diameter. On young stems, the bark is smooth, gray-brown, with resin blisters and chalky patches. On older trees, it is reddish brown, developing platelike ridges separated by deep furrows. Trees have long, branchless, columnlike boles and narrow, pointed crowns.

The needlelike leaves are $3/4$ to 2 inches long, spread in two rows that are nearly at right angles, with upper and lower needles being shorter than the lateral needles. This needle arrangement distinguishes Grand Fir from other firs. Needles are flat and flexible, with a shiny, dark green upper surface; silvery white below. On upper twigs, the needles appear to be crowded and curve upward. Slender twigs are brown and have tiny hairs when young. The 2- to $4^1/4$-inch cones are upright on the topmost twigs, long, cylindrical, and yellow-green or greenish purple. The bracts are shorter than the scales and not visible. Seeds are $3/8$ inch long, pale yellow-brown, with straw-colored, $3/4$-inch wings.

Grand Fir is found most frequently streamside, along gulches or on gentle mountain slopes on deep, moist soils. It can be found in pure stands, but it is most often found with mixed hardwoods and conifers. It is somewhat tolerant of shade and can reach 200 years of age.

Features: Grand Fir has some commercial value for lumber and pulp. The tree has an odor that some people find objectionable, hence its nickname "stinking tree."

Range: Southwest British Columbia and south to California along the Pacific coast. Also found inland in the Rocky Mountain region to central Idaho. Up to 1,500 feet in elevation along the coast and to 6,000 feet in inland areas.

Noble Fir, *Abies procera*
Red Fir, White Fir

Noble Fir is a large evergreen that grows to a height of 100 to 150 feet with a diameter of $2^1/2$ to 4 feet. It is the largest of the true firs. The bark is 1 to 2 inches thick, making the tree somewhat susceptible to fire. The bark on younger trees is gray and smooth, with prominent resin blisters. In older trees, the dark gray bark breaks into thin, rectangular plates separated by deep fissures. The tree forms a long, clear bole with a rounded crown and few lower horizontal branches.

Needlelike leaves are 1 to $1^5/8$ inches long and blue-green with whitish lines; they tend to curve upward on branches and appear crowded. On cone-bearing branches, needles are four sided and pointed compared to those on the flexible, non-cone-bearing or sterile branches, which are comparatively flat and rounded. Slender twigs are reddish brown with fine hairs. Four- to seven-inch cones stand upright on the uppermost branches and are $1^3/4$ to $2^1/4$ inches in diameter. Cones are olive-brown to purplish brown and are covered with long, papery, yellowish bracts that extend below the scales, giving the cones a fuzzy appearance. Seeds are $1/2$ inch long, dull brown, with light brown wings.

Noble Fir is found on moist soils, high in the mountains on ridges and slopes and in high valleys at elevations where growing seasons are short. It is found in mixed-conifer stands rather than pure stands. Trees can live for 600 to 700 years.

Features: Noble Fir produces quality timber used for exterior siding and interior house products. Middens of cone scales and bracts can be found under the trees where squirrels leave the piles after feeding.

Range: The Cascade Mountains and Coast Ranges in Washington, Oregon, and very northern California. Altitudes range from 3,500 to 7,000 feet, infrequently 200 to 8,900 feet.

Pacific Silver Fir, *Abies amabilis*
Amabilis Fir, Cascades Fir

Pacific Silver Fir is a large evergreen that grows to a height of 140 to 160 feet with a diameter from 2 to 4 feet. The bark is silvery white to ashy gray, with splotchy, chalk-colored blocks. Larger trees have a scaly appearance. The spirelike, conical crown and dense foliage, combined with the short, down-curved branches, make it an attractive tree.

The needlelike leaves are short, $^3/_4$ to $1^1/_2$ inches long, crowded at the ends of twigs, and pointed forward in two rows. Needles curve upward on the top branches. The upper sides of the needles are shiny, dark green, and grooved; needles are silvery white beneath. Stout twigs are yellow-brown and hairy. Cylindrical cones are $3^1/_2$ to 6 inches long, standing upright on the upper branches. Cones are purple when mature. Cone scales have white hairs and short bracts that are hidden.

Pacific Silver Fir grows well on moist soils on slopes with a western or southern exposure. It can be found in pure stands in many areas but also in mixed-conifer stands. It is the most abundant fir of the Pacific Northwest. Seedlings are very tolerant of shade and exhibit slow growth in the understory of forests. Trees can reach an age of 250 years.

Features: Pacific Silver Fir is a picturesque tree because of the shape of the crown and its dense foliage. It is often used in landscaping. The spirelike or pyramidal crown distinguishes it from the domelike crowns of Noble Fir or Grand Fir. Lumber manufactured from this tree is called "larch" but should not be confused with the true larches (or tamarack). Seeds are eaten by Blue and Spruce Grouse as well as squirrels.

Range: Found along the Pacific coast from southeast Alaska to Oregon at elevations of 1,000 to 5,000 feet. Also found locally in California.

Subalpine Fir, *Abies lasiocarpa*
Rocky Mountain Fir, Alpine Fir

Subalpine Fir is a medium-size evergreen that grows to a height of 60 to 100 feet with a diameter of 18 to 24 inches on protected sites. On exposed sites near timberline, it occurs as a sprawling shrub, often lying prostrate. The bark on young trees is smooth and gray with resin blisters. Older trees develop fissured, scaly bark. The crown forms as a long, thin spire with rows of short, horizontal branches. In wooded settings, the bole can be clear for 30 to 40 feet.

Needlelike leaves are 1 to 1³⁄₄ inches long, flat, spreading at right angles, appearing crowded, and curving upward on the higher branches. Needles are pale blue-green with white lines on both surfaces. Stout twigs are gray and sometimes hairy. Buds have reddish scales and a sharp tip. Dark purple cones are 2¹⁄₄ to 4 inches long, cylindrical, and upright on the uppermost branches. Cone scales are hairy with bracts that are shorter than the scale. Cones disintegrate on the tree.

As the name suggests, Subalpine Fir is widely distributed in high mountain settings and at exposed sites near timberline. It can be found in pure stands or mixed with Engelmann Spruce and other conifer species. Trees can reach 250 years of age.

Features: Open-grown trees in alpine meadows are quite scenic, with a crown that can drape to the ground. The lower branches can become weighted down with snow and then take root. New shoots provide browse for deer, elk, bighorn sheep, and moose.

Range: Central Yukon and southeast Alaska to New Mexico. Found at sea level in the most northern settings; at higher elevations from 2,000 to 12,000 feet in the southern extent of its range.

White Fir, *Abies concolor*
Silver Fir, Concolor Fir

White Fir is an evergreen found across much of the south-western U.S. It varies greatly in size depending on its location. In the Sierra Nevada, it is a very large tree that ranges in height from 130 to 150 feet and 3 to 4 feet in diameter. In the Rocky Mountains, trees are typically smaller, generally less than 100 feet tall with a diameter of 15 to 30 inches. Younger trees have an ashy gray bark with noticeable resin blisters. The bark on older trees can be 4 to 7 inches thick, ashy gray, with deep furrows and corky ridges. Trees have a narrow, pointed crown that can be half to two-thirds the length of the trunk. On older trees, the domelike crown may be misshapen by dwarf mistletoe.

The needlelike leaves are $1^{1}/_{2}$ to 3 inches long, flat, flexible, with almost no stalk, in two rows, at nearly right angles to the stem, and often curved upward on higher branches. They are light blue-green to bluish green, with whitish lines on both surfaces. Tips of the needles can either be short pointed, rounded, or even notched. Stout twigs are yellowish brown and hairless. Buds are resin covered. The cylindrical cones are 3 to 5 inches long and initially olive-green to purple before turning brown; they stand upright on the upper twigs. The bracts, shorter than the cone scales, are hidden from view.

White Fir grows in the warmest and driest climates of all the firs. It is commonly found in mixed stands with other conifers, most often on rich, moist, well-drained sites. It can also tolerate dry, exposed sites, where it is smaller and often malformed. Seedlings develop under the canopies of older trees. Trees can live to over 300 years.

Features: White Fir is often used as an ornamental and Christmas trees. It has some commercial value as construction lumber and plywood.

Range: From southeast Idaho to New Mexico, west to California and into the Baja, and north to southwest Oregon. At elevations from 5,500 to 11,000 feet in the south, to 2,000 feet in the north.

HEMLOCK

Hemlock are members of the Pine family, with two species found in the West.

Mountain Hemlock, *Tsuga mertensiana*
Black Hemlock, Alpine Hemlock

Mountain Hemlock is a medium-size evergreen that, in forested settings, can grow to heights of 75 to 100 feet with a diameter of $2^1/_2$ to $3^1/_2$ feet. On exposed, windswept sites, it is often a sprawling shrub. The bark on younger trees is dull purplish brown with narrow, flat plates. On older trees, it develops sharp ridges separated by deep furrows. In high alpine meadows, Mountain Hemlock has an extremely tapered trunk. Slender horizontal or drooping branches form a cone-shaped crown that has a characteristic slender, drooping leader. The bases of trees growing on steep canyon walls often curve upward or are pistol-butted.

Needlelike leaves are $^1/_4$ to 1 inch long, blue-green, with white lines on all surfaces, flattened, and grooved above and rounded beneath. They are blunt tipped and grow from all sides of the twigs or are crowded on the upper sides of short twigs. Needles have thin stalks that are attached to the stems with small pegs. Slender twigs are light reddish brown and have fine hairs. Cylindrical cones are 1 to 3 inches long, yellow-brown, hanging down from branches. Cone scales are rounded. Seeds are tiny ($^1/_8$ inch) and have $^1/_2$-inch wings.

Mountain Hemlock forms pure or almost-pure stands in high alpine meadows. On moist slopes and flats, or in north-facing ravines, it is found with other conifers. It matures at 200 to 300 years of age but can live as long as 500 years.

Features: Mountain Hemlock provides important cover for nesting birds; it is also a source of seeds. The needles are browsed by mountain goats and other animals. The tree has a shallow rooting system, making it susceptible to windthrow on steep side slopes or in canyons.

Range: Along the Pacific coast from southern Alaska to British Columbia, in the mountains south to central California; also in the Rocky Mountains in southeast British Columbia to northern Idaho and northeast Oregon. At elevations up to 3,500 feet in Alaska and 5,500 to 11,000 feet in the south.

Western Hemlock, *Tsuga heterophylla*
Pacific Hemlock, West Coast Hemlock

Western Hemlock is a large evergreen that grows to a height of 125 to 175 feet with a diameter of 2 to 4 feet. It is the largest of the American hemlocks. It has relatively thin, reddish brown to gray-brown bark, with long, flat plates separated by deep, narrow fissures. The inner bark is red, sometimes streaked with purple. The tree develops a long, slender trunk that tapers gently toward the top. The crown is short, narrow, and pyramidlike. The topmost terminal branch has a characteristic droop.

Needlelike leaves are $^1/4$ to $^3/4$ inch long, dark green, grooved above, with two faint white lines beneath, flat, uniform in width for their entire length, forming flat sprays. Needles are rounded or blunt at the tip and have very short basal stalks. Slender twigs are yellow-brown with fine hairs. Branches tend to be short and either horizontal or slightly drooping. Small light brown cones are $^3/4$ to 1 inch long, oval in shape, with elliptical scales and no stalk. Cones hang down at the end of twigs. Seeds are very tiny, only $^1/16$ inch, and have a large, straw-colored wing.

Western Hemlock likes moist sites where annual rainfall is at least 70 inches. It is found in pure, dense stands along the coast in the northern part of its range and also in the understory of mixed-hardwood or mixed-conifer forests. The seeds germinate easily on moist sites, and seedlings often develop on cut-over and burned-over areas. Trees can reach 500 years of age.

Features: Western Hemlock is the most important timber-producing species of the North American hemlocks and is one of the top timber-producing trees in the Northwest. It is used as contruction lumber and is an excellent source of pulpwood.

Range: Coastal areas from southwest Alaska to northwest California, also in the Rocky Mountains from southeast British Columbia to northern Idaho and northwest Montana, at elevations up to 2,000 feet in coastal areas, and up to 6,000 feet inland.

JUNIPER

Junipers, members of the Cypress family, are often short, stunted trees or bushy shrubs, mostly growing on dry sites. They have tiny, scalelike leaves that form rounded or four-angled twigs. Berrylike cones are either red or blue. Junipers are easily confused with cypresses.

Alligator Juniper, *Juniperus deppeana*

Alligator Juniper is a small evergreen that grows to a height of 20 to 50 feet with a diameter of 2 to 4 feet. It has thick, rough bark, blackish or gray, deeply furrowed in checkered plates resembling the hide of an alligator. The tree has a short, stout trunk and rounded, spreading crown made up of upright branches.

Scalelike leaves are opposite, $^1/_{16}$ to $^1/_8$ inch long, blue-green to silver-green, with sharp points, in four rows that form slender, four-angled twigs. They have a gland dot and often a whitish resin drop that gives the crown a silvery hue. Berrylike cones are $^1/_2$ inch in diameter, reddish tan to dark red-brown, with a whitish bloom when mature. They become hard, dry, and mealy. Maturing in the second year, they have three to five seeds.

Alligator Juniper grows on rocky hillsides and mountains in open oak/pinyon/juniper forests. It can sprout from the base of cut stumps.

Features: Alligator Juniper is one of the largest junipers and is easily recognized by its bark. The wood is used for fuel and fence posts.

Range: Found in the Trans-Pecos northwest to northern Arizona, also in Mexico, at elevations from 4,500 to 8,000 feet.

California Juniper, *Juniperus californica*

California Juniper is a small evergreen that grows to a height of 40 feet with a diameter from 1 to 2 feet. Gray bark is fibrous, furrowed, and shreddy. The tree is often multistemmed rather than growing from a single trunk and has a rounded crown made up of spreading branches. It also grows as a shrub.

Scalelike leaves are $1/16$ to $1/8$ inch long, usually in threes, blunt, forming stiff, rounded twigs. Scales do not usually overlap. They are light green and have a gland dot. Berrylike cones are $1/2$ to $3/4$ inch long, oval in shape, and bluish brown, with a bloom. They turn brown, become hard and dry, and usually have one or two seeds.

California Juniper is found on dry, rocky slopes and flats in semidesert areas, also on foothills and lower mountains, often with pinyons or Joshua Trees.

Features: California Juniper is found in hotter, drier areas than other junipers because of its ability to withstand heat and drought. It helps stabilize dry slopes. Native Americans ate the cones and ground them into meal.

Range: Found in the mountains of California, especially southwestern California, into northern Baja California, also in extreme southern Nevada and western Arizona, at elevations from 1,000 to 5,000 feet.

Drooping Juniper, *Juniperus flaccida*
Weeping Juniper, Mexican Drooping Juniper

Drooping Juniper is a small evergreen that grows to a height of 30 feet with a diameter up to 1 foot. It also grows as a shrub. The bark is cinnamon red-brown, with long, interlaced, fibrous, shreddy ridges. The tree has a rounded crown and is easily distinguished from other junipers by its drooping branches.

Scalelike leaves are opposite; $^1/_{16}$ to $^1/_8$ inch long; yellow-green; with long, pointed, spreading tips; in four rows that form slender, drooping twigs. Berrylike cones are $^3/_8$ to $^1/_2$ inch in diameter, cinnamon red-brown, with a bloom when mature. Cones are rough, slightly woody and dry, resinous, and contain 4 to 12 seeds. Male cones are found on separate trees.

Drooping Juniper grows with other junipers, pinyons, and oaks on rocky slopes and in mountain canyons.

Features: Drooping Juniper is the rarest juniper in the U.S., where it is found only in Big Bend National Park, in Texas. It is more widespread in Mexico. It is easily distinguished from other junipers by its drooping foliage.

Range: In the Chisos Mountains of the Trans-Pecos, and in Mexico, at elevations from 4,500 to 7,000 feet.

Oneseed Juniper, *Juniperus monosperma*

Oneseed Juniper is a small evergreen that grows to a height of 10 to 25 feet with a diameter up to 1 foot. It also grows as a shrub. The gray-brown bark is made up of thin, shreddy strips. The tree has a short trunk and branches near the base. The irregular crown is composed of upward-curving branches.

The scalelike leaves are opposite, $1/16$ inch long, green to dark green, with a gland dot, in four rows that form short, stout, crowded twigs. Scales do not overlap. The $1/4$- inch berrylike cones are reddish blue or dark blue with a bloom, resinous, soft, juicy, and sweet. Cones have one seed. Male cones are on separate trees.

Oneseed Juniper is found in open, parklike stands on dry plains, plateaus, hills, and mountains, on rocky soils. It often grows in pure stands.

Features: Oneseed Juniper is one of the most common small trees in New Mexico. The wood is used for firewood and fence posts. Native Americans used the bark to make mats and cloth.

Range: It is found from central Colorado through New Mexico and west to central Arizona, at elevations from 3,000 to 7,000 feet.

Rocky Mountain Juniper, *Juniperus scopulorum*
Rocky Mountain Redcedar, River Juniper

Rocky Mountain Juniper is a medium-size evergreen that grows to a height of 20 to 50 feet with a diameter of 1 to 2 feet. The brown bark is made up of thin, shredding strips. The tree has a straight trunk and narrow, conical crown made up of slender, upward-pointing branches; it resembles a teardrop.

Scalelike leaves are opposite, $1/16$ inch long, bluish to dark green, in four rows that form slender, four-angled twigs. Scales are somewhat pointed. Foliage droops at the ends of branches. Berrylike cones are $1/4$ inch in diameter, sweet, soft, and juicy, bright blue with a white bloom, becoming darker blue. They mature in two years and usually have two seeds.

Rocky Mountain Juniper is found in the mountains on rocky soils and on limestone and lava outcrops. In the southern portion of its range, it grows in the foothills with pinyons; in the north, it is found in open, scrub woodlands or on the edge of wooded areas.

Features: The wood is quite aromatic and favored for use in cedar chests. This juniper is also harvested for lumber, fence posts, and firewood. The tree is planted as an ornamental and for erosion control.

Range: From central British Columbia and generally southeast through the Rockies to southeastern New Mexico, at elevations from 5,000 to 7,500 feet.

Utah Juniper, *Juniperus osteosperma*

Utah Juniper is a small evergreen that reaches heights of 15 to 40 feet with diameters of 1 to 3 feet. The gray-brown bark is thin and fibrous, in long, shredded strips. The tree has a short, upright trunk that is either single or multi-stemmed and an open, rounded crown with upright, spreading branches.

The scalelike leaves are usually opposite, $1/16$ inch long, light yellow-green, in four rows that form stout twigs. Short-pointed scales are usually without gland dots. Berrylike cones are $1/4$ to $5/8$ inch in diameter; bluish brown with a bloom; becoming brown, woody, and dry; with only one or two seeds.

Utah Juniper is found on dry, rocky soils on plains, plateaus, hills, and mountains, growing in pure stands or with Singleleaf Pinyon.

Features: Utah Juniper is the dominant Juniper in Utah. It is also found on the south rim of the Grand Canyon, in Arizona. It grows slowly and becomes irregularly shaped with age. Parasitic mistletoe develops yellow twigs with whitish berries. Native Americans used the wood for bows and the bark to make sandals and woven bags.

Range: Found in Nevada, east to Wyoming, south to western New Mexico, and west to southern California, at elevations from 3,000 to 8,000 feet.

Western Juniper, *Juniperus occidentalis*
Sierra Juniper

Western Juniper is a small evergreen that grows to a height of 10 to 30 feet, but rarely exceeds 60 feet; it has a diameter from 2 to 3 feet. It also grows as a shrub. The bark is initially pinkish and smooth but turns reddish brown and shredded and develops furrows as the tree ages. The trunk is short with stout, upright branches that make up a broad, spreading crown. The tree can become gnarled and ragged as it ages. Roots can be exposed, often formed around rock outcrops. Giant trees on such outcrops in harsh climatic conditions can be as large as 16 feet in diameter and over 2,000 years old.

Scalelike leaves are $1/16$ inch long, often in threes, dark gray-green, forming stout, rounded twigs. Gland dots are noticeable. Twigs are three or four sided. Berries are $1/4$ to $3/8$ inch long and elliptical rather than round, blue-black, with a powdery appearance when mature. They mature in two years and have two or three seeds.

Western Juniper is found on shallow, rocky soils on mountain slopes and plateaus. It develops large roots that hug the rocks that support it.

Features: Western Juniper grows on rocky outcrops at high altitudes where there is little competition from other species.

Range: From central and southeast Washington to southern California, at elevations to 10,000 feet.

LARCH

Western Larch, *Larix occidentalis*
Hackmatack, Western Tamarack

Western Larch is a very large deciduous tree that grows to a height of 140 to 180 feet with a diameter of 3 to 4 feet. Younger trees have reddish brown, scaly bark. On older trees, the bark is 4 to 6 inches thick and develops flat plates divided by deep fissures. The thick bark makes older trees somewhat resistant to fire. The trunk is clear for most of its length. The slender crown appears fairly open, with short, horizontal branches.

The needlelike leaves are single, 1 to $1^3/4$ inches long, pale green, three angled, and arranged in clusters of several needles on short spurs. The twigs are stout, initially hairy, but soon turning orange-brown and hairless. The buds are chestnut brown. Cones are 1 to $1^1/2$ inches long, oblong, on a short stalk, and purplish red to reddish brown. Cones are persistent for many years. The cone scales are wider than they are long, sometimes with a fine tooth at the pointed tip. Bracts are visible and have a long spike. Seeds are tiny—only $1/4$ inch long—with short, $1/2$-inch, fragile wings.

Western Larch grows best on deep, moist, well-drained soil on mountain slopes and in high valleys with northern or western exposure. It grows in nearly pure stands and often is the most common tree found in mixed-conifer forests in the northern Rockies. It is fairly intolerant of shade so is often found in dominant crown positions in older stands of trees. It reaches maturity by 300 to 400 years of age but can survive for as long as 700 to 900 years.

Features: Western Larch, the largest of the American larches, offers a showy display of lustrous green in spring and summer that turns to brilliant yellow in fall. The wood is used for fine veneer, lumber, and pulp. Blue and Spruce Grouse feed on needles; twigs are occasionally browsed by deer.

Range: From southern British Columbia to northwest Oregon and central Idaho, at elevations from 2,000 to 5,500 feet in the north and to 7,000 feet in the south.

NUTMEG

California Nutmeg, *Torreya californica*
California Torreya, Stinking Cedar

California Nutmeg is a small- to medium-size evergreen that grows to a height of 16 to 70 feet with a diameter of 8 inches to 2 feet. It has thin, gray-brown bark broken into narrow, scaly ridges by irregular fissures. The crown is rounded or conical, with rows of slender branches.

Needlelike leaves are 1 to 2¼ inches long, in rows of two, flat, slightly curved, stiff, with a long, sharp point at the tip; leaves are almost stalkless at the base, shiny dark green above, having two whitish lines beneath. The paired twigs are initially yellow-green but turn reddish brown. The seeds and male cones (pollen cones) are found on separate trees. The elliptical seeds are 1 to 1½ inches long and have a green, fleshy outer layer with purplish markings that is shed. The inner layer is yellow-brown with thick walls. Seeds are stalkless and scattered on leafy twigs. The pale yellow, elliptical male cones are ⅛ inch long and found singly at leaf bases.

California Nutmeg is found along mountain streams, in shaded canyons, and on exposed slopes, often in mixed-conifer forests. It will sprout from stumps.

Features: The seeds are aromatic and smell like nutmeg. Crushed foliage has an unpleasant odor, hence the name Stinking Cedar. The attractive wood is fine grained and polishes well, although the tree is not logged commercially because of its limited distribution. Native Americans used the wood for bows. The tree is sometimes planted as an ornamental.

Range: Mountains of central and northern California, from 3,000 to 6,000 feet in elevation, and near sea level along the coast.

PINE

Pines are members of the Pine family and occupy vast acreages throughout the West. They have needlelike leaves usually in bundles of two or more (Single-leaf Pinyon is the only native pine with just one needle). Twigs are usually stout. Seeds are produced in cones. Many pines are commercially important producers of lumber and pulp.

Apache Pine, *Pinus engelmannii*
Arizona Longleaf Pine

Apache Pine is a medium-size evergreen that grows to a height of 50 to 70 feet with a diameter up to 2 feet. The thick, rough bark is dark brown or black-gray and breaks up into scaly ridges separated by deep furrows. The tree has a straight trunk with large, spreading branches that make up an open, rounded crown.

Needlelike leaves are three per bundle, 8 to 12 inches long, dull green, and stout. They appear crowded at the ends of very stout twigs, sometimes drooping or spread widely. They are, very rarely, in bundles of two or five. Cones are 4 to 5½ inches long, egg shaped, shiny, light brown, with almost no stalk. They are shed at maturity, although a few cone scales remain on the twig. Cone scales are thick, four sided, and have a prominent ridge with a stout, short prickle that curves backward.

Apache Pine grows on rocky ridges and slopes. It is often found with Ponderosa Pine, Arizona Pine, and Chihuahua Pine.

Features: Apache Pine seedlings grow in a grass phase for the first several years and then into a branchless stem with very long needles as the seedling develops a deep taproot.

Range: Southeastern Arizona and southwest New Mexico, south into Mexico, at elevations of 5,000 to 8,200 feet.

Bishop Pine, *Pinus muricata*
Santa Cruz Island Pine, Pricklecone Pine

Bishop Pine is a medium-size evergreen that grows to a height of 40 to 80 feet and 2 to 3 feet in diameter. The thick bark is dark gray with deeply furrowed, scaly plates. The tree has a rounded or irregular crown made up of spreading branches that retain spiny cones for many years.

Needlelike leaves are two per bundle, 4 to 6 inches long, yellow-green or dull green, rigid, slightly flattened, with a blunt point. The serotinous cones are 2 to $3\frac{1}{2}$ inches long, asymmetrical at the base, making the cone irregularly egg shaped. The cones have no stalks and grow in clusters that ring the branch. Cone scales are ridged with a flattened, spurlike prickle.

Bishop Pine grows in the coastal fog belt on low hills and plains, preferring wet areas such as peat bogs and swamps but also found on drier sites. It grows quickly and is relatively short lived. It forms pure stands but is very limited in its distribution.

Features: The cones of Bishop Pine remain closed and can become embedded in the bark as the wood on the trunk and branches expands. It depends on fire for seed dispersal. In areas where fire is suppressed, new generations of Bishop Pine will not be established.

Range: Found in widely scattered groves along the California coastline from northern California to the Baja, from sea level to 1,000 feet elevation.

Bristlecone and Foxtail Pines

The Bristlecone and Foxtail Pines include three species found in subalpine locations in the western Unites States and have a characteristic bushy form on young branches because of their tendency to retain needles for many years, thus creating a foxtail appearance. They rarely exceed 30 to 40 feet in height with a diameter from 12 to 24 inches. The bark is initially smooth, whitish to gray, becoming furrowed by scaly ridges and reddish brown. These pines develop short, stocky, malformed trunks and dense, irregular crowns. At timberline, they also grow as dense, low shrubs. Trees and shrubs form colonies that are connected to the same root system. The needles are $^3/_4$ to $1^1/_2$ inches long, stout, stiff, and found in groups of five.

Bristlecone

Bristlecone Pine, *Pinus aristata*. (not pictured) Bristlecone Pine can be distinguished by its bright blue-green needles, some having small drops of white resin on the outer surface and a noticeable groove. The brown or grayish brown cones are $2^1/_2$ to $3^1/_2$ inches long, cylindrical, and rounded at the base. The ends of the cone scales have a long, thin, stiff prickle that curves inward toward the scale.

Great Basin Bristlecone

These trees are found on the high ridges and slopes of Colorado, northern New Mexico, and northern Arizona at elevations from 7,500 to 11,200 feet on dry, rocky ridges.

Great Basin Bristlecone Pine, *Pinus longaeva*. Great Basin Bristlecone Pine has blue-green needles with only a few white resin deposits. Needles are not grooved. The cones have a rounded base and are rusty red. The ends of the cone scales also have a thin prickle that is shorter than the Bristlecone Pine's.

Foxtail

These trees are found in Utah, Nevada, and eastern California at elevations of 5,600 to 11,200 feet along rocky ridges and slopes. These are the oldest living things known to exist—trees found in the Inyo National Forest near Bishop, California, are more than 4,600 years old.

Foxtail Pine, *Pinus balfouriana*. (not pictured) Foxtail Pine has bright blue-green needles with no grooves. Cones are $3^1/_2$ to 5 inches long, ovoid to cylindrical, with a more conical base than either of the bristlecone pines. Cones are dark reddish brown. The ends of the cone scales have a very short, weak, deciduous prickle.

These trees are found in the mountains of northern California and the Sierra Nevada of central California at elevations of 5,000 to 11,500 feet, on high, rocky ridges in subalpine zones to timberline.

California Foothill Pine, *Pinus sabiniana*
Gray Pine, Bull Pine

California Foothill Pine is a small evergreen that grows to a height of 40 to 50 feet with a diameter of 1 to 2 feet. It has grayish brown bark that forms flat plates separated by reddish furrows, becoming shaggy on older trees. The trunk is crooked and often forked, with an open, irregular, gray crown.

Needlelike leaves are three per bundle, 8 to 12 inches long, gray-green with white lines, flexible, slender, and drooping. Brown cones are 6 to 10 inches long, egg shaped, and mostly symmetrical. They are heavy, sometimes over a pound, and bend downward from long stalks. Cone scales are irregularly shaped and have downward-pointing, $1/2$- to $3/4$-inch thorns.

California Foothill Pine is found on dry foothills and lower mountain slopes, in open stands, growing in pure stands or in combination with oaks. At higher elevations, it can be found with Ponderosa Pine. It is not tolerant of shade and easily damaged by fire.

Features: The wood is soft and lightweight and does not have any commercial value. Native Americans ate the seeds, and even the soft cones; they used the needles, cones, and resin to make baskets. The ghostly gray crown makes California Foothill Pine easy to identify at a distance.

Range: The Coast Ranges and western slopes of the Sierra Nevada in California, at elevations from 1,000 to 3,000 feet.

Coulter Pine, *Pinus coulteri*
Bigcone Pine, Pitch Pine

Coulter Pine is a medium-size evergreen that grows 40 to 70 feet tall and 15 to 30 inches in diameter. The bark is very dark brown, almost black, with rounded ridges separated by interlacing fissures. The single trunk is straight, with an open, irregular crown made up of rows of horizontal branches.

Needlelike leaves are three per bundle, 8 to 12 inches long, light gray-green, with many white lines, rigid, sharp pointed, and appearing crowded at the ends of stout, brown twigs. The cones are very large, 8 to 12 inches long, and can weigh 4 to 6 pounds when green. These are the heaviest and thorniest cones of the western pines. They are a shiny yellow-brown and bend downward from a short stalk. The cone scales open gradually while cones hang on the tree. Cone scales are very thick, with a sharp ridge that ends in a curved claw. The seeds have very hard coats with wings longer than the seed.

Coulter Pine is found in the mountains of southern coastal California. It often invades chaparral at lower elevations. The tree develops a large crown that can extend to the ground when open grown. It also can be found on dry, rocky slopes and ridges with other conifers. It is intolerant of shade and very slow growing.

Features: The wood is soft and lightweight and used for rough lumber and fuelwood. Native Americans ate the large seeds. Squirrels and other wildlife feed on them, too.

Range: Central and southern California and northern Baja California, from 3,000 to 6,000 feet elevation.

Jeffrey Pine, *Pinus jeffreyi*
Western Yellow Pine, Bull Pine

Jeffrey Pine is a medium-size to large evergreen that grows to heights of 90 to 130 feet with diameters from 3 to 5 feet. Young bark is gray, separated into flat plates with shallow cinnamon-red fissures. On older trees, the bark is thick, dark cinnamon-red, sometimes tinged with dark purple, and furrowed with large, scaly plates. The tree has a straight trunk and open, conical crown.

Needlelike leaves are three per bundle, 5 to 10 inches long, light gray-green or blue-green, with white lines on all surfaces, stout, stiff, and twisted. They sometimes grow in bundles of two or three on the same tree. Gray-green twigs are stout and hairless. Crushed needles and twigs have a noticeably pleasant scent that is often compared to vanilla, lemon, or pineapple. Cones are 5 to 10 inches long, egg shaped, light brown, and shiny. Cone scales are ridged and have a long, stout, inward-curved prickle. Seeds are $1/3$ inch long and have large wings.

Jeffrey Pine grows best in deep, well-drained soils on dry slopes. It is often found with, and confused with, Ponderosa Pine but usually does not attain the height or size of a Ponderosa. The bark of Jeffrey Pine has smaller, less-prominent plates and is less orange in color. Jeffrey Pine seedlings are resistant to frost damage.

Features: Jeffrey Pine is logged commercially and sold as yellow pine, as is Ponderosa Pine. Seeds are eaten by squirrels, chipmunks, grouse, and quail. It is susceptible to damage from needle blight, rusts, and dwarf mistletoe.

Range: From southwest Oregon through the Sierra Nevada, especially on eastern slopes, to western Nevada and southern California, from 6,000 to 9,000 feet.

Knobcone Pine, *Pinus attenuata*

Knobcone Pine is a small- to medium-size evergreen that grows to a height of 30 to 80 feet with a diameter from 1 to 2½ feet. The bark is gray, initially smooth but developing fissures that separate into scaly ridges with age. The trunk is often forked. The crown is narrow, egg shaped, with a pointed tip. Older crowns become irregular.

Needlelike leaves are three per bundle, 3 to 7 inches long, yellow-green, slender, and rigid. The 3- to 6-inch cones appear somewhat lopsided, with an asymmetrical base and very short stalk. They also have thorny scales. The clustered cones are serotinous—they remain closed after the seeds are mature. Cones can remain on the tree for many years.

Knobcone Pine grows on poor soils on dry slopes, rocky outcrops, and dry ridges. It is found in pure stands and also mixed with Sugar, Ponderosa, and Coulter Pines, and some chaparral oaks. It is not tolerant of shade and is usually short lived.

Features: The cones persist on the tree for many years and have been known to become imbedded in the trunk as it grows. Cones open after forest fires, releasing many, many seeds. For unknown reasons, feral pigs will damage the bark on tree trunks with their tusks, girdling the trees, sometimes causing them to die.

Range: Found in the mountains of southwestern Oregon along the Coast Ranges into northern and central California, at elevations from 1,000 to 4,000 feet.

Limber Pine, *Pinus flexilis*
White Pine, Rocky Mountain White Pine

Limber Pine is a small evergreen that grows to a height of 30 to 50 feet with a diameter up to 2 feet. The bark on younger trees is smooth and white to greenish gray but on older trees is reddish brown, almost black, with fissures that create rectangular or square, scaly blocks. The trunk is stout and tapered. It has a long, elliptical crown with many drooping branches that can reach the ground.

Needlelike leaves are five per bundle, 2 to 3$^1/_2$ inches long, light to dark green, with fine white lines on all surfaces, slender, flexible, and clustered at the ends of twigs. The yellow-brown cones are 3 to 6 inches long and egg shaped to cylindrical, with short stems. The cone scales are thickened and end in a blunt point. Cones open annually at maturity. The dark seeds are large, up to $^1/_2$ inch in diameter, and edible.

Limber Pine is found on dry, rocky ridges often near timberline. At that elevation, trees are often shaped into stunted shrubs from exposure to wind and snow. It often grows in pure stands and is relatively slow growing.

Features: Twigs are extremely tough and flexible and can be tied into knots. It has some commercial value for construction lumber and railroad ties.

Range: From Alberta southward through the Rocky Mountains and into southern California. This subalpine pine is found at higher elevations: 4,000 to 10,000 feet in the north, and up to 11,800 feet in southern California.

Lodgepole Pine, *Pinus contorta*
Shore Pine, Tamarack Pine

Lodgepole Pine is widely distributed through western North America and has at least four different varieties. Two coastal varieties are referred to as Shore Pine, and two inner mountain varieties are referred to as Lodgepole Pine. Differences between them are limited to bark, size, shape, and distribution. Shore Pine is a smaller evergreen, only 25 to 30 feet in height and 12 to 18 inches in diameter, with a much thicker bark ($^3/_4$ to 1 inch), reddish brown to black, with deep fissures separating thin scales. Shore Pine has a short, twisted trunk that ends in a crown of twisted branches, some of which may extend to the ground. It is seldom found far from tidal water. Shore Pine is found along the Pacific coast from Alaska to northern California. It has no commercial value.

The inner mountain form of Lodgepole Pine is a medium-size evergreen growing 70 to 80 feet tall with a diameter of 15 to 30 inches. The bark is thin ($^1/_4$ inch), orange-brown to gray, and covered with loose scales. The trunk is long, straight, and slender, ending in a short, narrow crown.

Both forms have needlelike leaves, two per bundle, 1 to 3 inches long, yellow-green to dark green, stout, and often twisted. Twigs are stout, dark red to almost black. Cones are generally oval to slightly cylindrical, $^3/_4$ to 2 inches long, asymmetrical at the base. Cone scales have a slender prickle. Cones characteristically stay on the tree for years, even though the seeds are fully developed.

Lodgepole Pine is a fast-growing tree and is quick to reestablish in cut- and burned-over areas. It forms dense stands, in some cases so dense that overcrowding stunts the growth of the entire stand. The tree often forms pure stands but will also grow mixed with other pines at lower elevations and with Engelmann Spruce, Subalpine Fir, Limber Pine, and Jeffery Pine at higher elevations.

Features: Lodgepole Pine takes its name from its use by Native Americans for tipi poles. It is not fire tolerant, but the serotinous cones are triggered to open with fire, releasing a tremendous number of seeds. Seedling densities of greater than 1 million seedlings to the acre have been documented.

Range: In the northern part of its range in Alaska and British Columbia, it is found from sea level to 2,000 feet; in Oregon and Washington up to 6,000 feet; to 11,500 feet in California. In the Rocky Mountains, it grows at 6,000 to 11,000 feet in elevation.

Monterey Pine, *Pinus radiata*
Insignis Pine

Monterey Pine is a medium-size evergreen that grows to a height of 50 to 100 feet with a diameter of 1 to 3 feet. It has thick, reddish brown bark that has scaly plates or ridges separated by deep furrows. It has a straight trunk with a crown that is narrow, irregular, and fairly open.

Needlelike leaves are three per bundle, 4 to 6 inches long, shiny green, slender, and flexible. Cones are 3 to 6 inches long, egg shaped, asymmetrical at the base, and pointed at the tip. They are shiny brown and resinous. Cones grow in clustered rings on short stalks and remain on the tree for many years without opening. The thick cone scales are slightly raised and rounded, with a tiny prickle.

Monterey Pine is relatively rare, found in only a few locations in California, on coarse soils on slopes. It is found in pure stands or with Monterey and Gowen Cypresses and California Live Oak.

Features: Monterey Pine has been successfully planted for commercial production in locations in the southern hemisphere where pines do not naturally occur. In the U.S., it is of limited commercial value. The cones of Monterey Pine are serotinous, remaining closed until heated by forest fire. Cones have been known to burst open with a loud snapping sound during hot weather.

Range: Rare, found in isolated locations in central California in the fog belt to about 6 miles inland, to 1,000 feet in elevation.

Ponderosa Pine, *Pinus ponderosa*
Western Yellow Pine, Blackjack Pine

Ponderosa Pine is the most widely distributed and common pine in North America. There are several varieties found in different geographical areas, each with differences in the number of needles and size of cones. Ponderosa Pine is a very large evergreen that grows to a height of 150 to 180 feet with a diameter of 3 to 4 feet. On young trees, the bark is black and deeply furrowed; on older trees, it has orange-brown or cinnamon brown, superficial, irregularly shaped, scaly plates separated by furrows, creating a jigsaw puzzle appearance. Even when open grown, the tree develops a long, clear trunk with an open, conical crown made up of spreading branches.

Needlelike leaves usually grow in bundles of two or three, although the different varieties can have between two and five needles per bundle. The needles are 4 to 8 inches long, yellow-green to dark gray-green, stout, and flexible, with a turpentine odor when crushed. Twigs are stout. The conical or egg-shaped cones are 2 to 6 inches long, light reddish brown, and have almost no stalk. They open and are shed when mature, leaving a few cone scales on the tree. Cone scales are raised and have a ridge with a short, sharp prickle.

Ponderosa Pine does not have specific soil requirements and is drought resistant. It grows best on moist, well-drained soils on the western slopes of the Siskiyou and Sierra Nevada. It often forms pure stands or is the most abundant tree in mixed-conifer stands. It is not particularly tolerant of shade and reproduces best in clearings following logging or fire. Trees can grow for 500 years.

The growth rate of individual trees affects the appearance of Ponderosa Pine. Young, vigorous growth develops dense crowns with dark green foliage. Slower-growing trees appear more yellow-green and develop the characteristic orange-brown or cinnamon brown, platy bark.

Features: Ponderosa Pine is the most commercially important timber tree in the West. Lumber is well suited for panel doors and window frames.

Range: Ponderosa Pine variety *ponderosa* is found in the mountains of the Pacific Coast region from southern British Columbia to southern California and western Nevada, from sea level to 7,600 feet in elevation. It has relatively large cones and needles mostly in bundles of three. Variety *scopulorum* (Rocky Mountain Ponderosa Pine) is found in the Rocky Mountains of southwest North Dakota, Montana, and Idaho, south to Arizona, New Mexico, and western Texas. It has shorter cones and needles, with needles in bundles of two.

Southwestern White Pine, *Pinus strobiformis*
Mexican White Pine, Border White Pine

Southwestern White Pine is a medium-size evergreen that grows to a height of 60 to 80 feet with a diameter from 1 1/2 to 3 feet. The smooth, gray bark becomes dark gray or brown with narrow, irregular ridges separated by deep furrows. The tree has a straight trunk with horizontal branches that make up a narrow, conical crown.

Needlelike leaves are five per bundle, 2 1/2 to 3 1/2 inches long, with a sheath that sheds the first year. Bright green with white lines only on inner surfaces, needles are slender and finely toothed near the tip. Yellow-brown cones are 6 to 9 inches long, cylindrical, and short-stalked. They open at maturity. Slightly thickened cone scales are very long, with a narrow, spreading tip. Seeds are large, edible, and have very short wings.

Southwestern White Pine is found at higher elevations on dry, rocky slopes and in canyons. It is a minor component of coniferous forests.

Features: Seeds of Southwestern White Pine were used by Native Americans as a source of food, although the shells are hard to crack. The tree is not found in great abundance and does not have much commercial use, although it is used locally for cabinetry and fence posts and as fuelwood.

Range: The Trans-Pecos to east-central Arizona to northern Mexico, at elevations from 6,300 to 9,900 feet.

Sugar Pine, *Pinus lambertiana*

Sugar Pine is the tallest member of the pines; it can grow to a height of 170 to 180 feet with a diameter from 30 to 42 inches. Young trees have smooth, dark green, thin bark, becoming grayish brown to purplish brown when mature. On older trees, the bark can be 1 to 4 inches thick and is broken into scaly ridges separated by deep fissures. Tree trunks are usually long, branchless, and cylindrical, with short, conical crowns made up of several massive, horizontal, or occasionally contorted branches.

Needlelike leaves are five per bundle, 2³/4 to 4 inches long, blue-green to gray-green, often silvery, with white lines on all surfaces. Needles are thin, stiff, pointed, and spirally twisted. Twigs are stout, initially hairy, becoming orange-brown to purplish brown, smooth, and hairless. Sharp-pointed, ovoid buds are ¹/3 inch long, with several tight, chestnut brown scales. Cones are huge—the largest produced by any pine—and can reach as much as 26 inches in length and 4 to 5 inches in diameter when open. They hang down on long stalks near the ends of upper branches. Thick, rounded cone scales end in a blunt point.

Sugar Pine is usually found on cooler, wetter western slopes. The extreme temperatures and drought conditions found on eastern slopes limit Sugar Pine's ability to grow there. Unlike some conifers, Sugar Pine does not form pure stands and is found with Ponderosa Pine, Incense Cedar, Douglas-fir, and Giant Sequoia.

Features: Sugar Pine is an important lumber tree. Early settlers used the wood for houses, shingles, shakes, and fences. Native Americans gathered and ate the sweet-tasting seeds. Today, the wood is used for cabinetwork, veneer backing, and house interiors.

Range: In the mountains of western Oregon south through the Sierra Nevada and into southern California, extending into northern Baja California. Found at altitudes of 1,000 to 5,000 feet in the north, 2,000 to 8,000 feet in California, and 4,000 to 10,000 feet in the south.

Torrey Pine, *Pinus torreyana*
Del Mar Pine, Soledad Pine

Torrey Pine is a small evergreen that grows to a height of 30 to 50 feet with a diameter of 1 to 2 feet. Black bark has broad, flat, scaly ridges separated by deep furrows. Branches are gray with smooth bark. The tree has a straight trunk with an open, spreading crown. On exposed sites, it has a more shrublike form.

The needlelike leaves are five per bundle, 8 to 13 inches long, dark gray-green with white lines, stiff, stout, and crowded in large clusters at the ends of very stout twigs. Egg-shaped, nut-brown cones are 4 to 6 inches long and bent downward on stout stalks. They take three seasons to mature and remain on the tree for several seasons thereafter. Cone scales are thick, with a sharp ridge and stout, straight spine. Elliptical seeds are very large and have a short, detachable wing. Although they have a thick wall, the seeds are edible.

Torrey Pine is found on dry, sandy bluffs and slopes. There are two native groves in southern California. It has been cultivated elsewhere in moist, warm climates. It is not tolerant of shade and has a short life span. Wood rats have been known to consume large quantities of seeds, thus reducing the amount of seed in the seed bank.

Features: Torrey Pine is a rare native conifer with only a few thousand trees, most of which are found in the Torrey Pines State Natural Reserve. In earlier geological times, it had a much broader distribution. Because it grows rapidly, it is cultivated in other climates for commercial timber purposes and shade.

Range: San Diego County in southern California and Santa Rosa Island.

Western White Pine, *Pinus monticola*
Idaho White Pine

Western White Pine is a large to very large evergreen that grows to a height of 150 to 180 feet with a diameter of $2^1/_2$ to $3^1/_2$ feet when mature. Young trees have thin, smooth, gray-green to light gray bark that, over time, breaks up into nearly square or rectangular, dark gray or purplish gray plates. The tree develops a long, slightly tapered trunk, often clear for half its length with a short, symmetrical, and somewhat open crown.

The needlelike leaves are five per bundle, 2 to 4 inches long, waxy, blue-green, with two to six rows of fine white lines on the lower side, and are straight, slender, and flexible. Needles persist for three or four years. Twigs are moderately slender, often with orange-brown hair during the first season, becoming thick and hairless and turning dark reddish to purplish brown. Buds are $1/_2$ inch long, cylindrical, and blunt. Narrow, cylindrical cones are 5 to 15 inches long, stalked, and often curved. Cone scales are thin, papery, and rounded.

Western White Pine grows best on northern exposures in valleys and on middle and upper slopes, with the largest trees found in northern Idaho, commonly in pure stands. In other areas, it grows on drier slopes as a minor component. It is susceptible to Pine Beetle damage and White Pine Blister Rust.

Features: Western White Pine is an important timber tree because of its uniform high grade with few knots, twisted grain, or discoloration. The trees are unusually wind-firm due to the development of a deep taproot as a seedling, which is supplemented in later life by a deep, wide-spreading system of lateral roots.

Range: Found along the Pacific coast from southwest British Columbia through the mountains of California to the Sierra Nevada, also in the northern Rocky Mountains from British Columbia southeast to Idaho and northwest Montana. In the north, from sea level to 3,500 feet; from 6,000 to 10,000 feet in the south.

Whitebark Pine, *Pinus albicaulis*
Scrub Pine, White Pine

Whitebark Pine is a small, subalpine evergreen that grows to a height of 50 feet with a diameter of 1 to 2 feet when found in the best growing conditions. On open, windswept sites, it can be sprawling and sometimes prostrate, barely resembling a tree. The thin bark is brownish to creamy white and smooth on immature trees. Older trunks become dark brown and scaly. The trunk is often twisted and distorted. On more protected sites, the trunk can be erect but tapers rapidly. The long, flexible, willowy branches form a spreading, irregular crown.

The needlelike leaves are five per bundle, 1 to $2^3/4$ inches long, dull green, with white lines on all sides, stiff, pointed, with clusters crowded together at the ends of twigs. The twigs are stout but flexible, brown, and when young have a dense covering of fine hair. The almost stalkless, roundish cones are $1^1/2$ to $3^1/4$ inches long, purple or purple-brown, with thick, pointed scales that do not open. The large, dark brown seeds (up to $1/2$ inch) are edible. Cone fragments are found beneath the tree.

Whitebark Pine is found in the rocky soils of exposed, subalpine ridges up to the treeline. In exposed areas, it may form pure stands and develop into thickets. This small tree can live to 350 years.

Features: Whitebark Pine is important for watershed protection but has little commercial value. Wildlife feed on the seeds. Clark's Nutcracker, a Rocky Mountain bird, tears the cones apart for the seeds. In most of the tree's range, the seeds are a primary food of the Grizzly Bear. Climatic changes in recent decades have led to outbreaks of White Pine Blister Rust and Pine Beetle infestations, which threaten to decimate the White Pine culture. This in turn could directly affect Grizzly Bear populations.

Range: Found from central British Columbia south to central California and from Alberta, Canada; through Montana; Idaho; and Wyoming. In the north, this subalpine species is found from 4,500 to 7,000 feet; from 8,000 to 12,000 feet elevation in the south.

PINYON

Several species of pinyons, or nut pines, occupy vast expanses of land in the intermountain region and arid southwestern U.S., in zones that lie between the deserts and forestlands. Pinyons are found on dry, rocky foothills, mesas, plateaus, and lower mountain slopes. Pinyon-juniper woodlands consist of small trees and shrubs found in scattered to densely mixed clusters, usually between 4,500 and 6,500 feet in elevation.

Pinyons have been an important source of food for both humans and wildlife. The nuts were consumed by Native Americans. Although pinyons are not cultivated, the nuts are harvested commercially and sold as pine nuts, Pinyon nuts, or pinyones. The wood was used by early settlers for building materials and fence posts. Many species of wildlife, including Wild Turkey, Pinyon Jays, wood rats, bear, and deer, consume the seeds.

The different species of Pinyon are easily distinguished by the number of needles present and the geographical region where they are found.

Mexican Pinyon, *Pinus cembroides*
Three-needled Pinyon, Nut Pine, Pinon

Mexican Pinyon is a small evergreen that grows to a height of 15 to 20 feet with a diameter of 1 foot or less. It also grows as a low shrub. When the tree is young, the bark is light gray and smooth. It turns dark gray to reddish brown, with scaly plates separated by furrows, when older. The tree has a short trunk with low, horizontal branches that form a spreading crown.

Needlelike leaves are three per bundle, 1 to $2^{1}/_{2}$ inches long, green with white lines on several surfaces, slender, and flexible. Rarely, there can be two needles per bundle. Needles are clustered at the ends of branches. Small, round or egg-shaped cones are resinous, 1 to 2 inches long, with almost no stalk. They can be orange-brown or reddish. Cone scales are thick, sometimes with a tiny prickle. The large, edible seeds are wingless, with thick, hard walls.

Mexican Pinyon is found with junipers and evergreen oaks on dry, rocky slopes of mesas, plateaus, and mountains.

Range: From the Trans-Pecos and southeast Arizona south into central Mexico, from 2,500 to 7,500 feet.

Parry Pinyon, *Pinus quadrifolia*
Four-needle Pinyon, Nut Pine

Parry Pinyon is a small evergreen that grows to a height of 15 to 30 feet and 1 to 1^1/$_2$ feet in diameter. It often grows as a shrub. When young, the bark is light gray and smooth, becoming reddish brown with furrowed ridges. It is a short tree with a rounded crown made up of low, horizontal branches.

Needlelike leaves grow four per bundle (Parry Pinyon is the only native pine with four needles), 1 to 2^1/$_4$ inches long, bright green with whitish lines on inner surfaces, sharp pointed, stout, and stiff. There are sometimes three or five needles per bundle. Egg-shaped cones are 1^1/$_2$ to 2^1/$_2$ inches long, dull yellow-brown, almost stalkless, and resinous. Cones scales are thick with a tiny prickle. Edible seeds are large and wingless.

Parry Pinyon is found on dry, rocky foothills and lower mountain slopes, often with junipers or in woodlands.

Features: Parry Pinyon has a very limited range, so the nuts are not harvested commercially. Wildlife species consume the nut crop each year. The wood is soft and grainy with many knots and has little commercial value. It is used for fence posts and firewood.

Range: Found in southern California and Baja California at elevations from 4,000 to 6,000 feet.

Singleleaf Pinyon, *Pinus monophylla*
Nut Pine, Singleleaf Pinyon Pine

Singleleaf Pinyon is a small evergreen that grows to heights of 15 to 30 feet with diameters from 1 to 1¹/₂ feet. It also grows as a shrub. The smooth bark is dark brown or gray, developing scaly plates. It has a rounded crown made up of low, horizontal branches.

Single, needlelike leaves are 1 to 2¹/₄ inches long and dull gray-green with whitish lines. Stout, stiff needles are resinous, sharp pointed, and can be either straight or slightly curved. Resinous, egg-shaped cones are 2 to 3 inches long, dull yellow-brown, almost stalkless. Cone scales are thick and have a small prickle. Large, edible seeds are wingless.

Singleleaf Pinyon is found on dry, rocky foothills, mesas, plateaus, and lower mountain slopes. It sometimes grows in widely scattered, pure stands, or mixed with junipers.

Features: Singleleaf Pinyon is the only native pine with just one needle. Native Americans in the Great Basin region relied on this pinyon for food, fuel, and shelter for thousands of years. Many species of wildlife eat the seeds and use the juniper-pinyon woodland for cover.

Range: Found in the Great Basin region in Nevada, southern California, and northern Baja California, from 3,500 to 7,000 feet in elevation.

Twoneedle Pinyon, *Pinus edulis*
Pinyon, Colorado Pinyon

Twoneedle Pinyon is a small evergreen that grows to a height of 15 to 35 feet and a diameter of 1 to 2 feet. Gray to reddish brown bark is rough, with furrowed, scaly ridges. The tree has a short trunk and bushy, rounded crown.

Needlelike leaves are $3/4$ to 2 inches long, two per bundle, light green, and stout. Needles may be tightly pressed against each other and appear as one needle. Occasionally, there may be only one needle, or three needles per bundle. Small, egg-shaped cones are $1^1/2$ to 2 inches long, yellow-brown, and resinous. They have thick, thornless scales. The large, oily seeds are wingless.

Twoneedle Pinyon is found on dry, rocky foothills, mesas, plateaus, and lower mountain slopes in open woodlands in pure stands or with junipers.

Features: Twoneedle Pinyon seeds are a commercial nut crop and are known as pinyon nuts, Indian nuts, pine nuts, and pinyones. They were once a staple food of many southwestern Native Americans and can be made into candies, eaten raw, or roasted. Most of the seeds are consumed by wildlife despite attempts to harvest them for commercial sale. Twoneedle Pinyon is commonly found on the south rim of the Grand Canyon National Park, in Arizona.

Range: Broadly distributed in the southern Rocky Mountains from Utah and Colorado south through New Mexico and Arizona, from 5,000 to 7,000 feet.

SEQUOIA

Redwood, *Sequoia sempervirens*
California Redwood, Coast Redwood

Redwood is the world's tallest tree, reaching heights over 350 feet, although more typically, it grows 200 to 275 feet in height with a diameter of 8 to 12 feet. The deeply furrowed cinnamon red to reddish brown, fibrous bark is 3 to 12 inches thick. The buttressed or swollen trunk is impressively long, straight, and slightly tapered. Swollen burls are often present on the trunk. Many sense a cathedral-like presence when entering groves of these majestic giants. The long trunk is topped by a rather small, irregular, narrow crown.

Redwoods have two kinds of leaves. On the tips of new growth, stems, and the flower/cone-bearing branches, scalelike leaves are $^1/_4$ inch long, pointed, keeled, and encircle the twig. In addition, there are single needlelike leaves $^3/_8$ to $^3/_4$ inch long, dark green above and whitish green beneath, flat, slightly stiff, pointed at the tip, in two rows on older twigs. The longer needles are twisted and blunt near the bases. The oval, brown to reddish brown cones are $^1/_2$ to $1^1/_8$ inch in diameter and are covered with 15 to 20 shield-shaped, wrinkled, pointed scales.

Redwoods are found on moist alluvial soils on flats or benches. It forms pure stands or is the dominant species in combination with Douglas-fir, Port Orford Cedar, and other conifers. The relatively thin bark makes these trees intolerant of fire. Redwoods live 500 to 2,000 years.

Features: The majestic Redwoods once covered nearly 2,000,000 acres, but extensive timber harvesting has resulted in fewer than 100,000 acres remaining today. The Redwood is one of the world's fastest-growing conifer trees, with leading branches growing up to 6 feet in length per year. Unlike most conifers, Redwood will sprout from cut stumps. These sprouts can reach heights of 50 feet and 8 inches in diameter in only 20 years, reaching marketable size in 50 years. The Redwood is still commercially harvested. Though environmentalists protest their harvest, the timber industry believes the rapid growth rate of new stands makes this tree a sustainable resource.

Range: Along the Pacific coast in a narrow band 25 to 40 miles wide, from sea level to 3,000 feet in the high-moisture fog belt that runs from extreme southwestern Oregon to just south of San Francisco Bay.

SEQUOIADENDRON

Giant Sequoia, *Sequoiadendron giganteum*
Bigtree

Giant Sequoia is a huge evergreen that can reach heights of 250 to 310 feet with diameters of 20 feet or more. The cinnamon red, 12- to 24-inch-thick bark is fibrous, with broad, rounded ridges separated by deep fissures. Young trees have a conical crown with lower branches that droop and can reach the ground. On larger trees, branches can reach diameters of 6 feet or more. As trees age, they lose the lower branches and develop a long, clear bole. Eventually, the conelike crown becomes more rounded and can be quite irregular on the oldest of trees.

Scalelike leaves are $1/8$ to $1/4$ inch long, blue-green, somewhat oval shaped, and either spreading or tightly covering drooping twigs. Twigs are initially green but turn brown and have a round cross-section. The 2- to 3-inch oval/oblong cones are covered with 25 to 40 shield-shaped, wrinkled scales. Cones take two years to mature and remain on the tree for many years. The $3/8$-inch seeds remain in the unopened cones until the cone dies, when they are finally released. The seeds are covered with a fine, reddish powder that assists seed germination and seedling development.

Giant Sequoia is found in scattered groves in canyons or slopes on rocky soils with other conifers. Seedling germination requires dry periods for cones to open and release their seeds. Germination occurs best on bare, disturbed soil. Giant Sequoia is extremely tolerant of fire; many larger trees show signs of past fire damage.

Features: The Giant Sequoia is a holdover from a group of ancient tree species, most of which have become extinct. The tree is named for a Native American (Sequoyah) who developed the Cherokee alphabet. Giant Sequoia were discovered in the 1830s but did not attract widespread attention until the 1850s. The Giant Sequoia is among the oldest living organisms on earth, with some specimens believed to be 3,000 to 3,500 years old. It is also considered to be one of the largest living organisms. Although it does not reach the heights attained by Redwood or Douglas-fir, the massiveness of the trunk and branches produces trees estimated to weigh 1,300 to 1,400 tons. In the 1930s, when these giant trees were still being logged, one tree is said to have taken 22 days to cut down and is believed to have produced more than 500,000 board feet of

lumber—equivalent to what mills of that time could process in five years. The wood is brittle but extremely durable. The heartwood of trees that have fallen more than 1,000 years ago is still solid.

It was common practice in the late 1800s to name these massive trees in honor of someone of importance. These names are still in use today. One of the largest known trees, found in Sequoia National Park, in California, is called the General Sherman. Its trunk measures over 30 feet in diameter at the base.

Range: These enormous trees are found on fewer than 25,000 acres, almost all of which are protected on state or federal land holdings in scattered groves on western slopes of the Sierra Nevada, from 4,500 to 8,000 feet in elevation.

SPRUCE

Spruce are members of the Pine family and can be recognized by the single, needlelike leaves that attach to the twig with a peglike base and the spiral arrangement of the needles. Spruce are usually large trees that have a classic conical shape.

Blue Spruce, *Picea pungens*
Colorado Spruce, Silver Spruce

Blue Spruce is a medium-size evergreen that grows to heights of 70 to 100 feet and 1 to 3 feet in diameter. The gray or brown bark is dark, thick, and furrowed on older trees. The tree has a short trunk and dense, narrow, conical crown made up of stout, horizontally arranged branches. The shape of wild-grown trees varies considerably from those used in landscaping.

The needlelike leaves are $^3/_4$ to $1^1/_4$ inches long, dull green to blue-green with whitish lines, spreading from all sides of the twig. Needles are four angled, sharp to the touch, stiff, with very short leafstalks, and have a pungent odor when crushed. The twigs are mostly hairless, yellow-brown, and somewhat stout. Cylindrical cones are $2^1/_4$ to 4 inches long, with almost no stalk, and hang down from the branches. They are a shiny light brown, with long, thin, flexible cone scales. Cone scales are somewhat rounded and irregularly toothed, giving them a ragged appearance. Paired seeds have long wings.

Blue Spruce is found in pure stands on moist soils along mountain streams, and on middle and upper mountain slopes. It can be easily confused with Engelmann Spruce (see page 236).

Features: Blue Spruce is often used in landscaping and for Christmas trees. Wild-grown trees are generally not as blue as ornamentals. It has little commercial value.

Range: Found in the Rocky Mountains from western Wyoming to Arizona and New Mexico, from 6,000 to 11,000 feet elevation.

Engelmann Spruce, *Picea engelmannii*

Engelmann Spruce is a large evergreen that grows to heights of 100 to 120 feet with diameters from 18 to 30 inches. Larger trees can reach heights of 165 feet and diameters up to 6 feet on favorable sites. Bark is very thin and broken into large, purplish brown to russet red scales that are thin and loosely attached. The crown is dense and narrow, with short branches spreading in close rows, often covered with light brown cones. Cones are commonly in abundance on the ground below the tree.

Needlelike leaves are ⅝ to 1 inch long, four sided, dark or blue green with whitish lines. They are often blunt and are slender and flexible. The needles tend to be pointed forward on the stem rather than at a right angle and encircle all sides of the twig from short, peglike leafstalks. Needles have a skunklike odor when crushed. Brown twigs are often fine haired. Cones are cylindrical, 1 to 2½ inches long, shiny brown, and hang at the ends of twigs. Cone scales are long, thin, flexible, narrowed, and irregularly toothed. Seeds are paired, blackish, and long winged.

Engelmann Spruce grows well on deep, rich loam with high moisture content. It is often found just below timberline. It is the principal spruce found in the inland mountains of the West. Often found in pure stands, it also occurs with other species, most commonly Subalpine Fir. It is tolerant of shade and can be found in the understory, where it can survive for many years.

Features: Engelmann Spruce has resonant qualities, making the wood suitable for pianos and other stringed instruments. It is also harvested for plywood and construction lumber and as pulpwood for paper products.

Range: In the Rocky Mountains, from central British Columbia and southwest Alberta, southeast to New Mexico, at elevations of 1,500 to 12,000 feet in British Columbia and Alberta and 9,000 to 12,000 feet in the central and southern Rockies.

Sitka Spruce, *Picea sitchensis*
Tidewater Spruce, Coast Spruce

Sitka Spruce is a large evergreen that grows to a height of 180 to 250 feet with a diameter from $3^1/_2$ to $4^1/_2$ feet. The smooth, thin, gray bark is rarely greater than 1 inch thick. As it ages, it develops dark purplish gray, concave, elliptical scales. Trees develop a long, clear, cylindrical bole, often from a buttressed or swollen base. The open crown has horizontal and ascending branches that end with drooping branchlets.

Needlelike leaves are $5/_8$ to 1 inch long, bright yellow-green above and blue-green and waxy beneath. They are flat, slightly keeled, and have a very sharp point. Needles spread outward at right angles from all sides of the twig. Twigs droop and are hairless, waxy, and orange-brown. Cones are 2 to $3^1/_2$ inches long, cylindrical, short stalked, and orange-brown. They hang at the ends of twigs and open and fall at maturity, in late autumn and early winter. Cone scales are long, stiff, thin, and irregularly toothed. Long, reddish brown, winged seeds are $1/_8$ inch long with $1/_3$- to $1/_2$-inch wings.

Sitka Spruce grows best in high-moisture, loamy soil. It can be found in pure stands in some parts of its range. Growth ring counts indicate ages of mature trees to be around 500 years, with some of the larger trees exceeding 800 years.

Features: Sitka Spruce is the world's largest spruce and one of the major timber-producing species in the Pacific Northwest. The best trees produce high-grade lumber. Sitka Spruce is used for musical instruments, and the pulpwood is used for newsprint. The strong, lightweight wood was used in airplane construction during World War II. Native Americans wove rootlets into baskets.

Range: Found along the West Coast from northern California northward, within 30 miles of the Pacific coast and in the foggy rain forest.

White Spruce, *Picea glauca*
Canadian Spruce, Skunk Spruce, Cat Spruce

White Spruce is a medium-size evergreen tree that grows to a height of 60 to 70 feet and 18 to 24 inches in diameter. It has thin, gray or black bark that can be either scaly or flaky. Recently exposed bark layers can have a silvery appearance. Open-grown trees have a picturesque, conical crown that reaches nearly to the ground.

The needlelike leaves are ¹/₂ to ³/₄ inch long, four sided, blue-green, and waxy. The tip is pointed but not sharp to the touch. Needles crowd the upper side of the branch. When crushed, they have a pungent odor. The smooth twigs appear waxy and are orange-brown or gray. Cones are 1¹/₂ to 2¹/₂ inches long, cylindrical, and light brown. Cone scales are thin and flexible, with nearly straight or slightly rounded, toothless edges. The seeds are only ¹/₈ inch long, pale brown, with short wings.

White Spruce grows best on moist loam or alluvial soils, although it can grow on many soil types and is often found along streams and lakeshores. It is found throughout Canada, forming almost pure stands, but is also found with Quaking Aspen, Paper Birch, Jack and Lodgepole Pine, Balsam Fir, and Black and Red Spruce. Trees can be 200 years of age or older.

Features: White Spruce is one of the most important commercial tree species in Canada, harvested for pulpwood and construction lumber. It is also used in musical instruments. Native Americans used the flexible roots for lacing birch-bark canoes and baskets. Birds and squirrels eat the seeds, and deer, moose, and Bighorn Sheep will browse the foliage in the winter.

Range: From the northernmost limits of tree cover in northern Canada and Alaska, east to Labrador, south to Maine, and west to northern Montana and British Columbia. Found from sea level to 5,000 feet in elevation.

YEW

Pacific Yew, *Taxus brevifolia*
Western Yew

Pacific Yew is a small evergreen or large shrub that grows to a height of 20 to 40 feet and from 12 to 15 inches in diameter. Larger trees are occasionally found on the better growing sites. The thin bark is smooth, with peeling, red-brown, papery scales. The largest trunks are often hollow-butted, sometimes twisted, with a spiral grain. The crown is large and conical, consisting of slender, horizontal branches.

Needlelike leaves are $1/2$ to $3/4$ inch long, linear, dark yellow-green to blue-green above and paler with two whitish lines beneath, odorless, flat, soft, and short pointed at both ends. They are generally in two rows and spirally arranged on the twig. Twigs are green on new growth, turning brown as they age, slender, and drooping. Male and female flowers are found on separate trees. The fruit is a fleshy, red cup surrounding a stalkless, brown seed and is found singly, scattered on leafy twigs.

Found on rich, moist sites, Pacific Yew has a root system that is deep and wide spreading. It is usually found in mixed-conifer forests as an understory tree. At higher elevations, near the treeline, it has a dwarfed or shrublike form. It is extremely tolerant of shade. It grows slowly, maturing in 250 to 350 years.

Features: Although the tree does not reach a large size and has limited distribution, the wood has some commercial value. It is strong and has been used for canoe paddles, bows, and cabinetry. The foliage and seeds are poisonous.

Range: From southeastern Alaska, along the coast to Monterey Bay, California. Also found in the Sierra Nevada and from British Columbia and Washington to the west slopes of the Rockies in Montana and Idaho, up to 8,000 feet in elevation.

HARDWOODS

ALDER

Alders, members of the Birch family, are deciduous trees with leaves that are simple and toothed. Drooping male catkins appear in spring; female catkins form hard, conelike fruits that persist through the winter until spring.

Arizona Alder, *Alnus oblongifolia*
New Mexico Alder, Mexican Alder

Arizona Alder is a medium-size deciduous tree that grows to a height of 80 feet with a diameter up to 2 feet. The thin, dark gray bark is smooth but with age becomes scaly or checkered with fissures. The tree has a long, straight trunk that supports an open, rounded crown.

The simple toothed leaves are alternate, $1^1/_2$ to $3^1/_4$ inches long, 1 to $1^1/_2$ inches wide, elliptical, and have seven to ten nearly parallel side veins. The margins are double sawtoothed. Leaves are dark green and essentially hairless above, paler and covered with fine hair beneath. Tufts of reddish fuzz are found in the angles between the veins. Slender, brown twigs have longitudinal ridges and fine hair when young. The pith is three angled. Male and female flowers are different: Male flowers are 2- to 3-inch-long, thin, cylindrical catkins. Female flowers are small, $1/_4$-inch, reddish cones that develop into persistent, $1/_2$- to $3/_4$-inch, hard, brown cones, found in clusters of three to eight.

Arizona Alder grows in moist soils along streams in canyons and on mountains with other riparian vegetation.

Features: Arizona Alder is one of the largest alders and a rather attractive tree, with its long, straight trunk. The wood is relatively soft and used for firewood.

Range: Found in Arizona and southwest New Mexico, from 4,500 to 7,500 feet elevation.

Red Alder, *Alnus rubra*
Oregon Alder, Western Alder

Red Alder is a medium-size deciduous tree that grows to a height of 80 to 120 feet with a diameter from 10 to 36 inches. The smooth, thin bark is pale gray to blue-gray and sometimes has thin, scaly, wartlike growths. On larger trees, the bark breaks up into large, flat plates. The inner bark is bright reddish brown. The straight-trunked tree has a crown that tends to be narrow when growing in dense stands but is broadly conical if open grown, where it may extend nearly to the ground.

The simple toothed leaves are alternate, 3 to 6 inches long, $1^1/2$ to 3 inches wide, oval, with 10 to 15 pairs of straight, parallel side veins. Leaf margins are slightly wavy and turn under slightly, with a deeply double sawtoothed edge. Leaves are dark green above, paler with rusty fuzz on the midrib and major veins beneath. The short, $1/4$- to $1/2$-inch leafstalk is grooved. Twigs are slender and covered with gray hairs when young and may be somewhat three angled. The pith is also somewhat triangular. Lateral buds are stalked. Male flowers are yellowish, drooping catkins, 4 to 6 inches long. Narrow, reddish female flowers are $3/8$ to $1/2$ inch long and develop into $1/2$- to 1-inch cones, found in groups of four to eight on short stalks.

Red Alder is found on moist, but not wet, soils along streams and on lower slopes. A pioneer species, it is often found in pure stands in recently burned or logged areas or other open areas where soil has been disturbed. It is a fast-growing tree that reaches maturity by 60 to 90 years. It is not tolerant of shade and dies if shaded out by other species.

Features: Red Alder is the largest western alder and the most important commercial hardwood in the Pacific Northwest. The wood is used for veneer, furniture, and tool handles. A red dye can be made from the red inner bark. The tree is also planted as an ornamental.

Range: Found within 50 miles of the Pacific coast from Alaska to California but also in some interior areas of Washington and Idaho, below 2,500 feet elevation.

White Alder, *Alnus rhombifolia*
Sierra Alder

White Alder is a medium-size deciduous tree that grows to a height of 50 to 80 feet with a diameter of 18 to 36 inches. Light brown or gray smooth bark divides into irregular, scaly plates with age. The long, clear, straight trunk supports an open, rounded crown.

The simple toothed leaves are alternate, 2 to $3^{1}/_{2}$ inches in length, $1^{1}/_{2}$ to 2 inches wide, oval to nearly round, with fine teeth. There are 9 to 12 pairs of parallel veins coming from the midvein. Leaves are dull dark green and nearly hairless above and may have tiny gland dots; they are light yellow-green and slightly hairy beneath. The slender twigs are orange-red. The buds are on short stalks. Narrow, cylindrical male catkins are between $1^{1}/_{2}$ to 5 inches long. Small female cones are $^{3}/_{8}$ to $^{3}/_{4}$ inch long. They remain clustered on the twigs, developing hard, black scales that remain closed until early spring. The nuts mature by late summer.

White Alder grows on moist soils in canyons and along streams. It is found in mixed-conifer forests and riparian zones in chaparral. It is a fast-growing tree and reaches maturity by 50 years.

Features: White Alder can be a good indicator of year-round water and does not grow near streams that are seasonally dry. It sometimes is planted as an ornamental but requires water. It is generally not found where Red Alder occurs. The wood is sometimes used for firewood. White Alder is the only native alder in southern California.

Range: Found in Washington and western Idaho and then south through the Coast Ranges of California and in the Sierra Nevada, to western Nevada and southern California. From sea level up to 8,000 feet elevation, but generally below 5,000 feet.

ASH

Ash are members of the Olive family. There are more than ten species of Ash in the West, most of which are found in relatively small geographical areas. They are easily recognized by their opposite, pinnately compound leaves and plentiful, winged fruits. One species, Singleleaf Ash, has simple opposite leaves.

California Ash, *Fraxinus dipetala*
Two-petal Ash, Flowering Ash

California Ash is a small deciduous tree that grows to a height of 20 feet with a diameter up to 4 inches. It also grows as a shrub. The light gray bark is rough and scaly. The tree has a single stem and an open crown.

The pinnately compound leaves are opposite and only $1^{1}/2$ to $4^{1}/2$ inches long. There are three to seven paired leaflets that are coarsely sawtoothed, $3/4$ to $1^{1}/2$ inches long, $1/4$ to $5/8$ inch wide. Leaflets are elliptical or obovate, short pointed at the base, and either blunt or short pointed at the tip. They are dark green above and paler beneath. Slender, green twigs are slightly four angled when young. Flowers have two broad lobes that hang on slender stalks, with many branched clusters up to 4 inches long. Flat, one-seeded, winged fruits mature in early summer.

California Ash is found on dry slopes in foothills, chaparral, and woodlands.

Features: "Two-petal Ash" refers to the tree's two white petals that form showy white flowers. It is planted as an ornamental.

Range: California and northern Baja California, up to 3,500 feet in elevation.

Fragrant Ash, *Fraxinus cuspidata*

Fragrant Ash is a small deciduous tree that grows to a height of 20 feet with a diameter up to 8 inches. It also grows as a shrub. It has smooth, gray bark that becomes fissured with scaly ridges. The small tree has a short trunk that disperses into many branches.

The pinnately compound leaves are opposite, 3 to 7 inches long. There are usually seven leaflets, $1^1/_2$ to $2^1/_2$ inches long and $^1/_2$ to $^3/_4$ inch wide, paired, with a single leaflet at the end. Leaflets are lancelike or oval and can be sharply sawtoothed or smooth on the margin. They are shiny, dark green above and paler with some hairs beneath when young. Slender twigs are gray. White, fragrant, $^5/_8$-inch flowers with four petals form in branched clusters, 3 to 4 inches long. Clusters of $^3/_4$- to $1^1/_4$-inch, flat, winged fruit mature in late spring.

Fragrant Ash is found in scattered locations in oak woodlands on rocky slopes in canyons and on mountains.

Features: The showy flowers and foliage make Fragrant Ash an attractive ornamental. It is the only ash with white flower petals found east of California. Native Americans used the wood for bows, arrow shafts, walking sticks, and weaving tools.

Range: Limited distribution at scattered locations from southern Texas through New Mexico and Arizona.

Oregon Ash, *Fraxinus latifolia*

Oregon Ash is a medium-size deciduous tree that grows to a height of 60 to 80 feet with a diameter of 2 to 4 feet. In very favorable growing situations, it can exceed this size. The bark is dark gray to gray-brown and typical of most ashes, with its interwoven, diamond-shaped, lace pattern made up of winding ridges with flat tops and sharp edges. The opposite branching of the leaves, twigs, and branches is quite apparent. The tree has a long, straight trunk with a compact, narrow crown.

The pinnately compound leaves are opposite, 5 to 12 inches long. There are five to nine stalkless leaflets, 2 to 5 inches long, 1 to 1$^1/_2$ inches wide, paired, with a single leaflet at the tip. Leaflets are elliptical and pointed; margins are smooth or slightly sawtoothed. Leaflets are light green above, paler and often hairy beneath. The terminal bud is small. Twigs are stout and densely woolly. Winged seeds, 1$^1/_4$ to 2 inches long, are produced prolifically every three to five years and are shaped like the blade of a canoe paddle.

Oregon Ash is most frequently found on rich, moist sites. It can occur in pure strips along streams and in canyons and is also found with a variety of hardwood and conifer species. Trees can live to be 200 to 250 years old.

Features: Oregon Ash is the only ash harvested commercially in the West. The wood is used for flooring, furniture, boxes, and fuel. The tree is planted for shade in parks and along roads near the Pacific coast. The wood of Oregon Ash was used by Native Americans for canoe paddles.

Range: Coastal British Columbia southward to the San Francisco Bay, also along the western slopes of the Sierra Nevada, up to 3,000 feet elevation.

Velvet Ash, *Fraxinus velutina*
Desert Ash

Velvet Ash is a small deciduous tree that grows to a height of 40 feet with a diameter up to 1 foot. The bark is gray and smooth when young, developing scaly ridges separated by deep furrows with age. The tree has a short trunk and branches that form a rounded crown.

The pinnately compound leaves are opposite, 3 to 6 inches long. There are usually five short-stalked leaflets (sometimes up to nine), 1 to 3 inches long, ³/₈ to 1¹/₂ inches wide, paired, with a single leaflet at the tip. Leaflets are lancelike to elliptical, with points at the ends, and can have either slightly wavy teeth or untoothed margins. They are shiny green above, paler with soft hairs beneath (sometimes hairless). Gray or brown twigs are often hairy when young. Small clusters of yellowish male and greenish female flowers form on separate trees. Winged seeds, ³/₄ to 1¹/₄ inches long, hang in dense clusters, maturing in summer and early fall.

Velvet Ash grows in moist soils along streambanks and arroyos in the mountains, canyons, and desert. It is found in oak woodlands and Ponderosa Pine forests.

Features: Velvet Ash is planted as an ornamental and is a fast-growing tree. It is an indicator of the presence of underground water in the desert. Native Americans used the branches as tools to pick fruit from Saguaro and pinyon trees.

Range: The Trans-Pecos across southern New Mexico, Arizona, and into southern California, from 2,500 to 7,500 feet in elevation.

ASPEN

Quaking Aspen, *Populus tremuloides*
Trembling Aspen, Golden Aspen, Popple

Quaking Aspen is a medium-size deciduous tree that grows to a height of 50 to 60 feet with a diameter of 1 to 1½ feet. On young trees, the bark is smooth, greenish white, or cream colored. Bark on older trees becomes dark brown or gray, with furrowed, long, flat-topped ridges toward the base. The open crown is narrow and rounded. The tree often grows in groves.

The simple toothed leaves are alternate, 1½ to 3 inches long, somewhat rounded, with an acute point, rounded base, and rounded teeth along the margin. Leaves are lustrous green above and paler beneath. They turn brilliant golden yellow in fall. Leafstalks are flat. Slender twigs are shiny, reddish brown, ending in a sharp-pointed bud covered with six or seven reddish brown scales. In early spring, 1- to 2½-inch-long brownish catkins develop. The fruit is a narrow, conical capsule that splits in two, with many tiny, cottony seeds. The seeds rarely sprout in the West, however. Propagation occurs from root suckers forming groves of trees that are clones.

Quaking Aspen is found on almost any kind of soil and is often found in pure stands at higher altitudes. It is very intolerant of shade. Quaking Aspen is a pioneer species that easily sprouts after logging or wildfire. It is a somewhat short-lived species; stands usually begin to die out after 30 or so years, although individual trees can reach ages of 150 years.

Features: Quaking Aspen gets its name from the rustling sound made by its leaves, trembling in the wind. It is one of the most widely distributed trees in North America. Its brilliant gold color in fall creates a spectacular landscape. The wood is used for pulp and as a source of fiber for composite boards. Higher grades are used for cabinets and flooring. The wood does not splinter easily.

Range: Across North America from Alaska to Newfoundland, south through British Columbia and in the Rocky Mountains south to southern Arizona and New Mexico, from sea level to 10,000 feet.

BIRCH

Members of the Birch family are small- to medium-size trees that are generally short lived and considered to be pioneer species. They have distinctive bark patterns. Trees are usually of poor form, with twisting trunks and open crowns.

Paper Birch, *Betula papyrifera*
White Birch, Canoe Birch

Paper Birch is a medium-size deciduous tree that grows to a height of 50 to 70 feet with diameters from 1 to 2 feet. The bark is dark brown when young but quickly turns to a chalky or creamy white, with long horizontal lines that separate into papery strips. The tree has a long, straight trunk, with a narrow, pyramidal, open crown made up of slightly drooping branches.

The simple toothed leaves are alternate, 2 to 4 inches long, 1¹/₂ to 2 inches wide, oval, with a long point. They are coarsely double sawtoothed and have a rounded base. Leaves are smooth and dull, dark green above; paler, light green, and nearly hairless beneath. They turn light yellow in the fall. Tiny flowers form in early spring. Male flowers are yellowish with two stamens and form long, drooping catkins near the tips of twigs. Greenish female flowers grow as short, upright catkins on the same twig. Narrow, cylindrical, 1¹/₂- to 2-inch brown cones hang on slender stalks and mature in the fall.

Paper Birch is found on moist soils, often in cut- or burned-over areas where mineral soil has been exposed. It can form pure stands and often serves as cover as more shade-tolerant, slower-growing species develop. It also is found in mixed conifer-hardwood forests.

Features: The waterproof bark of mature Paper Birch was used by Native Americans for canoes, wigwam covers, and utensils. It is also a good fire starter. The wood is used for veneer and pulp and a variety of specialty products, such as popsicle sticks, toothpicks, spools, and toys.

Range: Widespread across Canada and Alaska but also found in northern Washington, Idaho, and western Montana, to 4,000 feet in elevation.

Water Birch, *Betula occidentalis*
Red Birch, Black Birch

Water Birch is a small deciduous tree that grows to a height of 25 feet with a diameter of 6 to 12 inches. It grows in clumps and can form dense thickets. The red-brown bark is shiny, smooth, with white horizontal lenticels. Unlike that of Paper Birch, the bark of Water Birch does not peel. The crown is rounded, with spreading, drooping branches.

The simple toothed leaves are alternate, 1 to 2 inches long, 3/4 to 1 inch wide, ovate, pointed at the tip, with rounded leaf bases and four to five pairs of parallel side veins coming from the midvein. Margins are double sawtoothed. Leaves are dark green above, paler yellow-green with tiny gland dots beneath. Slender twigs are greenish and tend to be rough, warty, and hairless. Fruiting catkins are 1 to 1 1/4 inches long and upright or spreading on thin stalks. Catkins are sometimes persistent.

Water Birch grows well on moist sites along streams and in canyons. It is found in mixed hardwood-conifer forests and with other riparian vegetation.

Features: Water Birch is the only native birch in the southern Rocky Mountains and the Southwest. It is widespread geographically but uncommon within its range. Native Americans used the bark as a dye and made baskets from the wood. Flowers and leaves were used for medicinal purposes. The wood was also used for firewood.

Range: From British Columbia to southern Manitoba in Canada, and across the northern tier states from Washington to North Dakota and south to central California, Nevada, Arizona, and New Mexico, at elevations to 8,000 feet.

BOXELDER

Boxelder is a member of the Maple family and is the only one with pinnately compound leaves.

Boxelder, *Acer negundo*
Ash-leafed Maple, Manitoba Maple

Boxelder is a small- to medium-size deciduous tree that grows to a height of 30 to 60 feet with a diameter up to $2^{1}/_{2}$ feet. The light brown bark is thin, with narrow ridges between furrows that form a lacy pattern. The bark is coarser in older trees. The trunk is short and irregular, with a broad, spreading, bushy crown.

The pinnately compound leaves are opposite, 4 to 10 inches long, with three to seven leaflets that are 2 to 5 inches long and up to 3 inches wide. The leaflets are attached to the main leaf-stalk by short stalks. Leaflets are pointed at the tip but display considerable individual variability in shape, ranging from oval to lancelike. All are coarse toothed and may have one or more lobes. They are light green and smooth on top, but paler beneath, with some light fuzz, notably along the leaf veins. The green to purplish green twigs are stout, with small but noticeable lenticels, and covered with a waxy haze. Terminal buds are roundish, with four overlapping scales. The yellow-green flowers appear with the leaves in the spring. The winged seeds are 1 to $1^{1}/_{2}$ inches long, paired, and V shaped, as is typical of most maples.

Boxelder is often found on poor sites where it seems able to compete successfully with other species. It is frequently found along streams and on river-banks, floodplains, swamp margins, and moist upland slopes. It is fast growing but more often than not of rather poor form. It sprouts easily from cut trunks.

Features: Boxelder is a member of the Maple family but does not have the typical maple leaf. Despite being short lived and easily uprooted by strong winds, it is often planted as a shade tree. The sap can be used to make syrup. The leaves of seedlings bear a resemblance to Poison Ivy.

Range: Boxelder is one of the most common maples and can be found in nearly every state. It is widely scattered throughout the Southwest, where it can be found up to 8,000 feet in elevation.

BUCKEYE

California Buckeye, *Aesculus californica*

California Buckeye is a small deciduous tree that grows to a height of 40 feet with a diameter up to 2 feet. It also grows as a shrub and can form dense thickets. The smooth, thin bark is light gray. The tree has a short trunk and may have a swollen base. The crown is rounded and broad, made up of many crooked branches. It also grows in clumps.

The palmately compound leaves are opposite, 6 to 10 inches in diameter, the outline of which nearly forms a circle. Typically, five stalked leaflets are joined together at the long main leafstalk, like fingers on a hand; these are 3 to 6 inches long and 1 to 2 inches wide. The leaflets have sharp points and fine-toothed edges. They are dark green above, paler below, with whitish hairs. Reddish brown twigs are stout, with a tacky, resinous terminal bud. Fragrant flowers form showy white to rose-colored clusters that are 4 to 8 inches long. Individual flowers are 1 to 1 1/2 inches with four or five petals and have long, hairlike stamens. The tree blooms in late spring or early summer. The fruit is a 2- to 3-inch pear-shaped ball that splits into thirds, revealing the one, sometimes two, rounded, shiny, poisonous seeds.

California Buckeye is the only native buckeye found in the West. It is found on moist soils in canyons and on hillsides in the chaparral and oak woodlands.

Features: Although the seeds are toxic, Native Americans were able to grind flour from them by leaching out the toxins with boiling water. They used the unleached, ground seed meal to poison fish. Although some wildlife feeds on the seeds, they can be toxic to livestock. The flower's pollen and nectar is supposedly toxic to bees.

Range: Found only at lower elevations in California in the coastal mountains and in the Sierra Nevada, below 4,000 feet.

BUCKTHORN

Cascara Buckthorn, *Frangula purshiana*
Bearberry, Bitter-bark, Chittimwood

Cascara Buckthorn is a small deciduous tree that grows to a height of 30 to 40 feet with a diameter of 10 to 15 inches. It also grows as a large shrub. It has a smooth, thin, gray or brown bark that may develop thin, scaly, vertical ridges. The bark is very bitter to the taste. The trunk is short with a crown made up of numerous stout branches.

The simple toothed leaves are alternate, 2 to 6 inches long, 1 to 2½ inches wide, oblong to oval, with a very fine-toothed or wavy margin. There are 10 to 15 parallel side veins prominently raised on the underside. The leaf is dull green and nearly hairless above, paler and slightly hairy beneath. Young plants can be evergreen. Gray twigs are slender and hairy when young; they have scaleless buds covered with woolly hair. Greenish yellow, bell-shaped flowers are ³/₁₆-inch wide, have five petals, and are in a cluster. The ³/₈-inch berrylike fruit is red and turns a darker purple-black in fall, when it matures. It has two or three seeds.

Cascara Buckthorn often form groves in open bottomlands, burned-over areas, and along roadsides; it is also found in the understory of conifer and mixed-evergreen forests. It will produce multiple sprouts when trees are cut. A prolific seeder, it grows quickly on moist forest litter and wet soils, although it can be found on drier sites. Maturity is reached in about 50 years.

Features: Native Americans harvested the bark for its tonic and laxative properties. Many wildlife species feed on its berries.

Range: Within a few hundred miles of the Pacific coast from British Columbia to northern California and also in the Rockies in northern Idaho, Washington, and Montana, at elevations to 5,000 feet.

CERCOCARPUS

Cercocarpus are members of the Rose family and sometimes referred to as Mountain-Mahoganies. They grow as trees and shrubs, usually evergreen, with leathery leaves that are either toothed or nearly toothless. Inconspicuous flowers of mid to late summer develop into attractive 2- to 4-inch-long, feathered or tailed fruits. The dense, heavy wood is a rich mahogany color and used for carvings and ornaments. It will not float when fresh cut and makes good firewood. Mountain-Mahogany is not related to the true mahoganies.

Birchleaf Cercocarpus, *Cercocarpus montanus* var. *glaber*
Birchleaf Mountain-Mahogany, Hardtack

Birchleaf Cercocarpus is a small evergreen tree that grows to a height of 20 feet with a diameter of 6 inches. It is often a shrub. The gray bark is initially smooth but becomes scaly with age. It has an irregular, spreading crown.

The simple toothed leaves resemble birch leaves, are alternate, 1 to 1^1/4 inches long and ^{3}/8 to ^{1}/2 inch wide, elliptical, broadly rounded, and fine toothed toward the tip, with five to eight parallel side veins. Leaves are dark green above, pale green or grayish and slightly hairy beneath. Yellowish flowers develop in early spring in clusters of three at the base of leaves. They are ^{3}/8 inch long, funnel shaped, with five small lobes. They have no petals or stalks. The ^{1}/4-inch fruit has a 2- to 3^1/4-inch-long twisted tail covered with whitish hairs.

Birchleaf Cercocarpus is commonly found in the chaparral and on dry, rocky slopes. It is a pioneer plant—one that is first to appear after disturbances such as fire—and survives despite fires, heavy browsing, and cutting.

Features: The foliage is an important source of browse for cattle, deer, and sheep. The curly, hairy fruits are easily dispersed by wind. Native Americans used the wood for spears, arrows, and digging tools.

Range: From southern Oregon to Baja California and into Arizona, from 3,500 to 6,500 feet.

Curl-leaf Cercocarpus, *Cercocarpus ledifolius*
Curl-leaf Mountain-Mahogany

Curl-leaf Cercocarpus is a small evergreen that grows to a height of 40 feet with a diameter of 6 to 18 inches. Young stems have smooth, gray bark with raised lenticels that develops many scales separated by relatively deep fissures. The crown is rounded and made up of dense, spreading, twisted branches.

The simple untoothed leaves are alternate, $1/2$ to $1 1/4$ inches long and only $3/8$ inch wide, elliptical, with smooth margins that are slightly turned under. There are very prominent, grooved mid-veins on the leaves, but side veins are barely evident. The leaves are thick, leathery, shiny dark green above, pale with fine hairs beneath, and clustered in groups at the ends of branchlets. The twigs are reddish brown. Yellowish flowers develop in early spring in clusters of three at the base of leaves. They are $3/8$ inch long, funnel shaped, with five small lobes. They have no petals or stalks. The $1/4$-inch fruit has a $1 1/2$- to 3-inch-long twisted tail covered with whitish hairs.

Curl-leaf Cercocarpus grows on dry, rocky soils on lower mountain slopes with oaks, pinyons, and other conifers.

Features: Curl-leaf Cercocarpus is not a true mahogany although it has dense, reddish brown heartwood that has similar characteristics to mahogany. The wood is sometimes used for decorative pieces; in the past, it was used as firewood for mining operations. The roots were made into a red dye by Native Americans.

Range: Throughout the Great Basin and surrounding areas from 5,000 to 9,000 feet in elevation.

CHERRY

Cherry, members of the Rose family, are characterized by their clusters of white flowers, pulpy fruits with a hard stone, and dark bark covered with lenticels when young. They usually grow as small trees and shrubs and provide cover and food for wildlife.

Bitter Cherry, *Prunus emarginata*
Quinine Cherry, Wild Cherry

Bitter Cherry is a small deciduous tree that grows to a height of 20 feet with diameters up to 8 inches. It also grows as a shrub. The smooth, shiny bark is dark reddish brown with conspicuous horizontal lenticels and a very bitter taste. The tree has a short trunk with a rounded crown.

The simple toothed leaves are alternate, 1 to 2$^1/2$ inches long, $^3/8$ to 1$^1/2$ inches wide, elliptical or oblong, short pointed at the base, and rounded or blunt at the tip. Margins are finely saw-toothed. Leaves are dark green above, paler and sometimes hairy beneath. Slender twigs are shiny red and hairy when young. White flowers are $^1/2$ inch wide, with five notched, rounded petals; there are three to ten flowers on slender stalks. Flowers emerge in spring, with the leaves. Fruits are $^5/16$- to $^3/8$-inch cherries with thick, reddish black skin. They have a thin, juicy, bitter pulp and one pointed stone; they mature in summer.

Bitter Cherry is found on moist soils in valleys and on mountain slopes. It grows with conifers and in chaparral.

Features: This is the most widely distributed western cherry. Although the fruits are not edible by humans, many species of songbirds and mammals feed on them.

Range: British Columbia, Washington, and western Montana, south to southwest New Mexico and southern California, to 9,000 feet in elevation.

Black Cherry, *Prunus serotina* var. *virens*
Wild Cherry, Rum Cherry

Black Cherry is a medium-size deciduous tree that grows to a height of 60 feet with diameters from 2 to 3 feet. Young bark is initially dark gray and smooth, with conspicuous horizontal lenticels. With age, it becomes fissured with shiny, platy scales with upturned edges that expose reddish brown inner bark. The tree has a straight trunk and an oblong, rounded crown.

The simple toothed leaves are 2 to 5 inches long, $1^1/4$ to 2 inches wide, with one or two dark red glands at the base, elliptical, with margins that are finely sawtoothed with teeth that are curved or blunt. Slightly thickened leaves are dark green and shiny above, paler beneath, with dense pale or reddish brown hairs along the midvein. Slender twigs are reddish brown, hairless, and have a bitter taste. Flowers are $^3/8$ inch wide, with five white, rounded petals. Many flowers form on 4- to 6-inch-long stalks that droop at the ends of leafy twigs in late spring. Fruits are $^3/8$-inch-diameter reddish black cherries that have an edible, juicy pulp that is slightly bitter. They mature in summer.

Black Cherry grows best on deep, moist soils but can be found on many sites, except where very wet or dry. It grows in pure stands or mixed with other hardwoods and conifers.

Features: Black Cherry is often found along fencerows. Although it is closely related to eastern varieties that can produce high-quality, commercially valuable wood, this variety does not grow to comparable quality. Livestock can become ill or die from eating wilted leaves due to the presence of cyanide.

Range: The Trans-Pecos through New Mexico and Arizona, from 4,500 feet to 7,500 feet in elevation.

Chokecherry, *Prunus virginiana*
Western Chokecherry

Chokecherry is a small deciduous tree that grows to a height of 20 feet with a diameter of 2 to 6 inches. It also grows as a shrub. The bark is gray-brown, generally smooth, but may be scaly with shallow fissures. The tree has a short trunk that quickly breaks into many spreading branches, often forming dense thickets.

The simple toothed leaves are alternate, 1¹/₂ to 3¹/₄ inches long, egg shaped or elliptical, with a U- or heart-shaped base and 8 to 11 side veins. Leaf margins have fine, sharp-pointed teeth. Leaves are dark green and shiny above, lighter and sometimes hairy, especially along the midvein, beneath. The leafstalk is often reddish. Brown twigs are thin and have a very bitter taste. There are no spur branches. The rounded bud scales are hairless. White ¹/₂-inch flowers with five rounded petals hang in unbranched, 4-inch racemelike clusters, developing into ¹/₄- to ³/₈-inch, round, dark red to black, juicy fruits, each with a single, hard seed. Fruit is bitter, especially when not completely ripe. The seed is poisonous.

Chokecherry sprouts easily and grows on moist sites, along roadsides and borders of forest clearings.

Features: The fruit is consumed by a variety of birds and mammals and can be made into pies and jellies. The tree is used for erosion control.

Range: Widespread over much of the northern half of the U.S. and Canada and scattered throughout all the western states. Found up to 8,000 feet in elevation.

CHINQUAPIN

Giant Chinquapin, *Chrysolepis chrysophylla*
Giant Chinkapin, Golden Chinquapin, Goldenleaf Chestnut

Giant Chinquapin is a medium-size evergreen that grows 60 to 80 feet in height and reaches diameters up to 3 feet. It also grows as a shrub. Young trees have smooth, dark gray bark that develops into very wide, reddish brown plates. The inner bark is bright red. Trees develop a long, clear bole in forested settings, with a broad, rounded crown made up of large, spreading branches.

Simple leaves are alternate, 2 to 5 inches long, ⁵⁄₈ to 1¹⁄₂ inches wide, lance-like, with a sharp point, smooth margins, and slightly turned-under edges. Leaves are thick, leathery, shiny dark green with scales above and tiny yellow scales beneath. Leaves turn yellow in the fall. Twigs are stiff and initially covered with yellow scales, becoming reddish brown. Showy flowers are small, white, and have a strong odor. Flowers are found in 2- to 2¹⁄₂-inch catkins that stand upright on the end of twigs or in small clusters, usually in early summer. Fruits are 1- to 1¹⁄₂-inch-diameter spiny burs that split into four irregular parts, having one or two light brown, round, edible nuts.

Giant Chinquapin grows on poor, dry soils on slopes and dry ridges and in canyons. It can form pure stands but is also found in the understory of Redwood or Douglas-fir stands or mixed with other conifers. It is tolerant of shade when young but requires full sunlight for full growth. It can grow for 200 to 500 years.

Features: The wood is harvested for furniture and paneling. The nuts are eaten by many species of wildlife.

Range: Along the Pacific coast from southwest Washington to central California, also in the Sierra Nevada of central California from sea level to 1,500 feet elevation. The shrub form is found to 6,000 feet elevation.

COTTONWOOD

Cottonwoods, and Aspen, are members of the Willow family; they are widely distributed in the West. Leaves are oval to deltoid in shape, often toothed, and have long leafstalks that allow leaves to flutter in the wind. Hairy, cottonlike fruit are easily dispersed by the wind in spring. (Aspen is found on page 258).

Black Cottonwood, *Populus balsamifera* ssp. *trichocarpa*
California Poplar, Western Balsam Poplar

Black Cottonwood is a large deciduous tree that grows to a height of 125 to 150 feet with a diameter of 4 to 5 feet. On younger stems, the bark is brownish yellow or gray and smooth. On older trunks, the coarse bark has flat-topped, scaly ridges separated by deep, vertical fissures. These ridges are also separated horizontally by fissures every several inches. In a forest setting, the trunk is long and branchless, forming a round-topped crown that is narrow, cylindrical, somewhat open, with branches that reach upward.

The simple toothed leaves are alternate, 3 to 6 inches long, 2 to 4 inches wide, somewhat triangular, with a pointed tip and rounded base. The margin has fine, wavy, rounded teeth. Leaves are dark green and smooth above and a contrasting rusty brown, silver-white, or paler green underneath. Leafstalks are $1^{1}/_2$ to 3 inches long, have a round cross-section, and tend to be hairy. Brown twigs are slender to stout and slightly angular. The pointed, terminal buds are noticeably larger ($^3/_4$ inch) than the lateral buds ($^1/_2$ inch). When crushed, the buds are fragrant. Reddish purple male and female catkins, $1^{1}/_2$ to $3^{1}/_4$ inches long, form on separate trees in early spring. Fruits are globular capsules that contain many cottonlike seeds.

Black Cottonwood grows best on moist, sandy, or gravelly soils in valleys or on streambanks or floodplains. It forms pure stands and can be found with willow, Red Alder, Paper Birch, Douglas-fir, and White Pine. Black Cottonwood is very intolerant of shade and can be quickly overtaken by faster-growing trees of other species. It grows to be 150 to 200 years old.

Features: Black Cottonwood is the largest of the native cottonwoods and is the tallest broad-leafed tree of the Pacific Northwest.

Range: From Alaska along the Pacific coast to Baja California and also throughout the Rockies in Alberta, Montana, Idaho, Oregon, and Washington and scattered through Nevada. Found at sea level to 2,000 feet in the north, to 9,000 feet in the south.

Fremont Cottonwood, *Populus fremontii*
Rio Grande Cottonwood, Meseta Cottonwood, Alamo Cottonwood

Fremont Poplar is a medium-size deciduous tree that grows to a height of 40 to 80 feet with diameters of 2 to 4 feet. Young bark is gray and smooth with shallow fissures. Older trees have thick, rough bark that is gray and deeply furrowed. Open-grown trees have a wide, spreading crown with a flattened top made up of spreading branches.

The simple leaves are alternate, 2 to 3 inches long and wide, triangular, short pointed, and nearly straight across at the base, with short, irregularly curved teeth. Leaves are thick, shiny yellow-green, with long, flattened leafstalks. They turn bright yellow in the fall. Stout twigs are light green and hairless. Reddish 2- to $3^{1}/_{2}$-inch-long catkins appear in early spring. Egg-shaped fruits are $^{1}/_{2}$ inch long, light brown, and hairless. They split into three parts and have many cottony seeds.

Fremont Cottonwood is found along streams and river bottoms in deserts, grasslands, and woodlands, often with sycamores, willows, and alders. It grows only on wet soils and is an indicator of year-round water.

Features: Fremont Cottonwood can be identified in early spring by its burst of bright green foliage in riparian areas. It is easily propagated from cuttings and widely planted. Native Americans used the roots for carving. Clumps of mistletoe are often seen on branches. The wood is soft and rots easily. Wood shavings are used for livestock bedding and mulch.

Range: Southwest Colorado to California, south to the Mexican border, at elevations to 6,500 feet.

Narrowleaf Cottonwood, *Populus angustifolia*
Mountain Cottonwood, Black Cottonwood

Narrowleaf Cottonwood is a small deciduous tree that grows to heights of 50 feet with diameters up to 1½ feet. Smooth, yellow-green bark develops gray-brown furrows and ridges. The tree has a narrow, conical crown with upward-pointing branches.

The simple toothed leaves are alternate, 2 to 5 inches long, ½ to 1 inch wide, willowlike, lancelike, with a long narrow tip, rounded base, and short leafstalks. Leaf margins are finely sawtoothed. Leaves are shiny green above and paler beneath. They turn dull yellow in fall. The slender, yellow-green twigs are hairless. Narrow-pointed buds are resinous with shiny scales and a balsam odor. Flowers appear in early spring before leaves and are 1½- to 3-inch-long reddish catkins. Fruits are ¼-inch-long, rounded, light brown capsules.

Narrowleaf Cottonwood grows along watercourses on moist soils, often with willows and alders in conifer forests.

Features: Narrowleaf Cottonwood is the most common cottonwood in the northern Rockies, where it is planted as a yard tree. The wood is lightweight yet strong and used for pallets and crates.

Range: Southern Alberta south through the Rocky Mountains to the Mexican border, at elevations from 3,000 to 8,000 feet.

CHILOPSIS

Desert Willow, *Chilopsis linearis*
Desert Catalpa

Desert Willow is a small deciduous tree that grows to a height of 25 feet with a diameter up to 6 inches. Young bark is initially smooth. Older bark is dark brown, coarse, and furrowed into scaly ridges. The tree often has a forked, leaning trunk and an open, spreading crown.

The simple untoothed leaves are both opposite and alternate (on the same tree), linear, and 3 to 6 inches long, $^1/_4$ to $^3/_8$ inch wide. They are very long, pointed at each, end and can be straight or slightly curved. They have smooth margins, are light green, and can be hairy or sticky. The brown twigs are slender and sometimes hairy or sticky. Showy, bell-shaped flowers appear in 4-inch clusters from late spring to early summer. They are $1^1/_4$ inches long and wide, whitish, with purple or pink edges and a yellow throat. The dark brown fruit is a 4- to 8-inch-long, $^1/_4$-inch-diameter capsule that matures in early autumn, splits in half, and remains attached to the tree through winter. The capsule contains many flat, light brown seeds, each with two papery, hairy wings.

Desert Willow is found in desert washes and on plains and foothills, growing best on moist soils along streambanks.

Features: Desert Willow is planted widely as an ornamental for its showy spring foliage; it is also important for erosion control. It can be propagated from cuttings or grown from seed. The stiff, durable wood can be used for fence posts. Native Americans used it for bows. Despite its appearance and name, Desert Willow is not part of the Willow family.

Range: The Trans-Pecos and New Mexico west to southwest Utah and southern California, from 1,000 to 5,000 feet in elevation.

DOGWOOD

Pacific Dogwood, *Cornus nuttallii*
Flowering Dogwood, Mountain Dogwood

Pacific Dogwood is a small deciduous tree that grows to a height of 50 feet with a diameter from 12 to 20 inches. The thin bark is reddish brown, generally smooth, with thin, scaly plates at the base of the trunk. Layers of horizontal branches make up a dense, rounded crown.

The simple untoothed leaves are opposite, 2¹/₂ to 4¹/₂ inches long, 1¹/₄ to 2³/₄ inches wide, elliptical or egg shaped, with slightly wavy edges. There are five or six long, curved veins on each side of the midvein. Green leaves are shiny and nearly hairless above, paler with woolly hairs beneath. Leaves turn bright orange or red in autumn. Young twigs are slender, green, and hairy, turning dark red or black. Showy, off-white flowers are 4 to 6 inches in diameter and made up of a small, 1-inch, greenish yellow head bordered by six large, elliptical, petal-like bracts, 1¹/₂ to 2¹/₂ inches long, with short-pointed tips. Dogwoods bloom in spring and early summer and often a second time in late summer or autumn. Clusters of ¹/₂-inch long, elliptical, red or orange, berrylike fruits crowd the seed-head and mature in early autumn.

Pacific Dogwood is found on moist soils in valleys and on slopes in the understory of conifer forests. It is often found with the Giant Sequoia.

Features: Pacific Dogwood is well known for its beautiful flowers and widely planted as an ornamental. It is particularly pretty in late summer or fall when orange or red fruits appear and a second set of flowers blooms.

Range: Southwestern British Columbia to western Oregon and in the mountains to southern California, from sea level to 6,000 feet in elevation.

ELDERBERRY

Elderberry are members of the Honeysuckle family. They produce attractive displays of white flowers in spring. The berries of Blue Elderberry and some other species are edible and often used in baked goods, jams, and wine. The seeds of Red Elderberry are considered to be poisonous.

Blue Elderberry, *Sambucus nigra* ssp. *cerulea*
Blue Elder, Arizona Elder

Blue Elderberry is a small deciduous tree that grows to a height of 25 feet with a diameter up to 1 foot. It also grows as a shrub. The bark is light gray or brown and furrowed with a loose, woven pattern of long, scaly ridges. The trunk is short, with branches that form a rounded crown.

Pinnately compound leaves are opposite, 5 to 7 inches long. There are three to five leaflets, 1 to 5 inches long, $^3/_8$ to $1^1/_2$ inches wide, paired, with a single leaflet at the tip. Leaflets are elliptical, pointed at the tip, with an asymmetrical base, and have edges that are finely sawtoothed with sharp teeth. Green above and paler below, the leaflets are slightly thick and leathery. During periods of drought, they turn yellow. Twigs are light green and hairless, turning brown, and stout with ringed nodes. Small $^1/_4$-inch, yellow or white flowers form flat-topped clusters on the terminal branches. The clusters remain upright and can bloom throughout the year. Flowers turn into a dark blue to black $^1/_4$-inch berry that has a fine, white bloom.

Blue Elderberry is found along streams and drainages in woodlands, deserts, and desert grasslands. It also is often found on fencerows and along roadsides.

Features: Blue Elderberry is planted as an ornamental for its showy flowers. It is one of the largest elders and one of the few that grows in tree form.

Range: Throughout the West from western Alberta and southern British Columbia, south to northwest Mexico and the Trans-Pecos, at elevations to 5,000 feet.

Red Elderberry, *Sambucus racemosa*

Red Elderberry is a small deciduous tree that grows to a height of 20 feet with diameters up to 6 inches. It often grows as a shrub. The bark is smooth (sometimes with warts), light to dark gray or brown, and with age may become broken into scaly plates separated by shallow fissures. The tree has a short trunk and rounded crown. Open-grown trees have branches that reach to the ground.

Pinnately compound leaves are opposite, 5 to 10 inches long, with five or seven individual leaflets 2 to 5 inches long and 1 to 2 inches wide, paired, with a single leaflet at the tip. Leaflets are oval or lancelike, with a pointed tip and sometimes asymmetrical base; they have a toothed edge, with teeth varying from fine to coarse. Leaflets are green, with very few hairs above, paler and hairy beneath. Reddish brown twigs are stout, hairy when young, and have noticeable ringed nodes. The pith is thick and white on younger twigs but darkens to orange or brown with age. Small, creamy-white flowers form in upright, ball-like clusters up to 4 inches in diameter. Round, juicy, berrylike fruit is red or orange, each with a single, poisonous seed.

Red Elderberry grows in moist soils along streams and in ravines and swampy areas. It prefers open, sunny sites but can tolerate some shade.

Features: The fruit, eaten by birds, is generally considered toxic to humans, although it can be used to make wine. The tree is useful for soil stabilization.

Range: Coastal from southern Alaska to central California, up to 2,000 feet in elevation.

ELM

Siberian Elm, *Ulmus pumila*
Asiatic Elm, Dwarf Elm

Siberian Elm is a medium-size deciduous tree that grows to a height of 60 feet with a diameter up to 1¹/₂ feet. The bark can be gray or brown and is deeply furrowed. The tree has a short trunk with an open, rounded crown made up of spreading branches.

The simple toothed leaves are ³/₄ to 2 inches long, ¹/₂ to 1 inch wide, oval, with a slightly asymmetrical, blunt base and a sharp tip. Leaves are slightly thickened, have a saw-toothed margin and many straight side veins. They are dark green above, paler beneath. Leaves turn yellow in autumn. Twigs are slightly zigzagged, nearly hairless, and greenish brown. In winter, flower buds are nearly black, enlarged, and visible from a distance. Clusters of ¹/₈-inch-wide, greenish flowers form in early spring. Circular fruit is ³/₈ to ⁵/₈ inch long, hairless, with a broad, notched wing, forming in early spring.

Siberian Elm is found on drier sites and scattered along streams. It is not tolerant of particularly wet sites.

Features: Siberian Elm is a native of eastern Europe and Asia that has become naturalized in the western U.S. It is a fast-growing tree used as an ornamental or planted for hedgerows. It is resistant to Dutch elm disease.

Range: From Minnesota south to Kansas and west to Utah, from 1,000 to 5,000 feet in elevation.

EUCALYPTUS

Tasmanian Eucalyptus, *Eucalyptus globulus*
Bluegum, Tasmanian Bluegum, Bluegum Eucalyptus

Tasmanian Eucalyptus is a large evergreen that grows to a height of 120 feet with a diameter up to 3 feet. The mottled gray, brown, and green bark peels in shaggy strips, becoming gray and rough at the tree's base. The tree has a clear, straight trunk with characteristic drooping branches and narrow, irregular crown.

The simple untoothed leaves are both opposite and alternate (on the same tree), 4 to 12 inches long, 1 to 2 inches wide, narrowly elliptical, slightly curved, with a long, pointed tip. Leaves have smooth margins. Thick, leathery leaves are dull green and hairless on both surfaces. On young growth, leaves are opposite, more oval shaped, and have a blue or whitish bloom on the lower surface. Alternate leaves are found on older twigs. Slender, drooping twigs are yellow-green and hairless. Flowers are 2 inches wide with no petals and many white stamens. They have a noticeable camphor odor and appear in spring and winter. Fruits are $^3/_4$- to 1-inch, bell-shaped capsules that contain many seeds.

Tasmanian Eucalyptus originated in Australia but is widely planted in California as an ornamental. It has become naturalized and is now found in pure stands. It is highly invasive.

Features: Tasmanian Eucalyptus is favored as an ornamental because of its rapid growth and showy bark and leaves. Highly flammable twigs and leaves are a concern in areas prone to wildfire.

Range: Coastal California.

HACKBERRY

Netleaf Hackberry, *Celtis laevigata* var. *reticulata*
Western Hackberry, Sugarberry

Netleaf Hackberry is a small deciduous tree that grows to a height of 50 feet with a diameter up to 2 feet. The gray bark is initially smooth but becomes fissured with large, corky warts. The tree has a short trunk and an open, spreading crown.

The simple untoothed leaves are alternate, 1 to $2^1/_2$ inches long, $^3/_4$ to $1^1/_2$ inches wide, in two rows. Leaves are usually ovate with a short or long point. The base is asymmetrical and either rounded or slightly notched. Thick, dark green leaves have three main veins and sometimes coarse teeth. The undersides are yellow-green, with a pronounced network of raised veins, and slightly hairy. The slender twigs are light brown and hairy with a slight zigzag. Small, greenish flowers form at the base of young leaves in early spring. One-seeded, $^1/_4$- to $^3/_8$-inch-diameter, orange-red, sweet berries develop at the leaf bases, maturing in fall.

Netleaf Hackberry is found on moist soils along streams, in canyons, and on hillsides, usually in areas with a consistent water supply.

Features: The sweet berries were eaten by Native Americans and are an important source of food for many bird species. Witches'-broom—a deformed, brushy, fan-shaped growth caused by mites and fungi—can develop at the ends of branches. Leaves often have rounded galls caused by plant lice. There are several varieties of hackberry found in the Southwest.

Range: From Kansas to central Texas, west through New Mexico and Arizona, with more scattered occurrences in California, Oregon, Washington, Idaho, Utah, and Colorado, at elevations from 1,500 to 6,000 feet.

HAWTHORN

Black Hawthorn, *Crataegus douglasii*
Douglas Hawthorn, River Hawthorn

Black Hawthorn is a small deciduous tree that grows to a height of 30 feet with a diameter up to 1 foot. It also grows as a thicket-forming shrub. The smooth bark is brown or gray but may become broken into scales. Stout, spreading branches form a round, compact crown.

The simple toothed leaves are alternate, 1 to 3 inches long, $^5/_8$ to 2 inches wide, oval, and tend to be broader near the sharp-pointed tip. Leaf margins are sawtoothed, but some teeth have deeper cuts that create a lobed appearance. Leaves are dark green above, paler beneath. The base of the leaf is long, narrow, and pointed. Shiny red, slender twigs are hairless and may have straight, sometimes curved, strong, 1-inch spines. Flowers are clustered on long, slender stalks, and are $^1/_2$ inch in diameter, with five white petals. Clusters of red to shiny black, $^1/_2$-inch, round, miniature-apple-like fruits contain two or three small nutlets.

Black Hawthorn is found on moist soils in valleys and along mountain streams. It grows best in full sunlight. It often resprouts after wildfire and has been known to overtake pastures.

Features: Black Hawthorn is the most widespread of the western hawthorns and is found as far north as southern Alaska. Showy white flowers, rich green foliage, and shiny black fruit make this an attractive ornamental.

Range: From southern Alaska, throughout British Columbia and as far south as central California, and farther east between Saskatchewan and New Mexico. Near sea level in the north, up to 6,000 feet elevation in the south.

IRONWOOD

Desert Ironwood, *Olneya tesota*
Tesota, Arizona Ironwood

Desert Ironwood is a small evergreen that grows to a height of 30 feet with a diameter up to 2 feet. The gray bark is thin and smooth, becoming fissured, scaly, and shreddy. The tree has a short trunk and widely spreading crown and is often broader than it is high.

The pinnately compound leaves are alternate, 1 to 2¼ inches long, with two to ten pairs of tiny, oblong leaflets that have rounded tips and short, pointed bases. Blue-green leaflets are thick and have short stalks. Slender twigs are greenish, covered with gray hairs when young, and have ¼-inch, paired, straight spines at nodes. Fragrant clusters of purple flowers have five pea-shaped, unequal petals that appear in late spring, with the new leaves. Light brown, cylindrical pods, 2 to 2½ inches long, enclose one to five shiny, beanlike seeds, which mature in late summer and split into halves.

Desert Ironwood grows on desert washes and in rocky foothills. It is found in subtropical areas with warm, mild winters.

Features: Desert Ironwood has extremely dense, heavy wood that does not float. It polishes easily, and although it dulls most tools used to work it, it is made into bowls and small boxes. It is an excellent fuelwood. Native Americans roasted the beanlike seeds and ate them or ground them into flour. Desert animals eat the seeds and browse the leaves.

Range: The southwest corner of Arizona, southeast California, and northwest Mexico, to 2,500 feet in elevation.

LAUREL

California Laurel, *Umbellularia californica*
Oregon-myrtle, California Bay

California Laurel is a small- to medium-size evergreen that grows to a height of 40 to 80 feet with a diameter of 18 to 30 inches. It can reach heights of 100 to 175 feet with diameters of 3 to 10 feet on moist sites in southwestern Oregon. The bark is brown with thin, flat scales. The short trunk often divides near the ground into multiple stems and limbs that form a broad, round-topped crown. In rocky, shallow soils along the Pacific's windswept bluffs, it often grows in a low, shrubby thicket.

The simple untoothed leaves are alternate, 2 to 5 inches long, $1/2$ to $1^1/2$ inches wide, elliptical to lancelike, with a short-pointed or blunt tip and, usually, a V-shaped base. Thick, leathery leaves have a smooth, toothless margin that may turn under slightly. They are shiny dark green to yellow-green above, pale and hairless beneath. When crushed, the leaves give off a strong camphorlike odor. Stout twigs are green when young, turning reddish or brown, and also have a distinct odor when crushed. Small, $1/4$-inch, yellowish-green flowers are clustered at the leaf bases. Fruits are yellow-green to purple, 1-inch-round drupes with large seeds and thin pulp.

California Laurel is the only member of the Laurel family in the West. It is found on moist soils, on hillsides and in mountain canyons and valleys.

Features: The large burls that often form on the trunks of California Laurel are fashioned into bowls by wood turners; the largest burls are used to produce fine veneer. The wood is an attractive light brown with dark streaks and often marketed as "Oregon Myrtle." It was used for medicinal purposes by Native Americans. The tree is planted as an ornamental on the West Coast.

Range: Found from the Coos Bay area of southern Oregon along the coastal mountains and in the southern Sierra Nevada to the southern border of California, up to 1,500 feet in the north and from 2,000 to 6,000 feet in the south.

LOCUST

Locusts are members of the Legume family. They are easily recognized by their pinnately compound leaves; clusters of fragrant flowers in spring; long, flat seedpods; and rough, irregular bark. Most have poorly formed trunks and open, irregular crowns.

Black Locust, *Robinia pseudoacacia*
Yellow Locust, Locust

Black Locust is a medium-size deciduous tree that grows to a height of 40 to 60 feet with diameters of 1 to 2 feet. Thick, light gray bark is deeply furrowed with interlacing ridges. The bole is often forked and crooked, with an open, irregular crown. On good sites, the tree can develop a long, straight bole.

The pinnately compound leaves are alternate, 6 to 14 inches long, with 7 to 19 paired leaflets that are 1 1/2 to 2 inches long, 1/2 to 3/4 inch wide, elliptical or oval shaped, with smooth margins and a small, bristled tip. Leaf surfaces are dull, dark blue-green above, paler beneath. Leaves turn yellow in fall. Reddish brown twigs are somewhat zig-zagged, with stout, paired spines at nodes, 1/4 to 1/2 inch long. Fragrant, white, pealike flowers, 3/4 inch long, form a drooping raceme. Two- to four-inch-long, dark brown, narrow, oblong pods mature in autumn and persist into winter. They contain four to eight flattened, beanlike seeds.

Black Locust grows best on moist, rich, loamy soils but can thrive almost anywhere and is often found in old fields. A short-lived tree, it is fast growing and not tolerant of shade. Black Locust quickly establishes itself on disturbed sites and can displace native species.

Features: Black Locust is planted as an ornamental and often used for erosion control and shelter belts. The wood is extremely durable and was once used extensively for railroad ties and fence posts.

Range: Originally, Black Locust was found in the East, but it has become naturalized throughout the U.S. and southern Canada.

New Mexico Locust, *Robinia neomexicana*
New Mexican Locust, Southwestern Locust

New Mexico Locust is a small deciduous tree that grows to a height of 25 feet with diameters up to 8 inches. It also grows as a shrub. Thick, light gray bark has shallow furrows and flat, scaly ridges. Often growing in thickets, the tree has an open crown.

Pinnately compound leaves are alternate, 4 to 10 inches long, with 13 to 21 paired, elliptical leaflets that are $^1/_2$ to $1^1/_2$ inches long, $^1/_4$ to 1 inch wide. Pale blue-green leaflets are rounded at the ends and have a tiny bristle at the tip. They are finely hairy when young and have short stalks. Brown twigs are slightly zigzagged, with rust-colored hairs when young and stout, brown, $^1/_4$- to $^1/_2$-inch, paired spines. Showy, fragrant, purplish pink, pea-shaped flowers bloom in late spring and early summer. Fruits are $2^1/_2$- to $4^1/_2$-inch-long, narrow, oblong, flat, brown pods that contain three to eight flattened, beanlike, brown seeds.

New Mexico Locust forms thickets on moist soils in canyons but also grows on drier slopes, often with Gambel Oak, Ponderosa Pine, or pinyons.

Features: Flowery displays of the New Mexico Locust can be found on the north rim of the Grand Canyon in early summer. The tree is often planted as an ornamental and also for erosion control. It sprouts vigorously after cutting. Native Americans used the pods for food and the wood for a variety of purposes.

Range: Southeast Nevada to central and southern Colorado, south to western Texas and west to southeast Arizona, at elevations from 4,000 to 8,500 feet.

MADRONE

Madrone are members of the Heath family. Three species are locally common in the West. Smooth, red bark; white or pink flowers; and berrylike, red fruits are characteristic of all three. The trees grow on lower slopes in transition zones between desert grasslands and hardwood-conifer forests.

Arizona Madrone, *Arbutus arizonica*
Madroño

Arizona Madrone is a medium-size evergreen that grows to a height of 40 feet and up to 1 1/2 feet in diameter. The smooth, thin bark has a distinctive red-brown color, becoming divided into thin, scaly plates with age. Branches also have smooth, red bark. The trunk and stout branches tend to be crooked and support a rounded, irregular crown.

Simple untoothed leaves are alternate, 1 1/2 to 3 inches long, 1/2 to 1 inch wide, lancelike, with a V-shaped base and pointed tip. Leaves are thick, stiff, and shiny light green above, paler beneath. Twigs are light colored with fine hairs when young, turning red-brown. Jug-shaped flowers can be white or pink and are found in branched clusters at the ends of twigs. The small, orange-red, berrylike fruits (3/8 to 1/2 inch) have a finely warty exterior; they mature in autumn.

Arizona Madrone is found in oak woodlands with evergreen oaks and junipers.

Features: The wood of Arizona Madrone was used for charcoal and gunpowder. The dense crown provides cover for nesting birds.

Range: Found in southeast Arizona, extreme southwest New Mexico and northwest Mexico, at elevations from 4,000 to 8,000 feet.

Pacific Madrone, *Arbutus menziesii*
Madrone, Madroño

Pacific Madrone is a medium to large-size evergreen that grows 80 to 125 feet tall and 2 to 4 feet in diameter. The smooth, thin bark has a distinctive red-brown color and is divided into thin, scaly plates. Branches have smooth, red bark. The tree develops a clear, symmetrical trunk in forested stands as compared to the shorter, more crooked trunk found in more open settings. The narrow crown is somewhat rounded and open.

The simple untoothed leaves are alternate, 2 to 5 inches long, 1 to 3 inches wide, oval to oblong, with blunt tips. Leaf margins are usually smooth, although they sometimes can be finely to coarsely toothed on vigorous growth. Thick, leathery leaves are shiny dark green on upper surfaces, paler or whitish beneath. Leaves are shed in the summer of their second year, turning red before falling. The slender twigs are green, red, or brown. Large clusters of small, bell-shaped, white flowers appear in early spring. The small, orange-red fruits ($^3/_8$ to $^1/_2$ inch) are berrylike, with a finely warty exterior; they mature in autumn.

Pacific Madrone grows best on well-drained soils near sea level, although it can be found on a variety of soils. It also grows on upland slopes and in canyons. It becomes shrubby on poor, dry sites. It can be found in almost-pure stands and as an understory tree in Douglas-fir and Redwood forests.

Features: The contrast of the white flowers, glossy green foliage, vivid red bark, and orange-red fruits makes Pacific Madrone a very showy, attractive tree. Native Americans used it for medicinal purposes and also ate the fruits. The wood was used for charcoal and making weaving shuttles. Bees use the flower nectar for honey.

Range: In coastal areas from southwest British Columbia through Washington and Oregon to southern California, also in the Sierra Nevada and on Santa Cruz Island, at elevations up to 5,000 feet.

Texas Madrone, *Arbutus xalapensis*
Texas Madroño

Texas Madrone is a small evergreen that grows to a height of 20 feet and up to 8 inches in diameter. Branches have smooth, reddish or pinkish brown bark. The trunk develops thin, papery, square plates. The tree has a short, crooked trunk with twisted branches that form a rounded, spreading crown. It also grows as a shrub.

Simple untoothed leaves are 1 to $3^1/2$ inches long, $5/8$ to $1^1/2$ inches wide, elliptical, with blunt tips and uneven bases. Thick, stiff leaves can be wavy with smooth margins, sometimes sawtoothed, shiny green above, slender and slightly hairy beneath. Slender leafstalks are hairy. Red twigs are covered with dense hairs when young, turning dark reddish brown and developing scales. Jug-shaped flowers can be white or pinkish and are found in upright, branched clusters at the ends of twigs. The small, dark red to yellowish red, berrylike fruits ($3/8$ to $1/2$ inch) have a finely warty exterior; they mature in autumn.

Texas Madrone is found on rocky plains and mountain slopes and in canyons with evergreen oaks and junipers.

Features: The fruit of Texas Madrone is only slightly palatable to livestock. The tree does not reproduce well.

Range: From central Texas, the Trans-Pecos, and southeast New Mexico, at elevations from 2,000 to 6,000 feet.

MAPLE

Maples, members of the Soapberry family, are recognized by their opposite leaves, which are often lobed, with palmately arranged veins that run up each lobe. Leaf margins are often coarsely toothed.

Bigleaf Maple, *Acer macrophyllum*

Bigleaf Maple is a small- to medium-size deciduous tree that grows to a height of 75 feet with a diameter up to 1¹/₂ feet. On exceptional growing sites, in rich bottomlands, the tree can reach heights of 100 feet with diameters of 3 to 4 feet. The bark is light gray-brown and smooth on smaller trunks but darkens and becomes furrowed with flat plates as the tree ages. The bole may be clear for half or more of its length, but often the trunk divides into several vertical branches. In forested conditions, the crown is rather narrow.

The simple lobed leaves are opposite, 8 to 12 inches in diameter, and usually have five lobes. Including the very long leafstalk, the length can be 16 to 24 inches. The tips of the lobes and leaf are bluntly pointed, but the sinuses are rounded. Leaves are dark green above, paler beneath. Leafstalk joins the leaf blade in an inverted V. Except for the pointed tips and lobes, the leaf margins are smooth. A milky sap may exude from the leaf stem when it's torn from the twig. Stout twigs are green or reddish brown, often with numerous conspicuous lenticels. The terminal buds are blunt and have many scales. The ⁵/₁₆-inch, bell-shaped, light yellow flowers have five petals, are fragrant, and hang from hairy stalks in 4- to 6-inch, drooping clusters. The fruit of the Bigleaf Maple is a 1¹/₄- to 2-inch, double-winged samara with a noticeable V shape. The base of each wing contains a seed densely covered with stiff, yellowish hairs.

Bigleaf Maple grows well along streams and in canyons on moist soils and can be found in small groves or scattered among conifers and other broadleafed trees. It reaches maturity at 200 to 300 years.

Features: The leaves of the Bigleaf Maple are the largest of any maple and turn orange or yellow in the fall. It is one of the few commercial hardwood species on the Pacific coast. Old trees frequently develop large burls along the main bole, desirable for specialty wood products. The sap can be rendered for maple syrup.

Range: Generally a coastal tree found at sea level to 1,000 feet in British Columbia, and from 3,000 to 7,000 feet in the southern part of its range in southern California in the Sierra Nevada.

Bigtooth Maple, *Acer grandidentatum*
Canyon Maple

Bigtooth Maple is a small deciduous tree that reaches heights of 40 feet with diameters up to 8 inches. The thin bark can be gray or brown and either smooth or scaly. The tree has a short trunk with a dense, rounded, spreading crown. It also grows as a shrub.

The simple lobed leaves are opposite, 2 to 3¹/₄ inches wide and long, with three broad lobes and two smaller basal lobes with a few blunt teeth. There are three or five main veins. Leaves are shiny dark green above, paler with fine hairs beneath, turning red or yellow in autumn. Slender twigs are reddish and hairless. Five-lobed, yellow, ³/₁₆-inch flowers are bell shaped and hang in drooping clusters on long, hairy stalks. Fruits are in pairs, 1 to 1¹/₄ inch long, and reddish or green.

Bigtooth Maple is found on moist soils in mountain canyons and on plateaus.

Features: Bigtooth Maple is related to the eastern Sugar Maple and produces a sweet sap that can be used for syrup. The fall foliage makes it an attractive landscape tree; the wood is used for firewood.

Range: Found from southeast Idaho to northern Arizona, and east to southern New Mexico and the Trans-Pecos, at elevations of 4,000 to 7,000 feet.

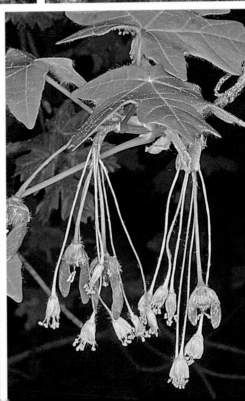

Rocky Mountain Maple, *Acer glabrum*
Dwarf Maple, Douglas Maple

Rocky Mountain Maple is a small deciduous tree that grows to heights of 30 feet with diameters up to 1 foot. The thin, smooth bark is brown or gray. The tree has a short trunk that abruptly turns into a mass of vertical branches, forming a rounded but irregular crown. It also grows as a shrub.

The simple lobed leaves are opposite, $1^1/2$ to $4^1/2$ inches in length and width, and palmately veined with three main veins. The leaf has three, sometimes five, short-pointed lobes with a double sawtoothed edge. In some instances, the lobes are so deep that the leaf is divided into a palmately compound leaf, with the leaflets joined together at the hairless, reddish leafstalk. The leaves are glossy green above, paler beneath. Buds and twigs, like the leafstalk, are reddish brown and slender. The small $1/4$-inch flowers hang in 1- to 3-inch-long clusters and bloom in the spring, when the leaves first appear. The fruit develops into a $3/4$- to 1-inch-long inverted V, typical of maples, and has one seed in each winged half of the V. The fruit does not mature until fall.

Rocky Mountain Maple grows best in moist soils and is found in coniferous forests in canyons and on mountain slopes.

Features: Native Americans used the wood to make snowshoes and various parts of the tree for medicinal purposes. It is the most northerly maple in North America, extending as far north as southern Alaska.

Range: From southeast Alaska through British Columbia into western Oregon and Washington. Also found throughout the Rockies from British Columbia, Idaho, and Montana to Arizona and New Mexico. Close to sea level in the north and from 5,000 to 9,000 feet in the south.

Vine Maple, *Acer circinatum*

Vine Maple is a small deciduous tree that grows to a height of 25 feet with a diameter up to 8 inches. It sometimes grows as a shrub. The bark can be brown or gray, smooth or finely fissured. The tree has a short trunk, often with several leaning branches that twist from the base, giving it a sprawling, vinelike appearance.

The simple lobed leaves are opposite, 2$^{1}/_{2}$ to 4$^{1}/_{2}$ inches wide and long, the outline of which almost forms a circle. There are 7 to 11 long-pointed lobes that are double sawtoothed, each lobe having a main vein that extends from a notched leaf base. Leaves are bright green above, paler beneath, with tufts of hair along vein angles. Leaves turn orange and red in autumn. Long leafstalks have enlarged bases. The slender twigs are green to reddish brown, often with a whitish bloom. Half-inch purple and white flowers form in clusters at the end of short twigs in the spring, as the leaves develop. The single fruits are paired, spread almost horizontally, and have reddish wings when young.

Vine Maple is found on moist soils in the understory of conifer stands and along shaded streams.

Features: Vine Maple is an attractive ornamental that provides color in spring, with its purple and white flowers; in early summer, with its showy, reddish fruit; and in fall, with foliage turning orange and red. The seeds are consumed by a variety of mammals and birds.

Range: Along the Pacific coast from southwest British Columbia to northern California, to 5,000 feet in elevation.

MESQUITE

Mesquite are members of the Legume family. They grow as small, spindly trees and have tiny, bipinnately compound leaves. Fragrant yellow flowers appear in spring and summer.

Honey Mesquite, *Prosopis glandulosa*

Honey Mesquite is a small deciduous tree that grows to a height of 20 feet and a diameter of 1 foot. It also grows as a thicket-forming shrub. The rough, thick, dark brown bark has shreddy plates separated by fissures. The trunk is short with a very open, spreading crown.

The bipinnately compound leaves are alternate and 3 to 8 inches long. The main stem splits in two, with each side stem having 7 to 17 pairs of short, $3/8$- to $1^1/4$-inch, stalkless, narrow, oblong leaflets, which are nearly hairless. Stout twigs are zigzagged, with pairs of yellowish thorns, $1/4$ to 1 inch long, growing from slightly swollen nodes. Two- to three-inch-long clusters of $1/4$-inch, light yellow, fragrant flowers bloom in spring and summer. The fruit is a $3^1/2$- to 8-inch long, narrow ($3/8$ inch) bean pod, which is slightly flattened and may contain anywhere from 3 to 15 seeds.

Honey Mesquite is found in desert and arid grasslands along sandy washes and in valleys.

Features: Honey Mesquite has a deep taproot that can be dug up and used as firewood or for smoking meats. The tree is considered a weed by ranchers. Native Americans used the seeds and pods for food. Bees frequent the flowers for nectar.

Range: From eastern Texas and southwest Oklahoma west to southwest Utah and southern California, to 4,500 feet in elevation. Also naturalized as far north as Kansas and southeast Colorado.

Velvet Mesquite, *Prosopis velutina*

Velvet Mesquite is a small deciduous tree that grows to a height of 20 to 40 feet with a diameter of 1 to 2 feet. Young bark is gray, thin, and smooth. The dark brown, older bark is thick and has vertical fissures separating long, flat plates. It has a short trunk that forks into many crooked branches, forming an open, spreading crown.

Bipinnately compound leaves are alternate, 5 to 6 inches long. The main stem splits into 1 or 2 pairs of side stems, each having 15 to 20 pairs of $1/4$- to $1/2$-inch, narrow, oblong leaflets that are dull green and stalkless. Light brown twigs are slightly zigzagged, covered with fine, velvety hair, and have paired thorns ($1/4$ to 1 inch) growing from enlarged nodes. Fragrant, light-yellow, $1/4$-inch flowers are crowded in 2- to 3-inch-long clusters in spring and summer. The fruits are 4- to 8-inch-long, slightly hairy, narrow ($3/8$ inch wide), slightly flattened pods containing several seeds.

Velvet Mesquite is found in valleys and along washes in desert and desert grassland, sometimes growing with oaks.

Features: Velvet Mesquite is used for fence posts and firewood. Native Americans used the pods for meal. Bees produce a fragrant honey from the nectar.

Range: Southwest New Mexico west to central Arizona and northwest Mexico, from 500 to 5,500 feet in elevation.

OAK

Oaks, members of the Beech family, are widely distributed in the West. They are divided into two major groups: white oaks and red oaks. The white oak group usually has leaves without bristles (although some live oaks have spiny teeth) and acorns that mature in one season. The red oak group has lobes or margins with bristles or spines and acorns that mature in two seasons.

Arizona White Oak, *Quercus arizonica*

Arizona White Oak is a small- to medium-size evergreen that grows to a height from 30 to 60 feet with a diameter of 2 to 3 feet. The light gray bark is thick on the trunk and has furrows separating scaly ridges, giving the bark a plated appearance. The trunk tends to be short, with stout branches that form a massive, rounded or irregular, spreading crown. At higher elevations near the treeline, the tree is stunted.

The simple toothed leaves are alternate, $1^{1}/_{2}$ to 3 inches long, and oblong. Leaf margins are somewhat wavy and spiny. Leaves are a dull blue-green, have sunken veins, are hairless above, with hairs and raised veins beneath. They are shed in the spring as new ones develop. Twigs are hairy with tiny buds. Small $^{3}/_{4}$- to 1-inch-long, yellowish acorns have a deep, cuplike cap and are found singly or in pairs on a short stem.

Arizona White Oak grows on moist benches and canyon walls in oak woodlands with other evergreen oaks. It is one of the largest southwestern oaks.

Features: The wood makes good firewood, although it is extremely hard and difficult to split or cut.

Range: The Trans-Pecos, New Mexico, and Arizona, also in Mexico, from 5,000 to 7,500 feet in elevation.

Blue Oak, *Quercus douglasii*
Mountain White Oak, Iron Oak

Blue Oak is a small- to medium-size deciduous tree that grows to a height of 20 to 60 feet with a diameter up to 1 foot. It sometimes grows as a shrub. The light gray bark is thin, with fissures separating narrow, scaly plates. The tree has a short, leaning trunk with a broad, rounded crown formed by short, stout branches.

The simple lobed leaves are alternate, $1^1/4$ to 4 inches long, $3/4$ to $1^3/4$ inches wide, elliptical or oblong, with rounded or blunt ends. Leaves have short leafstalks and can be lobed, shallowly indented, or unlobed, with toothed or untoothed margins. They are thin yet firm, pale blue-green, almost hairless above, paler and somewhat hairy beneath. Twigs are hairy. The acorns are $3/4$ to $1^1/2$ inches long, elliptical, and have no stalks. The cap has warty scales.

Blue Oak is found in low valleys and foothills on dry, loamy, or rocky soils. It may form dense, pure stands or be found in more open savannahs. It also grows with California Foothill Pine, Interior Live Oak, Valley Oak, and California Live Oak.

Features: The blue-green foliage makes this tree easily recognizable from a distance. The wood is used for firewood. Acorns are eaten by livestock and various wildlife species. Conversion of forestland to other uses has reduced the abundance of this species.

Range: Interior valleys from northern to southern California in the Coast Ranges and the Sierra Nevada, from 3,000 to 3,500 feet.

California Black Oak, *Quercus kelloggii*

California Black Oak is a small- to medium-size deciduous tree that grows to a height of 80 feet with a diameter of 1 to 3 feet. The bark is smooth and brown on younger trunks but dark brown on older trunks, with irregular plates and ridges separated by deep furrows. The short trunk is often crooked and defective. The stout branches form a rounded but often irregular crown.

The simple lobed leaves are alternate, 3 to 8 inches long, 2 to 5 inches wide, elliptical, with five to seven deep lobes that are bristled at the tips. They are dark green above, paler green and often hairy beneath. Twigs are sometimes hairy and end in clusters of ¼-inch-long, pointed, hairless buds. Leafstalks are 1 to 2 inches long. The 1- to 1½-inch-long acorn is covered up to two-thirds of its length by a thin, scaly cap. One or several acorns grow on short stalks.

California Black Oak is a common oak found in rocky or sandy soils of valleys and foothills. It often forms in pure stands but can also be found with Douglas-fir, California Foothill Pine, Ponderosa Pine, and Canyon Live Oak.

Features: California Black Oak is the only western oak having leaves with deep lobes and bristled tips. Acorn Woodpeckers drill holes into the trees and jam acorns into the holes so tightly that squirrels cannot remove them. This is a slow-growing tree used for firewood and also in landscaping.

Range: From southern Oregon south along the Pacific coast and in the Sierra Nevada to southern California, from 1,000 to 8,000 feet in elevation.

California Live Oak, *Quercus agrifolia*
Coast Live Oak, Encina

California Live Oak is a medium-size evergreen that grows to a height of 60 to 90 feet with diameters from 2 to 3 feet. In coastal areas, it usually grows as a shrub. Young bark is smooth and gray. The thick, dark, grayish brown bark is deeply furrowed. The trunk is short and stout. Large, crooked, spreading branches form a rounded crown. Larger California Live Oak trees can develop enormous, spreading crowns with branches that rest on the ground.

The simple toothed leaves are alternate, $3/4$ to 3 inches long, $1/2$ to $1\frac{1}{2}$ inches wide, hollylike, oblong or elliptical, and may be either short pointed or rounded at each end. Edges turn under and have spiny teeth. The thick, leathery leaves are shiny green above, yellow green and sometimes hairy beneath. The acorns are 1 to $1\frac{1}{2}$ inches long, narrow, and egg shaped. The cap covers a third of the acorn and has brownish scales with fine hairs on the outside and silky hairs on the inside. Acorns have no stalk.

California Live Oak is found on well-drained soils in foothills and valleys. It grows in open groves, quite often in pure stands or with Canyon Live Oak, California Black Oak, California Sycamore, and Bigcone Douglas-fir.

Features: California Live Oak acorns were a source of food for Native Americans, who ground the seeds into meal, washed it to remove the bitter taste, and boiled it into mush or baked it into bread. Early settlers used the wood for charcoal. Today, the tree is planted for erosion control.

Range: Coast Ranges from central California to Baja California, from sea level to 4,500 feet elevation.

Canyon Live Oak, *Quercus chrysolepis*
Canyon Oak, Goldcup Oak

Canyon Live Oak is a small- to medium-size evergreen that grows to a height of 20 to 100 feet with diameters from 1 to 3 feet. It sometimes grows as a bushy shrub. The bark is light gray and can be smooth or scaly. Trees have a short trunk with large, spreading branches that form a rounded crown. As is typical of live oaks, larger Canyon Live Oak trees can develop enormous, spreading crowns.

The simple toothed leaves are evergreen, 1 to 3 inches long, $1/2$ to $1 1/2$ inches wide, elliptical or oval shaped. Leaves on sprouts or young trees have hollylike spiny or prickly leaf margins whereas leaves on older trees have smooth margins. Initially, thick, leathery leaves are shiny, yellow-green and hairy above, turning dark blue-green and hairless in the second year, persisting for three or four years. Twigs are flexible and hairy, with blunt, hairless buds. The acorns are $3/4$ to 2 inches long and have hairy scales covering a thick, golden cap that resembles a turban.

Canyon Live Oak is found in cool, moist canyons and on dry mountain slopes along the California coast or in the foothills, either in pure stands or mixed with other oaks, Incense Cedar, and Ponderosa Pine. It is extremely slow growing and lives to 300 years or more.

Features: The dense, heavy wood was used for farm implements and wagon axles and wheels. It was used for wedges and the heads of mauls used to split wood and so was referred to as "Maul Oak."

Range: Southwest Oregon through the Coast Ranges and Sierra Nevada to Baja California at elevations of 1,000 to 6,000 feet, and east to central and southern Arizona and southwestern New Mexico at elevations of 5,500 to 7,500 feet.

Emory Oak, *Quercus emoryi*
Black Oak, Blackjack Oak

Emory Oak is a medium-size evergreen that grows to a height of 60 feet with a diameter up to $2^1/_2$ feet. It also grows as a shrub. Smooth, black bark becomes thick, rough, and deeply furrowed with blocky scales. The tree has a straight trunk and rounded crown.

The simple toothed leaves are alternate, 1 to $2^1/_2$ inches long, $^3/_8$ to 1 inch wide, somewhat lancelike, with a short, spiny point on the tip. Margins can be smooth but most are wavy with a few short, spiny teeth. Nearly hairless leaves are shiny yellow-green on both surfaces, thick, stiff, and leathery. Leaves are shed in spring as new leaves develop. Slender twigs are stiff with fine hairs. Acorns are $^1/_2$ to $^3/_4$ inch long, with a deep, scaly cap, and almost stalkless.

Emory Oak is found in canyons, foothills, and mountains. It is found with other oaks and evergreens and is one of the most common oaks within its limited range.

Features: Acorns are slightly bitter but can be eaten. Native Americans used the ground acorns as a thickening agent in cooking. The foliage is browsed by deer and livestock.

Range: From the Trans-Pecos to central Arizona, south to northwest Mexico, at elevations from 4,000 to 8,000 feet.

Gambel Oak, *Quercus gambelii*
Rocky Mountain White Oak, Utah Oak

Gambel Oak is a small- to medium-size deciduous tree that grows to a height of 20 to 70 feet with diameters of 1 to 2^1/$_2$ feet. It also grows as a shrub, forming dense thickets. The rough, gray bark is thick, with flat, scaly plates, and deeply furrowed. The tree has a rounded crown.

The simple lobed leaves are alternate, 2 to 6 inches long, 1^1/$_4$ to 2^1/$_2$ inches wide, elliptical or oblong, rounded at the tip, pointed at the base, with short leafstalks. Leaves have five to nine rounded lobes and deep sinuses. They are slightly leathery, shiny green above, lighter with soft hairs beneath. They turn yellow or red in the fall. Reddish twigs have fine hairs. Terminal buds are reddish brown and have distinct, overlapping scales. Acorns have short stalks and are ^{1}/$_2$ to ^{7}/$_8$ inch long. They are egg shaped and have a thick, scaly cap that covers much of the nut.

Gambel Oak is found in dense groves or shrubby thickets on dry slopes and valleys, foothills, mountains, and plateaus scattered with Ponderosa Pine or in pure stands.

Features: Gambel Oak is the most common oak in the southern Rockies and is found in the Grand Canyon. The wood is used for firewood and fence posts. Native Americans ate the acorns raw and used them in cooking. The root bark was used for medicinal purposes.

Range: Northern Utah east to southern Wyoming, south to west Texas and southern Arizona, at elevations from 5,000 to 8,000 feet.

Gray Oak, *Quercus grisea*
Scrub Oak, Shin Oak

Gray Oak is a medium-size deciduous tree that grows to a height of 60 feet with diameters up to 1 foot. It sometimes grows as a shrub. The light gray bark has fissures separating flat plates that can become shaggy. The tree has a short trunk and rounded crown, often growing in clumps.

The simple untoothed leaves are $3/4$ to 2 inches long, $3/8$ to $3/4$ inch wide, elliptical to ovate, sometimes with a few short teeth toward the tip, and slightly thickened or rigid. The base can be notched or rounded. Leaves are gray-green or blue-green, shiny, and slightly hairy above, dull and finely hairy with slightly raised veins beneath. Twigs are stout and hairy. Egg-shaped acorns are $1/2$ to $5/8$ inch long, with a deep, scaly cap.

Gray Oak is found on dry, rocky slopes of foothills and mountains and in canyons, growing in scattered groves with other oaks, pinyons, and junipers.

Features: The color of the foliage makes this an easy oak to identify. In New Mexico, Gray Oak most often grows as a shrub. Native Americans used the acorns for food. The wood is used for fence posts and firewood.

Range: The Trans-Pecos through New Mexico to central Arizona, at elevations from 5,000 to 7,000 feet.

Interior Live Oak, *Quercus wislizenii*
Highland Live Oak, Sierra Live Oak

Interior Live Oak is a small- to medium-size evergreen that grows to a height of 50 to 70 feet with a diameter of 1 to 3 feet. It also grows as a shrub. The dark gray bark is smooth on younger trees but becomes shallowly furrowed, leaving scaly ridges, as the tree ages. The trunks of larger trees are short and wide and have a wide, broad, but often irregular crown. As is typical of live oaks, larger Interior Live Oak trees can develop enormous, spreading crowns.

Simple toothed leaves are alternate, 1 to 2 inches long, $1/2$ to $1^1/4$ inches wide. The hollylike leaves on young trees are elliptical to lancelike, thick, and leathery, with a sharp point at the tip and often thick, spiny teeth on the margins. Larger trees have leaves with smoother margins. Both surfaces of hairless leaves are shiny dark green with a dense network of veins beneath; leaves remain on the tree for two years. The twigs tend to be hairy. The pointed buds are hairless. Acorns are oval shaped, 1 inch long, and oblong. They may have long dark lines and are half enclosed by a scaly cap. Acorns are either stalkless or attached, one or two together, by short stalks.

Interior Live Oak is found on rich, dry soils in river bottoms and washes and on slopes. It often forms pure stands but also is commonly found with California Foothill Pine and other oaks. It sprouts vigorously after fire.

Features: Interior Live Oak is sometimes planted as an ornamental and provides food for wildlife. The wood is of little value except as firewood. Native Americans used the acorns for food.

Range: Found in California on Mount Shasta and southward, primarily in the foothills of the Sierra Nevada and along the Coast Ranges, from 1,000 feet to 5,000 feet elevation.

Oregon White Oak, *Quercus garryana*

Oregon White Oak is a medium-size deciduous tree that grows 50 to 70 feet in height and 2 to 3 feet in diameter. The bark of younger stems is smooth. The bark on older trunks is gray or gray-brown, with narrow, shallow fissures that separate flat, scaly ridges. The trunk is short and often crooked. The branches spread into a wide, rounded crown.

The simple lobed leaves are alternate, 4 to 6 inches long, 2 to 4 inches wide, oblong or obovate, and either rounded or blunt at both ends. The leaf has five to seven lobes that are blunt or slightly toothed and separated by deep, narrow sinuses. Margins are smooth and slightly rolled under. Leaves are leathery, dark green, and smooth above, pale green with orange-brown hairs beneath. The leafstalk is $3/4$ inch long and hairy. Twigs are stout, and young ones are covered with a dense, orange-red pubescence. Twigs are tipped with clusters of $1/4$- to $1/2$-inch-long, fuzz-covered buds. Acorns are 1 to $1 1/4$ inches long, oval, and capped with a thin, scaly, saucerlike, densely pubescent cap. Acorns attach either singly or in pairs, directly or by short stems.

Oregon White Oak is found in dry, rocky soils in valleys and on mountain slopes, but it grows best on alluvial soils. It occasionally forms pure stands but usually grows as a single tree or in small groves mixed with various other trees.

Features: Unlike most western oaks, Oregon White Oak has some commercial value. It is the only native oak in British Columbia and Washington State. The wood is used for furniture, cabinet and interior finishing, ship building, and firewood. Acorns are sweet and eaten by livestock and wildlife. Native Americans used Oregon White Oak for medicinal purposes and ate the acorns.

Range: British Columbia southward to central California in the Coast Ranges and the Sierra Nevada, at elevations up to 3,000 feet in the north and from 1,000 to 5,000 feet in the south.

Silverleaf Oak, *Quercus hypoleucoides*
White-leaf Oak

Silverleaf Oak is a small- to medium-size evergreen that grows to a height of 30 to 60 feet with a diameter from 1 to 2^1/$_2$ feet. The black, blocky bark is separated into ridges and plates by deep furrows. The tree sometimes grows in clumps with twisted trunks and rounded, spreading crowns. It also grows as a shrub.

The simple untoothed leaves are alternate, 2 to 4 inches long, lancelike, with a sharp, pointed tip, rounded at the base, and with smooth margins that may be rolled under. Leaves are thick, leathery, shiny yellow-green above, with dense, white, woolly hairs beneath. Egg-shaped acorns are ^{1}/$_2$ to ^{5}/$_8$ inch long, with a deep, thick, scaly cap. There are one or two acorns on short stalks.

Silverleaf oak is found on mountain slopes and in canyons with other evergreen oaks, Mexican Pinyon, and Alligator Juniper.

Features: Silverleaf Oak is easily identified by the contrasting upper dark green leaf and silvery underside. Its colorful foliage makes this tree a popular ornamental.

Range: The Trans-Pecos to southeastern Arizona and northern Mexico, from 5,000 to 6,000 feet in elevation.

Valley Oak, *Quercus lobata*
California White Oak, Weeping Oak

Valley Oak is a medium- to large-size deciduous tree that grows to a height of 90 to 125 feet and a diameter of 3 to 5 feet. The light gray or brown bark has deep, vertical and horizontal fissures that break the bark into small, thick, flat blocks that resembles the hide of an alligator. The trunk is short, stout, and supports a broad, open, hemispherical crown formed by wide-spreading, drooping branches.

The simple lobed leaves are alternate, 2 to 4 inches long, 1¼ to 2½ inches wide, oblong or elliptical, with 7 to 11 deep lobes with sinuses that go halfway to the midvein. The lobes are rounded; the larger ones are notched at the end. Leaves are dark green and nearly hairless above, paler with fine hair beneath. They have short leafstalks. Twigs tend to droop and are slender and hairy, ending in clusters of ¼-inch hairy, scale-covered, pointed buds. The large acorns are 1¼ to 2½ inches long, conical, and have a cap that covers a third of the acorn. The light brown scales on the cap get thick and warty near the end. The underside of the cap is smooth.

Valley Oak is a handsome shade tree that grows in valleys, on lower slopes, and in the foothills. It is found on rich, loamy soils and sometimes forms pure groves. It is fast growing and lives only 200 to 250 years.

Features: Valley Oak is California's largest oak. Native Americans used the bark and other parts of the tree for medicinal purposes and ground the acorns into flour; they also roasted the acorns. Domestic animals and wildlife feed on the relatively sweet acorns. The wood has no commercial value because the heartwood often rots and is of little use other than as firewood.

Range: From northern to southern California from the Sierra Nevada to the coast, up to 5,000 feet in elevation. It is also found on Santa Cruz and Catalina Islands.

PALM

California Fan Palm, *Washingtonia filifera*
California Palm, California Washingtonia, Petticoat Palm

California Fan Palm is a medium-size evergreen that grows to a height of 75 feet with a diameter from 3 to 5 feet. The trunk is smooth and gray, with horizontal lines and fissures. The tree has a straight, unbranched trunk with a crown made up of large, fan-shaped leaves and a characteristic "skirt" of persistent, dried leaves.

Numerous fan-shaped leaves spread at the top of the tree. Leafstalks are 3 to 5 feet long, stout and have hooked spines along the edges. Gray-green leaf blades are 3 to 5 feet in diameter and split into many narrow, folded, leathery segments. Leaf margins are frayed, with threadlike fibers. Old, dead leaves hang down and form a thatchlike layer against the trunk. Flowers droop in 6- to 12-inch clusters from leaf bases and are 3/8 inch long, white, and slightly fragrant. Elliptical, black berries, 3/8 inch in diameter, are edible and have a thin, sweet pulp. There is only one elliptical, brown seed.

California Fan Palm is found in groves along alkaline streams and in canyons. It can be an indicator of water. The tree is found in southern California, with native groves located near Palm Springs and in Joshua Tree National Monument. It is widely cultivated as an ornamental.

Features: California Fan Palm is the largest native palm in the U.S. and the only native western palm. The name Petticoat Palm refers to the large mass of shaggy leaves that hangs from the crown. Dead leaves are often removed to reduce risks of wildfire. Native Americans ate the berries and ground the seeds into meal. They also used the stems to make cooking implements.

Range: Southeast California, southwest Arizona, and northern Baja California, from 3,000 to 5,000 feet.

PALOVERDE

Paloverde are members of the Legume family. Found in deserts and desert grasslands, this unusual tree has greenish yellow or greenish blue bark, is leafless for most of the year, and produces yellow flowers in the spring.

Blue Paloverde, *Parkinsonia florida*

Blue Paloverde is a small deciduous tree that grows to a height of 30 feet with a diameter up to 18 inches. It remains leafless for most of the year. The smooth bark on the trunk and branches is blue-green. The base of larger trees becomes brown and scaly. The tree has a short trunk and an open, airy crown made up of widely spreading branches.

The bipinnately compound leaves are alternate, few, and scattered, appearing in spring, and quickly shed. Leaves are 1 inch long and have a short main stem that forks into two side stems. Each side stem has two or three pairs of oblong leaflets that are ¼ inch long and pale blue-green. The smooth twigs are blue-green, can be slightly zigzagged, and have a short, straight, slender spine at each node. Flowers are ¾ inch wide with five bright yellow petals. The largest petals may have a few red spots. Two-inch clusters of four or five flowers cover the tree in spring. Trees may reflower in late summer. Yellowish brown fruits develop as 1½- to 3¼-inch narrow, oblong, flat, thin pods with two to eight beanlike seeds. Fruits mature and drop in summer.

Blue Paloverde is found along washes and in valleys, deserts, and desert grasslands with other arid-land vegetation.

Features: The showy yellow flowers and blue-green bark make this an attractive tree in spring. It is used for erosion control along drainages. Native Americans ground the mature seeds for meal and cooked and ate the immature pods. Photosynthesis occurs through the blue-green bark as leaves are absent for most of the year.

Range: Southeast California and central and southern Arizona, also northwest Mexico, at elevations up to 4,000 feet.

Yellow Paloverde, *Parkinsonia microphylla*

Yellow Paloverde is a small deciduous tree that grows to a height of 25 feet with diameters up to 1 foot. It is leafless most of the year. The smooth bark on the trunk and branches is yellow-green. The tree has a short trunk and an open, airy crown made up of widely spreading branches.

The bipinnately compound leaves are alternate, few, scattered, appearing in spring, and quickly shed. Leaves are 1 inch long and have a short main stem that forks into two side stems. Each side stem has three to seven pairs of tiny, elliptical leaflets that are pale yellow-green. Twigs are short, stout, and end in a 2-inch-long, straight spine. Clusters of flowers, 1/2 inch wide with five petals (three are pale yellow and the two largest are white or cream colored), appear in spring. Yellowish brown fruits develop as 2- to 3-inch thin pods ending in a long, narrow point, constricted between seeds. Fruits remain on the tree.

Yellow Paloverde grows with Saguaro in the desert and desert grasslands, and on dry, rocky slopes in the foothills.

Features: The showy, yellow flowers and yellow-green bark make this a very attractive tree in spring. It is useful for erosion control along drainages. Native Americans ground the mature seeds for meal and cooked and ate the immature pods. Although leaves are absent for most of the year, photosynthesis continues to occur through the yellow-green bark and twigs.

Range: From Arizona to southeast California and northwest Mexico, at elevations from 500 to 4,000 feet.

SERVICEBERRY

Saskatoon Serviceberry, *Amelanchier alnifolia*
Western Serviceberry, Western Shadbush

Saskatoon Serviceberry is a small deciduous tree that grows to a height of 30 feet with a diameter up to 8 inches. The thin bark can be gray or brown. It is often smooth but can also develop slight fissures. It also grows as a thicket-forming shrub with several stems that fork into many branches. The tree has a rounded crown.

The simple toothed leaves are alternate, $3/4$ to 2 inches in diameter, almost round, with coarse teeth above the middle of the leaf. Seven to nine straight veins are visible on each side of the midvein. Leaves are dark green above, lighter and hairy beneath. Slender, hairless twigs are red-brown. Small, pointed buds are deep red. Bud scales usually have a fringe of white hairs. Star-shaped flowers are $3/4$ to $1 1/4$ inches wide and have five white petals. They appear in spring with the leaves and form as clusters at the ends of twigs. Small applelike edible fruits develop in early summer and are $1/2$ inch in diameter, purplish or black, and can be sweet and juicy.

Saskatoon Serviceberry is found on moist soils in thickets, openings, along wood edges, and in forests; it is a common understory shrub. It is more abundant on lower slopes, although it is found at higher elevations, almost to timberline.

Features: The tasty fruits of Saskatoon Serviceberry are often used fresh or prepared in baked goods. They are an important food for many species of wildlife. The tree's spring foliage is very picturesque. Folklore assigns the name serviceberry because the flowers were collected and used in church services at the same time of year when circuit-riding preachers traveled through the mountains. The name shadbush is given because the flowers bloom at about the same time as the shad run occurs in coastal streams.

Range: From coastal Alaska to northern California and east to western Minnesota, at elevations to 6,000 feet.

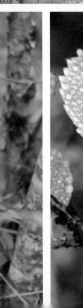

SILKTASSEL

Wavyleaf Silktassel, *Garrya elliptica*
Tasseltree, Quininebush

Wavyleaf Silktassel is a small evergreen that grows to a height of 20 feet with a diameter of 4 inches; it also grows as a multitrunked, thicket-forming shrub. It has smooth, gray bark that may develop small fissures and scales that look like flaws. The crown is rounded and egg shaped.

Simple untoothed leaves are opposite, 2 to 3$^{1}/_{4}$ inches long, elliptical or egg shaped. The leaf margins are wavy and uneven. Leaves are leathery, dark, shiny green, and hairless above, paler and covered with a coat of woolly hair beneath. The twigs are four sided, green, and hairy when young, turning brown to black with age. Twigs, bark, and fruit are bitter to the taste. The tree blooms in late winter, with thin, drooping clusters of many small, green, scaly flowers. These tiny flowers develop into $^{3}/_{8}$-inch, purple to black, berrylike fruits covered with white hairs and dangling in clusters.

Wavyleaf Silktassel is found on dry slopes and ridges, in chaparral and mixed evergreen forests. It is the only species of this genus that reaches tree size.

Range: Found along the Pacific coast from southern Oregon to southern California, to 2,000 feet in elevation.

SOAPBERRY

Western Soapberry, *Sapindus saponaria* var. *drummondii*
Wild Chinatree, Jaboncillo

Western Soapberry is a small deciduous tree that grows to a height of 40 feet with a diameter up to 12 inches. It also grows as a spreading shrub. The light gray bark becomes furrowed with scaly ridges. The crown is rounded, formed with upright branches.

Pinnately compound leaves are alternate, 5 to 8 inches long, with 11 to 19 paired leaflets that are not quite opposite, 1¹/₂ to 3 inches long, ³/₈ to ³/₄ inch wide. Leaflets have very short stalks, are curved, lancelike, with a toothless margin and pointed tip. Leathery leaflets are dull green above, hairy with noticeable veins beneath. Yellow-green twigs may be hairy and have no terminal bud. Pith is solid. Small, yellow-white flowers on a vertical stalk develop into ³/₈- to ¹/₂-inch, nearly transparent, leathery, berrylike fruits that turn from yellow-orange to black and remain on the tree through winter. Fruits have a single, hard seed.

Soapberry prefers moist streamside soils near hardwood forests and in open grasslands in the upper desert.

Features: Although the fruits are poisonous, they have been used as a soap substitute but can cause a skin rash for those who are allergic. The wood splits easily and is used for weaving baskets. Native Americans used it for arrow making and the seeds for jewelry beads.

Range: From Missouri south to Louisiana and then westward to southern New Mexico, Arizona, and north to Colorado, at elevations to 6,000 feet.

SYCAMORE

Sycamore, members of the Sycamore family, are easily identified by their distinctive mottled bark made up of a patchwork of brown, green, and cream-colored patches. Trees often grow in clumps and have massive branches that make up a twisted crown. Their long-pointed, lobed leaves are also somewhat unique.

Arizona Sycamore, *Platanus wrightii*
Arizona Planetree, Alamo

Arizona Sycamore is a medium-size deciduous tree that grows to a height of 40 to 80 feet with a diameter of 2 to 4 feet. Smooth, white bark develops brownish peeling flakes and becomes mottled with shades of white, green, and brown. Bark at the base of larger trees becomes rough and furrowed, turning dark brown or gray. Stout trunks often branch near the base, forming clumps up to 10 feet in diameter. The crown is broad and irregular with large, crooked, spreading branches.

The simple lobed leaves are alternate, 6 to 9 inches long and wide, star shaped, with three or five long, narrow, sharp-pointed lobes with sinuses that extend nearly halfway into the leaf, which has five main veins. Leaf margins are wavy and may have a few large teeth. Leaves are light green above, lighter and hairy beneath. Slender, light brown twigs are zigzagged, have noticeable ring scars, and are hairy when young. Small flowers hang in ball-like clusters. Fruits are $7/8$-inch balls made up of many nutlets that hang in groups of two to seven on long stalks.

Arizona Sycamore is found on wet soils along streambanks and in valleys and canyons and on foothills and mountains. It is also found in the desert and desert grasslands.

Features: The mottled bark, coarse green foliage, and sprawling appearance make Arizona Sycamore an attractive shade tree. It also helps prevent erosion along streambanks.

Range: Found in Arizona, southwest New Mexico, and northwest Mexico, from 2,000 to 6,000 feet in elevation.

California Sycamore, *Platanus racemosa*
Western Sycamore, Aliso

California Sycamore is a medium-size deciduous tree that grows to a height of 40 to 80 feet with a diameter from 2 to 4 feet. Smooth, white bark develops peeling flakes and becomes mottled with shades of white, green, and brown. Bark at the base of larger trees becomes rough and furrowed, turning dark brown or gray. Stout trunks branch near the base, often forming clumps up to 10 feet in diameter. The crown is broad and irregular with crooked, spreading branches.

The simple lobed leaves are alternate, 6 to 9 inches long and wide, star shaped, with five long, narrow, sharp-pointed lobes with sinuses that extend nearly halfway into the leaf. Leaf margins are wavy and may have a few large teeth. Leaves are light green above, lighter and hairy beneath. Slender, brown twigs are zigzagged, have noticeable ring scars, and are hairy when young. Small flowers hang in ball-like clusters. Fruits are $7/8$-inch balls made up of many nutlets that hang on long stalks in groups of two to seven.

California Sycamore is found on streambanks in valleys and on foothills and mountains on wet soils.

Features: The mottled bark, coarse green foliage, and sprawling appearance make California Sycamore an attractive shade tree and ornamental. Native Americans used the bark for medicinal purposes.

Range: Found in the Sierra Nevada and California Coast Ranges and Baja California, to 4,000 feet.

TANOAK

Tanoak, *Notholithocarpus densiflorus*
Tanbark-oak

Tanoak is a medium-size evergreen that grows to a height of 70 to 90 feet with a diameter of 2 to 3 feet. It sometimes grows as a shrub. Smooth, gray bark develops irregular, broken, flat ridges separated by deep fissures over time. In forest settings, the tree has a long, clear trunk with a narrow, pyramidlike crown. Open-grown trees have rounded crowns, with branches covering the trunk.

The simple toothed leaves are alternate, 2^1/$_2$ to 5 inches long, and generally oblong or lancelike. Straight, sunken side veins are nearly parallel. Leaf margins have wavy, coarse teeth and can be curled under. The base of the leaf is rounded and has a short leafstalk. Leaves are leathery, shiny, dark green above; brownish and covered with woolly hair, especially in the spring, beneath. In the fall, leaves become bluish white and lose much of their pubescence. Stout twigs are initially yellowish and hairy, becoming dark reddish brown and covered with a thin, white, almost waxy, coating. Whitish flowers are in an erect catkin that grows from the base of the leaf and have a disagreeable odor. Trees may bloom a second time in the fall. The fruit is a ^{3}/$_4$-inch-long, egg-shaped, pointed acorn, bitter to taste, with a saucer-shaped, shallow cap with long, slender, spreading scales, lined with lustrous, red fuzz.

Tanoak grows best on rich, moist, well-drained soils and is often found in nearly pure stands or with oaks. It is tolerant of shade but responds well to light when overstory trees are removed. It reaches maturity by 200 to 300 years of age.

Features: The bark was once collected commercially as the main source of tannin in the West. Although the acorns are very oaklike, the flowers more closely resemble those of the chestnut. The acorns are edible, but, as with many of the red oaks, they have a bitter taste. Native Americans used the bark and acorns for medicinal purposes.

Range: From southern Oregon to southern California along the Coast Ranges and also in the Sierra Nevada, at sea level to 5,000 feet elevation.

WALNUT

Walnuts are members of the Walnut family. There are only six different kinds of walnuts native to the U.S., four of which are found in the West. Walnuts are characterized by their long, pinnately compound leaves with numerous leaflets; the brown, chambered pith in twigs; and their fruits—edible walnuts.

Arizona Walnut, *Juglans major*
Arizona Black Walnut, Nogal

Arizona Walnut is a small deciduous tree that grows to a height of 30 to 50 feet with a diameter of 1 to 2 feet. It has gray-brown bark that is initially smooth, becoming thicker as it ages, developing ridges separated by deep furrows. The tree often has a forked trunk with widely spreading branches and a rounded crown.

The pinnately compound leaves are alternate, 7 to 14 inches long, with 9 to 13 lancelike leaflets that are 2 to 4 inches long, slightly wavy, and coarsely sawtoothed. The yellow-green leaves are hairy when young, becoming hairless. Stout twigs are brown, have large, raised, shield-shaped leaf scars and chambered pith. Small, green flowers appear in early spring, in drooping catkins at the tips of twigs. The fruits are walnuts, 1 to 1¹/₂ inches in diameter, with a thin, hairy, brown husk and thick, grooved shell. The seed is edible.

Arizona Walnut is found on moist soils along streams and in canyons in mountains, deserts, desert grasslands, and oak woodlands.

Features: The wood of Arizona Walnut is used for furniture and gunstocks. The large burls and bases of trunks are used for tabletops and veneer. Native Americans used the nuts for food and the nut hulls for dye.

Range: From central Texas to central Arizona and south into Mexico, at elevations from 2,000 to 7,000 feet.

Little Walnut, *Juglans microcarpa*
Texas Walnut, Nogal

Little Walnut is a small deciduous tree that grows to a height of 20 to 30 feet with a diameter of 6 to 18 inches. It also grows as a shrub. The gray bark is smooth when young but with age turns darker and becomes deeply furrowed. The tree branches near the ground and has a broad, rounded crown.

The pinnately compound leaves are alternate, 8 to 13 inches long, and have 11 to 25 narrow, lancelike leaflets that are 2 to 3 inches long. Leaves are yellow-green, sharp pointed, and usually curvy, with finely sawtoothed edges. Leafstalks on leaflets are very short. Slender twigs are gray and have large, raised, shield-shaped leaf scars and brown, chambered pith. Small, greenish flowers appear in early spring, in drooping catkins at the tips of twigs. Fruits are $^1/_2$ to $^3/_4$ inch in diameter, with a thin, hairy husk that turns brown. The nut has a thick, hard, grooved shell and very small, edible seed.

Little Walnut is found along streams in plains and on foothills, and in grasslands and deserts.

Features: Little Walnut has the smallest fruit of all walnuts. The wood can be used in cabinetmaking. Rootstock is used for growing non-native walnuts. The seeds are eaten by wildlife.

Range: From southwest Kansas through Oklahoma and Texas and southward into northeastern Mexico, at elevations from 1,500 to 4,000 feet.

Northern California Walnut, *Juglans hindsii*
Hinds Walnut

Northern California Walnut is a medium-size deciduous tree that grows to a height of 70 feet with a diameter of 1 to 2 feet. The gray-brown bark is broken into long plates separated by narrow ridges. The trunk is tall, with a narrow, rounded crown formed by dense branches.

The pinnately compound leaves are alternate, 7 to 12 inches long, with 15 to 19 leaflets, 2½ to 4 inches long, with sawtoothed margins. The leafstalk is covered with soft hairs. The green, stalkless leaflets are shiny on upper surfaces, paler and hairy below, with a tuft of hair along the leaf veins. Twigs are stout, brown, occasionally hairy, and have large, raised, shield-shaped leaf scars and chambered pith. Green catkins, 3 to 5 inches long, hang from the tips of twigs in early spring. Fruits are 1½ to 2 inches in diameter and have a thin husk and thick, dark brown shell that is nearly smooth. The edible seed matures in early fall.

Northern California Walnut is found on moist soils along streams in canyons and foothills, with other riparian species.

Features: Groves of this tree were originally found in limited areas east of the San Francisco Bay. It is now planted as a shade tree and used as rootstock for grafting English Walnuts. Southern California Walnut is similar to Northern California Walnut but is found with limited distribution in southwest California, often growing as a small shrublike tree.

Range: Central California, at elevations to 500 feet.

WILLOW

Willows grow as trees or shrubs, typically on wet soils, especially along streams, where they help stabilize the banks. They often grow with several stems from the same base and can form dense thickets. The narrow, lancelike leaf and flowering catkins (commonly referred to as pussy willow) make willow fairly easy to identify. Identification of a particular species can be quite challenging, however.

Goodding's Willow, *Salix gooddingii*

Goodding's Willow is a medium-size deciduous tree that grows to a height of 60 to 80 feet with diameters from $1^{1}/_{2}$ to $2^{1}/_{2}$ feet. The bark is gray-brown to black and has deep furrows with thick, scaly ridges. The tree tends to grow in clumps, with one or more straight and leaning trunks, and has a spreading, irregular crown. Clumps can be massive.

Simple toothed leaves are 2 to 5 inches long, $^{3}/_{8}$ to $^{3}/_{4}$ inches wide, lancelike, often with a slight curve to one side and a long point. Leaf margins are finely sawtoothed. Leaves are shiny dark green above, lighter green beneath. Slender twigs are grayish brown and detach easily from the base. Tiny, yellowish green flowers form on 1- to 3-inch-long catkins in early spring. Male and female flowers form on separate trees. Cone-shaped capsules mature in late spring and contain many small, cottony seeds.

Goodding's Willow is found on wet soils on banks along streams and lakes and on floodplains, often growing in pure stands or with cottonwoods and other riparian vegetation.

Features: Goodding's Willow twigs were split and woven into waterproof baskets by Native Americans. The tree indicated sources of water for early travelers in desert regions. Snapped branches root easily and can be used to establish new trees.

Range: The Trans-Pecos, west through New Mexico and Arizona to northern California, at elevations to 5,000 feet.

Pacific Willow, *Salix lucinda* ssp. *lasiandra*
Shining Willow, Western Black Willow, Yellow Willow

Pacific Willow is a small deciduous tree that grows to a height of 50 feet with a diameter up to 2 feet. The bark can be gray or brown, developing flat ridges separated by deep, rough furrows. The tree has a crooked trunk, with an open, irregular crown, and can also grow as a thicket-forming shrub.

Simple toothed leaves are alternate, 2 to 5 inches long, $^1/_2$ to 1 inch wide, narrow, lancelike, with very long points and a rounded base. They are finely sawtoothed, initially hairy, becoming hairless. Leaves are shiny green above, white beneath. Leafstalks are slender. Twigs can be a shiny red, brown, or yellow. The flowering catkins are $1^1/_2$ to 4 inches long and have hairy, yellow or brown scales. Flowers mature into tiny, $^1/_4$-inch-long, light reddish brown, hairless capsules that contain numerous cottony seeds.

Pacific Willow grows on wet soils along streams and lakes, and along roadsides. It can be found in valleys or on mountains.

Features: Pacific Willow wood was once used to make charcoal. The bark and twigs were used by Native Americans for medicinal purposes.

Range: From central and southeast Alaska east to Saskatchewan and then south to southern New Mexico and southern California, mostly in the mountains, at elevations to 8,000 feet.

Scouler's Willow, *Salix scouleriana*
Black Willow, Fire Willow

Scouler's Willow is a small deciduous tree that grows to a height of 50 feet with a diameter up to 1¹/₂ feet. The gray bark is thin and smooth, becoming dark brown and developing flat ridges separated by fissures. The tree has a straight trunk and a rounded crown.

Simple untoothed leaves are alternate, 2 to 5 inches long, ¹/₂ to 1¹/₂ inches wide, elliptical to oval, widest at the tip, with a short, blunt point. Leaf margins can be smooth or have sparse, wavy teeth. Leaves are dark green above, whitish with gray or red hairs beneath. Stout twigs are yellow to reddish brown. Flowering catkins are 1 to 2 inches long, stout, almost without stalks, having black, long-haired scales. This is a true pussy willow; flowers appear in spring before leaf-out. Fruits are ³/₈-inch, light brown, hairy capsules that mature in fall and contain many seeds.

Scouler's Willow is found in upland settings in the understory of conifer forests, in cut-over areas, and in clearings. It can be found on dry sites.

Features: Scouler's Willow is also called Fire Willow because of its tendency to grow on recently burned-over areas, forming dense thickets. Diamond-shaped patterns caused by fungi form on its stem, making the wood desirable for canes and furniture posts. Native Americans used the bark for medicinal purposes and the wood to make baskets and water jugs.

Range: Central Alaska south to Idaho and California and east to the Black Hills of South Dakota, also in the mountains of southern New Mexico, at elevations to 10,000 feet.

Glossary

Alluvial. Describing soil that is deposited from rivers or floods.

Alternate. Having only one leaf or bud to a node. Compare to *opposite,* in which there are pairs of buds or leaves at each node.

Angiosperms. Flowering plants, including trees that have flat leaves.

Angled. Describing a twig that has ridges and is not smooth or rounded. (A "four-angled twig" would have a square-shaped cross-section.)

Bark plates. Somewhat flat or scaly pieces of bark separated by vertical and horizontal fissures.

Bark ridge. Narrow, raised bark separated by vertical fissures.

Base. The lower part of the leaf where it meets the leafstalk.

Berry. A fleshy fruit with more than one seed (such as a raspberry or grape).

Bipinnately compound. Describing a leaf arrangement with a central leafstalk that further divides into two or more side axes, with two or more leaflets per side axis. Also called *twice compound* or *twice cut.*

Blade. The broad, flat portion of a leaf.

Bloom. A light, powdery or waxy covering, such as the whitish covering on blueberries.

Bole. The trunk of a tree.

Bract. A scalelike structure, usually at the base of a leaf or flower or between cone scales.

Bristle. A pricklelike, stiff hair, often found on cone scales.

Bud. A young, undeveloped leaf or flower. Usually covered with one or more scales.

Burl. A deformed growth on a tree trunk or branch, commonly in the form of a rounded outgrowth. The grain patterns found in a burl are prized for woodworking and furniture making.

Capsule. A dry, thin-walled fruit containing one or more seeds that splits along a groove when mature.

Catkin. A compact, usually drooping cluster of nondescript flowers, which are usually stalkless and more often either male or female, and not both.

Chaparral. A plant community or zone between the grassland and forest in the California foothills. Common chaparral trees are evergreen oaks with thick, leathery leaves.

Clear. Describing the portion of a tree trunk that is branchless.

Clones. A group of individuals, all genetically identical, that were reproduced asexually from another individual.

Compound leaf. A leaf made up of three or more leaflets.

Cone. A fruit or flower with overlapping scales, such as a pinecone.

Cone scale. One of the scales of a cone.

Conifer. Referring to cone-bearing, usually evergreen, trees.

Crown. The top of the tree, consisting of branches, twigs, and leaves.

Deciduous. Not persistent; describing trees that shed their leaves annually.

Deltoid. Triangularly shaped.

Double sawtoothed. Toothed margin of a leaf in which smaller and larger teeth alternate.

Elliptical. Describing a leaf shape that is generally twice as long as wide.

Entire. Having a margin that is smooth and toothless (as in a leaf that is entire).

Evergreen. Referring to trees that have leaves all year.

Exotic. Not native; introduced.

Fissures. Deep cracks in bark; also called *furrows.*

Form. The shape of a tree.

Fruit. The part of a plant that bears the seed or seeds.

Furrows. Deep cracks in bark; also called *fissures.*

Gall. A swollen growth on leaves and/or twigs, usually caused by insects.

Glabrous. Without hair.

Gland. A dot or pore that usually secretes fluid.

Gymnosperms. Plants with naked, exposed seeds (such as the conifers).

Hardwood. A general term that refers to trees with leaves to distinguish them from conifers.

Invasive. A species that is not native to an area that grows aggressively and often outcompetes other species.

Keeled. Ridged; usually referring to a leaf, cone scale, or seed that has a ridge down its center.

Lancelike. Narrowly elliptical; shaped like a lance. Usually in reference to a leaf.

Lateral bud. A bud that grows from the side of the twig.

Leader. The highest terminal shoot of a plant; also called *terminal shoot.*

Leaf. The green, chlorophyll-containing part of a tree; leaves can be scalelike (as in cedars and junipers), thin and needlelike (pines), or flat and broad (hardwood trees).

Leaf blade. The flat portion of the leaf of hardwood trees.

Leaflet. One of several leaflike parts on a compound leaf.

Leaf margin. The edge of a leaf.

Leaf scar. A mark or scar left on a tree after the leaf is shed.

Leafstalk. The portion of a leaf that attaches to the twig; also called *petiole.*

Leaf veins. The vascular tissues in a leaf; can be netlike or riblike.

Leathery. Describing leaves that are thick and tough.

Legume. Bean.

Lenticel. A small, corky spot or line on twigs and bark that allows for gas exchange.

Linear. Describing a leaf with nearly parallel margins—a very long and narrow leaf.

Lobe. A protrusion, either rounded or pointed, from the leaf edge.

Lobed. Describing leaves that have lobes and sinuses.

Midrib. The main rib or central vein of a leaf.

Naked bud. A bud without scales. (Close examination reveals tiny leaf edges in the bud.)

Naturalized. Describing a plant that has escaped from cultivation, reproduced in the wild, and become part of the established natural flora; or a non-native, invasive species that has become established in natural flora.

Node. The part of the stem or twig that usually bears the leaf or leaves.

Nut. A dry fruit with one seed and, usually, a hard shell that does not split along a natural line (an acorn, for example).

Oblong. Describing a leaf shape that is longer than wide.

Open grown. Describing a tree that grows without competition from other trees (a single tree growing in the middle of a field, for example).

Opposite. Describing a leaf arrangement in which the leaves or leaflets are in pairs at the nodes, one on each side of the twig or stem. Compare to *alternate,* in which there is only one leaf or leaflet at a node.

Ornamental. A tree cultivated and planted for landscaping purposes.

Palmately compound. Describing a leaf in which multiple leaflets are attached at one point on a single leafstalk, like the fingers on a hand.

Parallel veins. Leaf veins that are parallel.

Parasitic. Describing a plant that feeds on another plant (mistletoe, for example).

Pendulous. Hanging or drooping.

Persistent. Evergreen, long lasting, or continuous.

Petiole. Leafstalk.

Photosynthesis. The chemical process in which the chlorophyll in leaves converts light and water into food for the plant.

Pinnately compound. Describing a leaf that has a central leafstalk with two or more leaflets arranged in two rows on either side of the stem, often in a featherlike arrangement. Compare to *palmately compound,* in which leaflets join at a single point.

Pistol butted. Describing a tree with a curved base, often the result of an attempt to grow straight after shifting land has tilted the tree.

Pith. The soft, spongy, innermost part of a stem. A smooth pith is homogenous; a chambered pith is divided into chambers.

Pod. A beanlike fruit containing one or more seeds.

Pubescence, Pubescent. Fuzzy, with fine hair.

Raceme. Clusters of flowers in which individual flowers are attached singly along a single unbranched central stem.

Ranked. Describing alternately arranged leaves, which are actually in a spiral arrangement around the twig. ("Two-ranked leaves" are at 180 degrees, "three-ranked" are every 120 degrees, "four-ranked" at 90 degrees, and so on.)

Recurved. Curved downward or backward.

Resin. A plant secretion that is usually sticky and often aromatic.

Resinous. Describing a plant or plant part that has a sticky secretion.

Rib. A prominent vein or extended edge of a seed or husk.

Ringed. Describing twigs that have leaf scars at the nodes that appear to encircle the twig.

Riparian. Referring to the margin of land that meets water; land along streams or lakes.

Sap. The resinous fluid that seeps out of some trees on the bark.

Sawtoothed. Having evenly spaced teeth along the leaf margin.

Scales. Very short, overlapping needles on some conifers; tiny leaflike structures on acorn caps; small, rough plates on bark.

Scaly bark. Bark with small, rough, and often peeling flakes.

Serotinous. Describing pinecones that remain closed even after the seeds inside have matured. The cones often open and release seeds after exposed to the heat of a forest fire.

Serrate. With sharp teeth.

Sessile. Stalkless.

Shade intolerant. Describing trees that do not survive in the shade of taller trees.

Shade tolerant. Describing trees that can survive in the shade of taller trees.

Sheath. A paperlike tube that surrounds the base of needle bundles in some conifers.

Shreddy. Describing bark that separates into thin strips.

Shrub. A woody plant with multiple stems.

Sinus. A dip or cleft between lobes of a leaf, sometimes nearly to the midvein of a leaf.

Simple leaf. A leaf that is a single whole leaf, not made up of multiple leaflets, as in a *compound leaf.*

Specialty wood products. Manufactured or crafted items made from wood.

Spur branch. A small, compact branch (generally shorter than a few inches) that supports leaves and/or flowers.

Stalk. The stem that attaches the leaf to the twig, also called a *leafstalk* or *petiole.*

Subalpine. Referring to the zone on a mountain where dense forest transitions to alpine tundra as elevation increases. Subalpine trees gradually get smaller and more stunted as they are influenced by harsh weather and growing conditions.

Succulent. Juicy or pulpy.

Terminal bud. The bud at the end of the twig.

Thorn. A modified branch with a sharp point.

Three angled. Triangle shaped, as in a "three-angled" cross-section of a twig.

Timberline. The elevation on a mountain where trees cease to grow because of the harsh growing conditions. Tundra is found above timberline. See *subalpine.*

Veneer. A thin, usually decorative, sheet of wood used to cover coarser wood.

Wing. A thin, flat, dry projection on a seed or twig.

Woody. Hard, not fleshy or succulent.

Woolly. Covered with matted hairs.

National Park and Seashore Tree Lists

Our national parks and seashores are wonderful places to visit, not only for their scenic beauty, but also for the opportunity to practice your tree identification skills. These tree lists identify the trees included in this book that are present, or probably present, at a particular national park. Take the time for a brief visit to the information desk at a visitor center to ask a few questions on where the most likely areas are to find your trees of interest.

ARCHES NATIONAL PARK
Boxelder
Fremont Cottonwood
Red Elderberry
Siberian Elm
Rocky Mountain Juniper
Utah Juniper
Black Locust
Gambel Oak
Pinyon
Goodding's Willow

BIG BEND NATIONAL PARK
Fragrant Ash
Velvet Ash
Quaking Aspen
Birchleaf Cercocarpus
Black Cherry
Fremont Cottonwood
Narrowleaf Cottonwood

Arizona Cypress
Blue Elderberry
Siberian Elm
Douglas-fir
Alligator Juniper
Drooping Juniper
Oneseed Juniper
Texas Madrone
Bigtooth Maple
Honey Mesquite
Emory Oak
Gambel Oak
Gray Oak
Ponderosa Pine
Mexican Pinyon
Western Soapberry
Arizona Walnut
Little Walnut
Desert Willow
Goodding's Willow

BLACK CANYON OF THE GUNNISON NATIONAL PARK
Quaking Aspen
Boxelder
Narrowleaf Cottonwood
Douglas-fir
Siberian Elm
Rocky Mountain Juniper
Utah Juniper
Rocky Mountain Maple
Gambel Oak
Ponderosa Pine
Pinyon
Saskatoon Serviceberry
Blue Spruce

BRYCE CANYON NATIONAL PARK
Quaking Aspen
Water Birch
Curl-leaf Cercocarpus
Chokecherry
Fremont Cottonwood
Narrowleaf Cottonwood
Douglas-fir
Blue Elderberry
Red Elderberry
Siberian Elm
Subalpine Fir
White Fir
Rocky Mountain Juniper
Utah Juniper
Bigtooth Maple
Rocky Mountain Maple
Gambel Oak
Great Basin Bristlecone Pine
Limber Pine
Ponderosa Pine
Pinyon
Saskatoon Serviceberry
Blue Spruce
Englemann Spruce

CANYONLANDS NATIONAL PARK
Water Birch
Boxelder
Curl-leaf Cercocarpus
Chokecherry
Fremont Cottonwood
Douglas-fir
Siberian Elm
White Fir
Utah Juniper
Bigtooth Maple
Rocky Mountain Maple
Gambel Oak
Pinyon
Ponderosa Pine
Singleleaf Pinyon
Goodding's Willow

CAPITOL REEF NATIONAL PARK
Quaking Aspen
Water Birch
Boxelder
Curl-leaf Cercocarpus
Fremont Cottonwood
Narrowleaf Cottonwood
Douglas-fir
Blue Elderberry
Siberian Elm
White Fir
Rocky Mountain Juniper
Utah Juniper
Black Locust
Rocky Mountain Maple
Gambel Oak
Great Basin Bristlecone Pine
Limber Pine
Ponderosa Pine
Pinyon
Saskatoon Serviceberry
Blue Spruce
Englemann Spruce
Goodding's Willow

CARLSBAD CAVERNS NATIONAL PARK
Velvet Ash
Black Cherry
Chokecherry
Narrowleaf Cottonwood
Douglas-fir
Siberian Elm
Alligator Juniper
Oneseed Juniper
Rocky Mountain Juniper
New Mexico Locust
Arizona Madrone
Texas Madrone
Bigtooth Maple
Honey Mesquite
Arizona White Oak
Gambel Oak
Gray Oak
Ponderosa Pine
Southwestern White Pine
Pinyon
Western Soapberry
Little Walnut
Desert Willow
Goodding's Willow

CHANNEL ISLANDS NATIONAL PARK
Birchleaf Cercocarpus
Black Cottonwood
Fremont Cottonwood
Monterey Cypress
Tasmanian Eucalyptus
Black Locust
Pacific Madrone
Bigleaf Maple
Blue Oak
California Black Oak
California Live Oak
Canyon Live Oak
Valley Oak
Bishop Pine
Torrey Pine
California Sycamore
California Fan Palm
Pacific Willow

CRATER LAKE NATIONAL PARK
Quaking Aspen
Cascara Buckthorn
Incense Cedar
Western Red Cedar
Bitter Cherry
Giant Chinquapin
Black Cottonwood
Pacific Dogwood
Douglas-fir
Blue Elderberry
Red Elderberry
California Red Fir
Grand Fir
Noble Fir
Pacific Silver Fir
Subalpine Fir
White Fir
Mountain Hemlock
Western Hemlock
Pacific Madrone
Bigleaf Maple
Rocky Mountain Maple
Oregon White Oak
Lodgepole Pine
Ponderosa Pine
Sugar Pine
Western White Pine
Whitebark Pine
Saskatoon Serviceberry
Englemann Spruce
Pacific Willow
Scouler's Willow

DEATH VALLEY NATIONAL PARK
Velvet Ash
Water Birch
Curl-leaf Cercocarpus
Fremont Cottonwood
Blue Elderberry
Utah Juniper
Western Juniper

Black Locust
Rocky Mountain Maple
Honey Mesquite
California Fan Palm
Great Basin Bristlecone Pine
Limber Pine
Singleleaf Pinyon
Goodding's Willow
Desert Willow
Pacific Willow

GLACIER NATIONAL PARK
Quaking Aspen
Water Birch
Western Red Cedar
Bitter Cherry
Chokecherry
Black Cottonwood
Douglas-fir
Blue Elderberry
Grand Fir
Subalpine Fir
Black Hawthorn
Western Hemlock
Rocky Mountain Juniper
Western Larch
Rocky Mountain Maple
Limber Pine
Lodgepole Pine
Ponderosa Pine
Western White Pine
Whitebark Pine
Saskatoon Serviceberry
Englemann Spruce
White Spruce
Scouler's Willow

GRAND CANYON
NATIONAL PARK
Fragrant Ash
Velvet Ash
Quaking Aspen
Water Birch
Boxelder
Curl-leaf Cercocarpus

Bitter Cherry
Chokecherry
Fremont Cottonwood
Narrowleaf Cottonwood
Douglas-fir
Red Elderberry
Siberian Elm
Subalpine Fir
White Fir
Oneseed Juniper
Rocky Mountain Juniper
Utah Juniper
New Mexico Locust
Bigtooth Maple
Rocky Mountain Maple
Honey Mesquite
Gambel Oak
Gray Oak
Pinyon
Ponderosa Pine
Singleleaf Pinyon
Western Soapberry
Blue Spruce
Englemann Spruce
Arizona Sycamore
Arizona Walnut
Desert Willow
Goodding's Willow
Pacific Willow
Scouler's Willow

GRAND TETON NATIONAL PARK
Quaking Aspen
Water Birch
Curl-leaf Cercocarpus
Chokecherry
Narrowleaf Cottonwood
Douglas-fir
Subalpine Fir
Black Hawthorn
Rocky Mountain Juniper
Rocky Mountain Maple
Limber Pine
Lodgepole Pine
Whitebark Pine

Saskatoon Serviceberry
Blue Spruce
Englemann Spruce
Scouler's Willow

GREAT BASIN NATIONAL PARK
Quaking Aspen
Water Birch
Curl-leaf Cercocarpus
Chokecherry
Narrowleaf Cottonwood
Douglas-fir
Blue Elderberry
Red Elderberry
White Fir
Rocky Mountain Juniper
Utah Juniper
Rocky Mountain Maple
Great Basin Bristlecone Pine
Limber Pine
Ponderosa Pine
Singleleaf Pinyon
Englemann Spruce

GREAT SAND DUNES NATIONAL PARK AND PRESERVE
Red Elderberry

GUADALUPE MOUNTAINS NATIONAL PARK
Velvet Ash
Quaking Aspen
Birchleaf Cercocarpus
Black Cherry
Chokecherry
Douglas-fir
Siberian Elm
Alligator Juniper
Drooping Juniper
Oneseed Juniper
Rocky Mountain Juniper
New Mexico Locust
Texas Madrone
Bigtooth Maple
Honey Mesquite

Gambel Oak
Gray Oak
Ponderosa Pine
Southwestern White Pine
Pinyon
Western Soapberry
Little Walnut
Desert Willow
Goodding's Willow

JOSHUA TREE NATIONAL PARK
Velvet Ash
Desert Ironwood
California Juniper
Honey Mesquite
California Fan Palm
Singleleaf Pinyon
Desert Willow
Goodding's Willow

LASSEN VOLCANIC NATIONAL PARK
Quaking Aspen
Incense Cedar
Curl-leaf Cercocarpus
Bitter Cherry
Black Cottonwood
Douglas-fir
Red Elderberry
California Red Fir
White Fir
Mountain Hemlock
Western Juniper
Rocky Mountain Maple
California Black Oak
Limber Pine
Lodgepole Pine
Ponderosa Pine
Sugar Pine
Western White Pine
Whitebark Pine
Pacific Willow
Scouler's Willow

MESA VERDE NATIONAL PARK
Quaking Aspen
Water Birch
Boxelder
Bitter Cherry
Chokecherry
Fremont Cottonwood
Narrowleaf Cottonwood
Douglas-fir
Blue Elderberry
Red Elderberry
Siberian Elm
Rocky Mountain Juniper
Utah Juniper
Bigtooth Maple
Rocky Mountain Maple
Gambel Oak
Ponderosa Pine
Pinyon
Saskatoon Serviceberry
Pacific Willow

MOUNT RAINIER NATIONAL PARK
Red Alder
Alaska Cedar
Western Red Cedar
Bitter Cherry
Chokecherry
Black Cottonwood
Pacific Dogwood
Douglas-fir
Blue Elderberry
Red Elderberry
Grand Fir
Noble Fir
Pacific Silver Fir
Subalpine Fir
Mountain Hemlock
Western Hemlock
Bigleaf Maple
Rocky Mountain Maple
Vine Maple
Lodgepole Pine
Ponderosa Pine

Western White Pine
Whitebark Pine
Saskatoon Serviceberry
Englemann Spruce
Sitka Spruce
Pacific Willow
Scouler's Willow

NORTH CASCADES NATIONAL PARK
Red Alder
Quaking Aspen
Paper Birch
Water Birch
Boxelder
Cascara Buckthorn
Alaska Cedar
Western Red Cedar
Bitter Cherry
Chokecherry
Black Cottonwood
Pacific Dogwood
Douglas-fir
Blue Elderberry
Red Elderberry
Grand Fir
Pacific Silver Fir
Subalpine Fir
Black Hawthorn
Mountain Hemlock
Western Hemlock
Rocky Mountain Juniper
Western Larch
Black Locust
Bigleaf Maple
Rocky Mountain Maple
Vine Maple
Lodgepole Pine
Ponderosa Pine
Western White Pine
Whitebark Pine
Saskatoon Serviceberry
Englemann Spruce
Sitka Spruce
Scouler's Willow

OLYMPIC NATIONAL PARK
Red Alder
Oregon Ash
Quaking Aspen
Cascara Buckthorn
Alaska Cedar
Western Red Cedar
Bitter Cherry
Black Cottonwood
Pacific Dogwood
Douglas-fir
Blue Elderberry
Red Elderberry
Grand Fir
Pacific Silver Fir
Subalpine Fir
Black Hawthorn
Mountain Hemlock
Western Hemlock
Rocky Mountain Juniper
Black Locust
Pacific Madrone
Bigleaf Maple
Rocky Mountain Maple
Vine Maple
Lodgepole Pine
Western White Pine
Whitebark Pine
Saskatoon Serviceberry
Englemann Spruce
Sitka Spruce
Pacific Willow
Scouler's Willow

PETRIFIED FOREST NATIONAL PARK
Fremont Cottonwood
Narrowleaf Cottonwood
Siberian Elm
Oneseed Juniper
Honey Mesquite
Pinyon
Goodding's Willow

PINNACLES NATIONAL PARK
California Ash
California Buckeye
Birchleaf Cercocarpus
Fremont Cottonwood
California Juniper
Blue Oak
California Live Oak
Canyon Live Oak
Interior Live Oak
Valley Oak
California Foothill Pine
Redwood
California Sycamore
Northern California Walnut

POINT REYES NATIONAL SEASHORE
Red Alder
Boxelder
California Buckeye
Incense Cedar
Giant Chinquapin
Monterey Cypress
Pacific Dogwood
Douglas-fir
Red Elderberry
Tasmanian Eucalyptus
California Laurel
Black Locust
Pacific Madrone
Bigleaf Maple
California Live Oak
Canyon Live Oak
Bishop Pine
Lodgepole Pine
Monterey Pine
Redwood
Wavyleaf Silktassel
California Sycamore
Tanoak
Pacific Willow

REDWOOD NATIONAL PARK
Red Alder
White Alder
Oregon Ash
Cascara Buckthorn
Incense Cedar
Port Orford Cedar
Western Red Cedar
Birchleaf Cercocarpus
Bitter Cherry
Giant Chinquapin
Chokecherry
Black Cottonwood
Monterey Cypress
Pacific Dogwood
Douglas-fir
Red Elderberry
Grand Fir
White Fir
Western Hemlock
California Laurel
Black Locust
Pacific Madrone
Bigleaf Maple
Vine Maple
California Black Oak
Canyon Live Oak
Oregon White Oak
Knobcone Pine
Limber Pine
Lodgepole Pine
Monterey Pine
Sugar Pine
Redwood
Saskatoon Serviceberry
Wavyleaf Silktassel
Sitka Spruce
Tanoak
Pacific Willow
Scouler's Willow

ROCKY MOUNTAIN NATIONAL PARK
Quaking Aspen
Water Birch
Chokecherry
Narrowleaf Cottonwood
Douglas-fir
Red Elderberry
Subalpine Fir
Rocky Mountain Juniper
Rocky Mountain Maple
Limber Pine
Lodgepole Pine
Ponderosa Pine
Sasaktoon Serviceberry
Blue Spruce
Englemann Spruce
Scouler's Willow

SAGUARO NATIONAL PARK
Arizona Alder
Velvet Ash
Quaking Aspen
Boxelder
Black Cherry
Chokecherry
Fremont Cottonwood
Arizona Cypress
Douglas-fir
White Fir
Desert Ironwood
Alligator Juniper
New Mexico Locust
Arizona Madrone
Rocky Mountain Maple
Honey Mesquite
Velvet Mesquite
Arizona White Oak
Canyon Live Oak
Emory Oak
Gambel Oak
Silverleaf Oak
Blue Paloverde
Yellow Paloverde
Apache Pine

Ponderosa Pine
Southwestern White Pine
Mexican Pinyon
Pinyon
Western Soapberry
Arizona Sycamore
Arizona Walnut
Desert Willow
Goodding's Willow
Scouler's Willow

SEQUOIA AND KINGS CANYON NATIONAL PARKS
White Alder
California Ash
Quaking Aspen
Water Birch
California Buckeye
Incense Cedar
Birchleaf Cercocarpus
Curl-leaf Cercocarpus
Bitter Cherry
Chokecherry
Black Cottonwood
Fremont Cottonwood
Pacific Dogwood
Red Elderberry
California Red Fir
White Fir
Mountain Hemlock
Western Juniper
California Laurel
Bigleaf Maple
Rocky Mountain Maple
Blue Oak
California Black Oak
Canyon Live Oak
Interior Live Oak
Oregon White Oak
California Foothill Pine
Foxtail Pine
Limber Pine
Lodgepole Pine
Ponderosa Pine
Sugar Pine

Western White Pine
Whitebark Pine
Singleleaf Pinyon
Giant Sequoia
Saskatoon Serviceberry
California Sycamore
Goodding's Willow
Pacific Willow
Scouler's Willow

YELLOWSTONE NATIONAL PARK
Quaking Aspen
Water Birch
Boxelder
Chokecherry
Narrowleaf Cottonwood
Douglas-fir
Black Hawthorn
Rocky Mountain Juniper
Rocky Mountain Maple
Limber Pine
Lodgepole Pine
Whitebark Pine
Saskatoon Serviceberry
Englemann Spruce
White Spruce
Scouler's Willow

YOSEMITE NATIONAL PARK
White Alder
Oregon Ash
California Ash
Quaking Aspen
California Buckeye
Incense Cedar
Birchleaf Cercocarpus
Bitter Cherry
Chokecherry
Black Cottonwood
Fremont Cottonwood
Pacific Dogwood
Douglas-fir
Red Elderberry
California Red Fir
White Fir

Mountain Hemlock
Western Juniper
California Laurel
Bigleaf Maple
Rocky Mountain Maple
Blue Oak
California Black Oak
Canyon Live Oak
Interior Live Oak
Oregon White Oak
Valley Oak
Gray Oak
Knobcone Pine
Limber Pine
Lodgepole Pine
Ponderosa Pine
Sugar Pine
Western White Pine
Whitebark Pine
Singleleaf Pinyon
Giant Sequoia
Saskatoon Serviceberry
Tanoak
Pacific Willow
Scouler's Willow

ZION NATIONAL PARK

Velvet Ash
Quaking Aspen
Water Birch
Boxelder
Curl-leaf Cercocarpus
Chokecherry
Fremont Cottonwood
Narrowleaf Cottonwood
Arizona Cypress
Douglas-fir
Blue Elderberry
Red Elderberry
Siberian Elm
Subalpine Fir
White Fir
Rocky Mountain Juniper
Utah Juniper
Black Locust
New Mexico Locust
Bigtooth Maple
Rocky Mountain Maple
Honey Mesquite
Gambel Oak
Ponderosa Pine
Pinyon
Singleleaf Pinyon
Saskatoon Serviceberry
Goodding's Willow
Scouler's Willow

Information on trees located in the western national parks was obtained from:
   NPSpecies: The National Park Service Biodiversity Database. IRMA Portal version. https://irma.nps.gov/npspecies/ (accessed 9/15/2014).

NPSpecies Data Use and Liability Disclaimer

NPSpecies provides information on the presence and status of species in our national parks. Although the data have been reviewed using the best information available at the time of disclosure, these species lists are works in progress and the absence of a species from a list does not necessarily mean the species is absent from a park. The level of effort spent on species inventories or researching historical reference information varies from park to park, which may result in data gaps. Also, species taxonomy changes over time and can reflect regional variations or preferences; as a result, information may be listed under a different species name.

The National Park Service shall not be held liable for improper or incorrect use of the data described or contained in NPSpecies. These data are not legal documents and are not intended to be used as such. The information contained in NPSpecies is dynamic and may change over time. It is the responsibility of the data user to use the data appropriately and in a manner consistent with the data's limitations.

The National Park Service gives no warranty, expressed or implied, as to the accuracy, reliability, or completeness of the information in NPSpecies. It is strongly recommended that these data be acquired directly from an NPS server or source and not indirectly through non-National Park Service sources.

For more information, please visit:
1) Inventory and Monitoring Program: http://science.nature.nps.gov/im/about.cfm
2) NPSpecies: https://irma.nps.gov/NPSpecies/
3) NPSpecies help page: https://irma.nps.gov/content/npspecies/Help/ (includes link to User Guide)

Help Improve NPSpecies

All park species lists are a work in progress. They represent information currently in the NPSpecies data system and records are continually being added or updated by National Park Service staff. If you believe you found a species not currently included in the NPSpecies database, please let them know. Use the following link to submit your information:
   Make a suggestion: https://irma.nps.gov/NPSpecies/Suggest

References

Books

Cafferty, Steve. *Trees: West.* New York: HarperCollins, 2007.

Cope, Edward A. *Muenscher's Keys to Woody Plants.* Ithaca, NY: Comstock Publishing, 2001.

Harlow, William M. *Fruit Key and Twig Key to Trees and Shrubs.* New York: Dover Publications, 1959.

Harlow, William M., Ellwood S. Harrar, James W. Hardin, and Fred M. White. *Textbook of Dendrology.* 5th ed. United States: McGraw Hill, 1969.

Harlow, William M., Ellwood S. Harrar, James W. Hardin, and Fred M. White, *Textbook of Dendrology.* 8th ed. United States: McGraw Hill, 1996.

Little, Elbert L. *National Audubon Society Field Guide to Trees, Western Region.* New York: Alfred A. Knopf, 2013.

National Audubon Society. *Familiar Trees of North America: West.* New York: Alfred A. Knopf, 2013.

Paruk, Jim. *Sierra Nevada Tree Identifier.* San Francisco: Yosemite Association, 1997.

Petrides, George A. *A Field Guide to Western Trees.* Peterson Field Guide Series. Boston: Houghton Mifflin, 1998.

Watts, Tom. *Pacific Coast Tree Finder.* 2nd ed. Rochester, NY: Nature Study Guild, 1973.

Williams, Michael D. *Identifying Trees: An All-Season Guide to Eastern North America.* Mechanicsburg, PA: Stackpole Books, 2007.

Websites

Key to the Flora of North America
    www.efloras.org
"Field Guide for the Identification and Use of Common Riparian Woody Plants of the Intermountain West and Pacific Northwest Regions." 2008.
    http://www.nrcs.usda.gov/Internet/FSE_PLANTMATERIALS/publications/idpmcpu7428.pdf
Montana State University Extension svc tree identifier.
    http://store.msuextension.org/publications/OutdoorsEnvironmentandWildlife/2B0323.pdf
Oregon Wood Innovation Center.
    http://owic.oregonstate.edu/information-oregon-wood-species.OregonState University
"Native American Uses of Utah Forest Trees."
    http://extension.usu.edu/files/publications/publication/NR_FF_018pr.pdf/
CalPhotos.
    http://calphotos.berkeley.edu/
Evergreen.edu Winter Twig Flash Cards.
    http://blogs.evergreen.edu/naturalhistory/files/2012/10/Winter-Twig-Flashcards.pdf/
Center for Disease Control Poisonous Plants.
    http://www.cdc.gov/niosh/topics/plants/
Native Plants PNW.
    http://nativeplantspnw.com/author/habitatdana/
USDA Forest Service database.
    http://www.fs.fed.us/database/feis/plants/tree
USDA database.
    http://plants.usda.gov
California Plant Database.
    http://www.calflora.org
The Gymnosperm Database.
    www.conifers.org
University of Michigan Ethnobotany.
    http://herb.umd.umich.edu/
The National Park Service Biodiversity Database. IRMA PORTAL version.
    https://irma.nps.gov/npspecies/(access9/15/2014).NPSpecies
Forest types of North America, SAFopedia.
    http://www.safnet.org
Virginia Tech Dendrology.
    http://dendro.cnre.vt.edu/

Photo Credits

Page 18 (right): Susan Penny

Page 30 (top): Dr. Mark S. Brunell

Page 33 (top): Doug Von Gausig

Page 36 (top left): Susan McDougall

Page 43 (top): Kathe Frank

Page 50 (top): Gary A. Monroe

Page 53 (top): John Seiler

Page 53 (bottom): Robert A. Howard Collection, courtesy of Smithsonian Institution

Page 54 (top): T. F. Niehaus, courtesy of Smithsonian Institution

Page 58 (bottom center): Susan Penny

Page 61 (bottom): Patrick J. Alexander

Page 62 (top): Kathe and Jack Frank

Page 64 (bottom): T. F. Niehaus, courtesy of Smithsonian Institution

Page 78 (top): Al Schneider, www.swcoloradowildflowers.com

Page 80 (bottom): Kathe and Jack Frank

Page 93 (bottom): Susan Penny

Page 95 (bottom right): John Seiler

Page 96 (bottom left): John Seiler

Page 103 (bottom): Al Schneider, www.swcoloradowildflowers.com

Page 123 (top right): John Seiler

Page 126 (top): John Seiler

Page 127 (bottom left and right): John Seiler

Page 129 (bottom left): John Seiler

Page 129 (bottom right): T. F. Niehaus, courtesy of Smithsonian Institution

Page 133 (top left, extreme top right, and bottom three): Kathe and Jack Frank

Page 133 (middle right): Robert A. Howard Collection, courtesy of Smithsonian Institution

Page 137 (bottom middle): Susan McDougall

Page 139 (top right): Susan McDougall

Page 145 (top left): Gary A. Monroe

Page 145 (top right and bottom): Susan McDougall

Page 145 (middle right): Dr. Mark S. Brunell

Page 149 (top): Gary A. Monroe

Page 151 (top right): Susan McDougall

Page 153 (top right): J. Zylstra, courtesy of Smithsonian Institution

Page 159 (top left, bottom center, and bottom right): Kathe and Jack Frank

Page 173 (top and bottom left): Gary A. Monroe

Page 173 (bottom right): Doug Von Gausig

Page 185 (top left and right): Susan McDougall

Page 185 (bottom left and bottom right): Kathe and Jack Frank

Page 193 (top left): Gary A. Monroe

Page 193 (top right, third photo clockwise from top left, and bottom middle): T. F. Niehaus, courtesy of Smithsonian Institution

Page 197 (top left): J. Zylstra, courtesy of Smithsonian Institution
Page 197 (top right): Gary A. Monroe
Page 219 (top left, bottom left, and bottom right): Marilyn Darling
Page 223 (all photos): John Seiler
Page 229 (third photo clockwise from top left): Susan McDougall
Page 241 (top right): John Seiler
Page 243 (top right): Susan McDougall
Page 251 (bottom left): J. Zylstra, courtesy of Smithsonian Institution
Page 253 (top right): T. F. Niehaus, courtesy of Smithsonian Institution
Page 253 (bottom right): G. A. Cooper, courtesy of Smithsonian Institution
Page 261 (top): D. E. Herman, North Dakota Tree Handbook, USDA NRCS PLANTS database
Page 261 (middle right): Robert A. Howard Collection, courtesy of Smithsonian Institution
Page 263 (top right): Al Schneider, www.swcoloradowildflowers.com
Page 263 (middle right): Susan McDougall
Page 267 (top right and middle right): Kevin Elliott
Page 275 (middle right): T. F. Niehaus, courtesy of Smithsonian Institution
Page 279 (top left): Dave Powell, USDA Forest Service (retired), Bugwood.org
Page 279 (top right): Robert A. Howard Collection, courtesy of Smithsonian Institution
Page 279 (middle right): G. A. Cooper, courtesy of Smithsonian Institution
Page 281 (bottom left and middle): Susan McDougall
Page 281 (top right): Robert A. Howard Collection, courtesy of Smithsonian Institution
Page 283 (top left): Susan McDougall

Page 287 (top left and bottom): Al Schneider, www.swcoloradowildflowers.com
Page 287 (top right): John Seiler
Page 297 (middle right): D. E. Herman, North Dakota Tree Handbook, USDA NRCS PLANTS database
Page 301 (bottom center): Susan Penny
Page 303 (top left and middle): Kathe and Jack Frank
Page 303 (top right): Dave Powell, USDA Forest Service (retired), Bugwood.org
Page 303 (bottom left and bottom center): Ed Jensen
Page 307 (top right): Mark W. Skinner, USDA PLANTS
Page 311 (middle right): Patrick J. Alexander
Page 321 (top left): Russ Kleinman and Shawn White
Page 321 (top right): Robert Sivinski
Page 321 (middle right): Al Schneider, www.swcoloradowildflowers.com
Page 321 (bottom left): Patrick J. Alexander
Page 321 (bottom right): Russ Kleinman, Richard Felger, Sarah Johnson, and Kevin Keith
Page 323 (top, middle right, bottom left, and bottom right): Kathe and Jack Frank
Page 327 (middle right): Robert Sivinski
Page 329 (top right): Paul B. Moore, Shutterstock
Page 357 (bottom middle): John Seiler
Page 359 (middle right and bottom left): John Seiler
Page 361 (fourth photo clockwise from top left and bottom right): Ed Jensen
Page 361 (bottom left): Al Dodson
Page 375 (bottom center): Susan Penny
Page 383 (top right): Ed Jensen
Page 383 (bottom left): John Seiler

Index